Exploring the Relationship Between Media, Libraries, and Archives

Collence Takaingenhamo Chisita
Harare Polytechnic, Zimbabwe & University of South Africa, South Africa

Alexander M. Rusero
Harare Polytechnic, Zimbabwe

A volume in the Advances in Library and Information Science (ALIS) Book Series

Published in the United States of America by
IGI Global
Information Science Reference (an imprint of IGI Global)
701 E. Chocolate Avenue
Hershey PA, USA 17033
Tel: 717-533-8845
Fax: 717-533-8661
E-mail: cust@igi-global.com
Web site: http://www.igi-global.com

Library of Congress Cataloging-in-Publication Data

Names: Chisita, Collence Takaingenhamo, 1965- editor. | Rusero, Alexander M., editor.
Title: Exploring the relationship between media, libraries, and archives / Collence Takaingenhamo Chisita and Alexander M. Rusero, editors.
Description: Hershey, PA : Information Science Reference, [2019] | Includes bibliographical references.
Identifiers: LCCN 2017058884| ISBN 9781522558408 (hardcover) | ISBN 9781522558415 (ebook)
Subjects: LCSH: Digital media. | Library cooperation. | Libraries and mass media. | Collective memory.
Classification: LCC ZA4045 .E97 2019 | DDC 302.23/1--dc23 LC record available at https://lccn.loc.gov/2017058884

This book is published in the IGI Global book series Advances in Library and Information Science (ALIS) (ISSN: 2326-4136; eISSN: 2326-4144)

British Cataloguing in Publication Data
A Cataloguing in Publication record for this book is available from the British Library.

All work contributed to this book is new, previously-unpublished material.
The views expressed in this book are those of the authors, but not necessarily of the publisher.

For electronic access to this publication, please contact: eresources@igi-global.com.

Advances in Library and Information Science (ALIS) Book Series

ISSN:2326-4136
EISSN:2326-4144

Editor-in-Chief: Alfonso Ippolito, Sapienza University-Rome, Italy & Carlo Inglese, Sapienza University-Rome, Italy

MISSION

The **Advances in Library and Information Science (ALIS) Book Series** is comprised of high quality, research-oriented publications on the continuing developments and trends affecting the public, school, and academic fields, as well as specialized libraries and librarians globally. These discussions on professional and organizational considerations in library and information resource development and management assist in showcasing the latest methodologies and tools in the field.

The **ALIS Book Series** aims to expand the body of library science literature by covering a wide range of topics affecting the profession and field at large. The series also seeks to provide readers with an essential resource for uncovering the latest research in library and information science management, development, and technologies.

COVERAGE

- Discovery Tools
- Outreach, Promotion, and Advocacy
- Future of Computing in Libraries
- Databases
- Conservation
- Outsourcing of Library Services
- Blogging in Libraries
- Alternatives to Dewey Decimal System
- Gaming in Libraries
- Ethical Practices in Libraries

The Advances in Library and Information Science (ALIS) Book Series (ISSN 2326-4136) is published by IGI Global, 701 E. Chocolate Avenue, Hershey, PA 17033-1240, USA, www.igi-global.com. This series is composed of titles available for purchase individually; each title is edited to be contextually exclusive from any other title within the series. For pricing and ordering information please visit http://www.igi-global.com/book-series/advances-library-information-science/73002. Postmaster: Send all address changes to above address.

Titles in this Series

For a list of additional titles in this series, please visit:
https://www.igi-global.com/book-series/advances-library-information-science/73002

Library and Information Science in the Ag of MOOCs
Anna Kaushik (University of Kota, India)
Information Science Reference • ©2018 • 309pp • H/C (ISBN: 9781522551461) • US $185.00

Changing the Scope of Library Instruction in the Digital Age
Swati Bhattacharyya (University of California – Riverside, USA) and K Rama Patnaik (Indian Institute of Management Bangalore, India)
Information Science Reference • ©2018 • 286pp • H/C (ISBN: 9781522528029) • US $175.00

Handbook of Research on Innovative Techniques, Trends, and Analysis for Optimized ...
Victor X. Wang (Grand Canyon University, USA) and Thomas G. Reio Jr. (Florida International University, USA)
Information Science Reference • ©2018 • 445pp • H/C (ISBN: 9781522551645) • US $275.00

Measuring the Validity of Usage Reports Provided by E-Book Vendors Emerging Research ...
Aiping Chen-Gaffey (Slippery Rock University of Pennsylvania, USA) and Heather Getsay (Slippery Rock University of Pennsylvania, USA)
Information Science Reference • ©2018 • 130pp • H/C (ISBN: 9781522532385) • US $135.00

Examining the Emotional Dimensions of Academic Librarianship Emerging Research ...
Megan Lowe (University of Louisiana – Monroe, USA) and Lindsey M. Reno (University of New Orleans, USA)
Information Science Reference • ©2018 • 168pp • H/C (ISBN: 9781522537618) • US $145.00

Handbook of Research on Managing Intellectual Property in Digital Libraries
Adeyinka Tella (University of Ilorin, Nigeria) and Tom Kwanya (The Technical University of Kenya, Kenya)
Information Science Reference • ©2018 • 461pp • H/C (ISBN: 9781522530930) • US $245.00

For an entire list of titles in this series, please visit:
https://www.igi-global.com/book-series/advances-library-information-science/73002

IGI Global
DISSEMINATOR OF KNOWLEDGE

701 East Chocolate Avenue, Hershey, PA 17033, USA
Tel: 717-533-8845 x100 • Fax: 717-533-8661
E-Mail: cust@igi-global.com • www.igi-global.com

Table of Contents

Detailed Table of Contents

The study provided an open access model for quality scientific outputs in a quasi-linear information society: a pareto optimality approach. The qualitative research method was used and involved a three-stage sampling technique to select participants. The findings of the study revealed that respondents were of the opinion that paying APC or publishing costs constitute burden for authors and that the publishers should have other ways of making profits in business such as library subscription, among others. Thus, all stakeholders should collaborate and be involved in the maintenance of the information society to enhance open access initiatives, especially in developing countries.

The chapter seeks to discuss the role played by library consortia in resource sharing among libraries, media organizations, and archives. It will outline the existing models that are functioning effectively especially in the developing countries and discuss the best practices. The target audience being libraries, archives, and media. While unravelling the economics of resources sharing among the information players, the chapter will address the challenges and opportunities in supporting research, teaching, and learning. The value of the book chapter is that it will give an insight into the development of library consortia and their significance as opportunities to provide equal access to research in libraries, archives, and media. The chapter will also provide a comprehensive comparison between library consortia in developing countries and developed countries highlighting how resource sharing in developing countries has helped to bridge the gap of information access, thereby showing progressive development.

INFLIBNET (information library network) has gradually emerged as the backbone of the higher education sector of India. The remarkable initiatives taken by the INFLIBNET strive for strengthening and supporting information needs of the students, scholars, teachers, scientists, and peers. Scholars all around the world would be thankful to the INFLIBNET for their marvelous and ambitious project in the direction of bringing millions of theses and dissertation under the umbrella of OA. With 166,675 full-text ETD items and growing, it qualifies to be called a massive digital library (MDL). This chapter discusses the salient features, significance, and implications of the Shodhganga. It also discusses Shodhgangotri, a database consisting of approved research proposal submitted by the research scholars. The chapter concludes with discussion on the evaluation report of the Shodhganga website with the web-analyzer software Nibbler.

Botswana government uses ICT to deliver services and communicate with the public to increase access and usage of services. One of the platforms for such communications is social media which generates liquid communication. Liquid communication is defined as a type of communication that can easily go back and forth between participants involved which is neither restricted by time nor space. This can be shared and re-tweeted many times beyond the control of the creating agency, resulting in challenges regarding its management. The question that arises is, How do government agencies ensure governance of such records? Using literature review, this chapter explores governance of liquid communications by Botswana government. The study established that there are no guidelines for managing liquid communications. The chapter recommends that Botswana government should design a governance framework to guide ministries in the management of liquid communication. Failure to regulate this environment would result in trouble for the country such as loss of memory.

The major focus of this chapter is to discover how the media can be a subordinate of cultural heritage and at the same time pose a threat to cultural heritage. It explores the link between media and cultural heritage. Attention is also on the use of the internet in the promotion of cultural heritage in Zimbabwe. Media use of internet permit cultural heritage of different groups to be uploaded, downloaded, and accessed by other people around the world, presenting opportunities for cultural exchange.

There is growing concern among information science practitioners and librarians on their relevance in the constantly changing world of technology where their work is seemingly under threat. This has been caused by increase in technological advancement and processes that are automating the processes which basically entailed their work. This chapter thus seeks to provide these practitioners, particularly their trainers, with some insight into the future prospects and the place of LIS and media in the coming years by attempting to define roles and processes that they may play for them to remain as relevant as they have always been.

Media and information literacy skills are critical contemporary skills to enable the 21st century citizen to effectively and efficaciously function in the information glut economy. This chapter explores what MIL is, outlining the relationship between media literacy and information literacy. The chapter builds a case for adoption of MIL by organizations, educators, and information practitioners. Significance of MIL against the backdrop of media convergence is interrogated. Various ways in which MIL can be integrated into the curriculum and necessary competencies required

Foreword

Exploring the Relationship Between Media, Libraries, and Archives is a collection of multidisciplinary essays by young and established scholars, exploring various aspects of the interface between information technologies, libraries and its often undervalued sister facility, archives, to function as open memory, as well as memorial, to the communities that it serves. The book begins, in the opening chapter by O. G. Omiunu, with a discussion of the challenges of embracing open access model for quality scientific outputs, both in terms of provenance and implications for research property ownership. This is a critical paper to begin this very interdisciplinary monograph, as capacity to control information dissemination also means loss of property right – the bane of African indigenous knowledge systems.

The second chapter by Arnold Mwanzu explores the creative possible solutions of resource sharing, through library consortia, linking libraries, archives and media organizations. The chapter gives an insight on the development of library consortia and their significance as opportunities for providing equal access, especially in an African environment of resource scarcity and inadequate attention to the development of libraries as repositories of knowledge and as avenues for research for development.

Chapter 3 examines the curation, digitization and use of research efforts of young scholars, in the form of dissertations in India. This effort, by Rupak Chakravarty, is very timely, as it shows how much value the proper storage, curation and accessibility of research by fresh, young and dynamic researchers can contribute to national and global development.

Chapter 4, by Tshepho Mosweu and Mpho Ngoepe, examines how the global liberalization of information communications technology has led to the fluidity of information on Botswana public sector, due to the deliberate government embrace of e-government. The challenge, however, remains, as the chapter points out, that there are no guidelines for managing such unbridled liquid communications, which could, inadvertently lead to memory loss.

Chapter 5 undertakes an exploration of how postmodernism has advocated the use of archival science to challenge the dominant narrative discourse by including the voices of the minority, the marginalised, the ordinary people in the efforts of National Archives of Zimbabwe and Botswana respectively. Lazarus Sauti utilizes insights from practitioner and researcher perspectives to advert our attention to the easy to forget dangers of failure to proactively influence the narratives that matter to people, their cultures and their futures.

Chapter 6, by Walter Luvungu and Purity Kavuri Mutuku, examines the prospects of Library and Information Science and Media Training in the era of globalization. It provides library and media practitioners, particularly their trainers, with some insight into the prospects and the place of LIS and media in the coming years by attempting to define roles and processes that they may play for them to remain relevant as they have always been.

Chapter 7, by Darlington Musemburi and Collen Nhendo, deals media information literacy, with a view to building a case for adoption of MIL by organisations, educators and information practitioners by suggesting various ways in which MIL can be integrated into the curriculum and necessary competencies required to deliver MIL by teachers and librarians are explored.

Chapter 8 presents a snapshot of the challenges and opportunities faced by selected school libraries in Zimbabwe. The major observation by Sindiso Bhebhe in this clearly insightful essay, is that the school's library system in Zimbabwe, including rural schools, is plagued by a plethora of challenges ranging from neglect in relation to funding and policy issues, with negative consequences relating to manpower and resource availability to spark the curiosity to learn and harness knowledge at the early stages in the life of Zimbabwean youth.

Chapter 9, by Sindiso Bhebhe and Tshepho Lydia Mosweu, presents a very insightful and deep exploration of how postmodernism has advocated the use of archival science to challenge the dominant narrative discourse by including the voices of the minority, the marginalised, the ordinary people in the efforts of National Archives of Zimbabwe and Botswana, respectively.

In the final chapter, Floribert Edong examines the curation, digitization and use of research efforts of young scholars, in the form of dissertations in India, while chapter nine discusses the efforts to document the social and cultural history of Nigeria, through the cinema, examining the controversy over the nature of film as a historical document. It goes further to explore the issue of historical film making in Nollywood and ends with a reading of Biyi Bandele's *Half of a Yellow Sun* and Kunle Afolayan's *October 1* as forms of historical films.

The editor of this monograph, Collence Chisita, has brought to the intellectual domain an auspicious volume, and in the process, he has been a catalyst for the better utilization and appreciation of the critical relationships between medial, libraries and archives in Africa.

John Ayotunde
University of the West Indies – Mona, Jamaica

Isola Bewaji
University of the West Indies – Mona, Jamaica

Preface

The dawn of the new millennium in the 21st century has positively and negatively disrupted the free-flow of information, preservation and conservation; largely due to the advent of digitalisation and proliferation of digital media technologies which have revolutionalised the way messages are transmitted as well as breaking the traditional monopolisation of information by fully fledged and well-established institutions. It is against this realisation, that the Editors of this volume initiated the need to come out with a compilation pertaining the nexus between, the media, library and archives – a 'holy trinity' whose presence makes it possible to originate, process, discover, retrieve, share, preserve the nexus of libraries, media and archives encapsulate the life-cycle of record from birth, use, and disposal or archiving.

In 1992, UNESCO (n.d.) established the Memory of the World initiative aimed at creating deep and wider access and awareness to the 'parlous state of preservation of, and access to, documentary heritage in various parts of the world.'

It was through this global realisation felt at the level of UNESCO that as Editors we felt the glaring gap of the reluctance in Africa for the need to keep alive the dream of conservation, preservation and access of information heritage in as much as scholarship in that area is concerned. Realising the dearth of scholarship in that regard and the niche gap of establishing the correlation of media, libraries and archives, the two of us combined our talents, and experiences hailing from the critical sectors of the media, libraries and archives to come out with this inexhaustible title.

Media, Libraries, and Archives seeks to create the missing link between the three critically interrelated disciplines by exposing the hidden truth that the media is the first draft of history which needs adequate libraries and archives for preservation and conservancy of information for the umpteenth time. The exciting dimension of the theme is that it seeks to undertake a holistic and multi-disciplinary approach of correlating media, archives and libraries whose common denominator is that the trinity are all sources of accessing, storing and restoring information.

This text shall be critical in the contribution of knowledge as it draws insights, experiences as well scholarship from across the globe transcending states such as Nigeria, Botswana, Zimbabwe, India, Kenya and South Africa among others. The relevance of the media, libraries and archives in the 21st Century will depend on their ability to provide a balanced epistemic experience for users. National development is impossible without prioritising indigenous knowledge and clothing citizens with new mental costumes to achieve epistemic justice for inclusive development.

It is becoming imperative for media practitioners, librarians and archivists to rethink, reinvent and re-profile their services to meet the dynamic needs of users. In this contemporary epoch of intelligence present there is an opportunity to innovate, reinvent and re-profile in order to effectively disseminate research and scholarly communication as well as keeping abreast of current technological development in ICTs. The survival of media, libraries and archives consortia is hinged upon renewal and reinvention through innovation and creativity and collaboration. It is through these insights that this volume has successfully come out well.

In this volume, one author, Omiunu, provides insights on the open access model for quality scientific outputs in a quasi-linear information society, postulating that publishing costs are a conduit for the creation of burden for authors and proffers collaboration for the maintenance of the information society to enhance open access initiatives especially in developing societies.

True to Omiunu's realisation, often talent of authorship and scholarship has fallen prey to predatory publishers and publishing mills who on a daily basis dupe authors and rob them of their talent. Mwanzu takes the debate further through discussing the role played by library consortia in resource sharing among libraries, media organisations and archives through outlining the existing models that are effectively functioning especially in the developing countries, unearthing the political-economic dynamics that largely impinge on the viability of the consortium.

Because of the diversified nature of the volume, Chakravarty brings in a different but related dimension through the unpacking of the status of electronic thesis and dissertations (ETD) in India, openly claiming that the INFLIBNET (INFormation LIBrary NEtwork) has gradually emerged as the backbone of the higher education sector of India. The remarkable initiatives taken by the INFLIBNET strive for strengthening and supporting information needs of the students, scholars, teachers, scientists and peers. This is done by a way of highlighting the salient features, significance, the implications of the Shodhganga and also discusses Shodhgangotri, a database consisting of approved research proposal submitted by the research scholars. The ETD culture in India provides lessons for those still developing effective or sound systems for the management of scholarly content.

Mosweu and Ngoepe critically unpack the governance of liquid communications in the Botswana public sector, arguing that because liquid communication can be shared and re-tweeted many times beyond the control of the creating agency, resulting in challenges regarding its management. A veteran journalist, Lazarus Sauti also shares his insights pertaining the media as a threat and subordinate of cultural heritage in Zimbabwe, claiming that the Media use of internet permit cultural heritage of different groups to be uploaded, downloaded and accessed by other people around the world, presenting opportunities for cultural exchange whilst at the same time threatening the same.

Indeed these reflections are appealing given the proliferation of internet usage through other digital devices such as cell phones. Social media platforms have successfully managed to converge and diverge cultures at one goal in a split of a second across the globe.

This realisation is worth furthering through interrogating the future of LIS and Media Training in the Global Era, an avenue Musimbi and Matuku explored very well through outlining the challenges and prospects LIS and Media Training. The duo argues that technological advancement has had both negative and positive implications of LIS and Media training but also provides trainers with some insight into the future prospects and the place of LIS and media in the coming years by attempting to define roles and processes that are critical if they are to remain relevant. Musemburi and Nhendo drive the argument further, charging that Media and Information Literacy skills are critical contemporary skills to enable the 21st century citizen to effectively and efficaciously function in the information glut economy. Bhebhe takes a Snapshot of the status-quo of the selected Zimbabwe's school libraries through discussing the challenges and opportunities faced by the selected school libraries in Zimbabwe. The line of argument is based on the observation that the school's library system in Zimbabwe including rural schools is plagued by a plethora of challenges ranging from neglect in relation to funding and policy issues. The authors bring into perspective the idea that the school library plays a critical role in the teaching and learning experiences. They view the school library as an entity central to the learning activities within the aegis of the school environment. The article also reflects the value of the school library in promoting or championing radical independent learning (heutagorgy) through its innovative role as a Socratic mid-wifely status in bridging the gap between luminosity and dimness

In addition, Bhebhe and Mosweu carries the debate further, indulging in a comparison study of oral history programmes at National Archives of Zimbabwe and Botswana through the application of the postmodernism approach to oral history. The pair interrogates how the postmodernism school of thought cutting across many disciplines has also touched the archival science. Endong brings in a related humanistic perspective and exciting dimension of documenting Nigeria's Social and Cultural History through Cinema, claiming that cinema has emerged as an alternative technology to document reality. This could be seen in the fact that, both fictional and non-fictional films are increasingly deployed to chronicle various aspects of history.

From the reflections submitted above, it is clear that the future of the world shall be hinged on the critical role played by the trichotomous linkage between the media, libraries and archives in championing creativity and innovation (creagement) with regards to generation, processing, provision and preservation of scholarly communication. Such progressive and proactive activities shall be indispensible to sustain the information needs of students, educators and researchers as well as support evidence based decision making in the public and private sector from across the world.

Collence Takaingenhgamo Chisita
Harare Polytechnic, Zimbabwe

Alexander M. Rusero
Harare Polytechnic, Zimbabwe

May 2018

REFERENCES

UNESCO. (n.d.). *Memory of the world.* Retrieved from https://en.unesco.org/programme/mow

Acknowledgment

The deep and wide coverage of articles covered in this book could not have been possible without the contributions from educators and PR actioners from different parts of the world. Contributors were drawn from Zimbabwe, South Africa, New Zealand, Australia, India, Italy, Kenya, Nigeria, South Africa and Botswana. My warmest regards goes to the authors and reviewers drawn as far as the United States of America who helped to bring ideas into reality. The team of excellent reviewers included Grace Msauki (Zimbabwe Economic Policy Analysis and Research Unit, ZIPARU), Thembani Malapela (Italy), Dr. Rupak Chakravarty (India), Dr. Tapiwa Gomo (North East Africa), Dr. Nkem Osuigwe (Nigeria), Joseline Chigwada (Zimbabwe), Darlington Musemburi (Zimbabwe), Dr. Bhojaraju Gunjal (India), Dr. Shri Ram (India), Blessing Chiparausha (Zimbabwe), Dr. Stewart Sutherland (Canberra, Australia), Professor Tunde Baweji (University of West Indies), MacDonald Nhakura (Zimbabwe), Munyaradzi Shoko (Zimbabwe), and Collete Mak (United States of America). This spirit, drive and positive energy to give an invaluable gift like knowledge and expertise is greatly appreciated by the editors since it is a great contribution to a better world. The idea of putting together this book was a result of interdisciplinary, intercultural and intergenerational dialogue that did spun over a year. The wide array of articles give credence to collaborative workmanship among the academia, it is a clear testimony that there is immense potential that can be realised when people from m different cultural and professional backgrounds work together to share the best of human experiences. Furthermore the articles are a confirmation of the validity and authenticity of the great African Proverb that "knowledge is like a baobab tree, no one person can embrace it with both arms".

I would also like to thank Dr. Engineer Mudondo from Harare Polytechnic for his strong support and boundless enthusiasm for the development of scholarly artefacts to support teaching, learning and research.

I dedicate this book to all those key contributors to the knowledge industry, namely, the librarians and archivists both educators and practitioners and media experts who took their time to meticulously explore the interface between memory workers and institutions. Contibutors brought in interesting and though provoking insights on the library, archives and media nexus. I also dedicate the book to students in the media, library and information science and related disciplines. My thanks also goes to main and co-authors of jointly written articles not only for contributing to the book but also for your predilection to share with others such priceless experiences. Our editorial team is highly grateful for comments and contributions received from our esteemed reviewers from all parts of the globe, Africa, India and United States. Your contributions in the form of comments, criticism and suggestions added value to the scholarly content. All the authors who contributed book, the editorial team would like to thank you for your corporation which reflects a high level of communication in the true spirit of tsunagaru.

Lastly, let me thank Alexander Madanha Rusero for bringing this idea into culmination and Jordan Tepper for the animated responses to our ideas.

Chapter 1
An Open Access Model for Quality Scientific Outputs in a Quasi-Linear Information Society:
A Pareto Optimality Approach

Ojinga Gideon Omiunu
University of Ibadan, Nigeria

ABSTRACT

The study provided an open access model for quality scientific outputs in a quasi-linear information society: a pareto optimality approach. The qualitative research method was used and involved a three-stage sampling technique to select participants. The findings of the study revealed that respondents were of the opinion that paying APC or publishing costs constitute burden for authors and that the publishers should have other ways of making profits in business such as library subscription, among others. Thus, all stakeholders should collaborate and be involved in the maintenance of the information society to enhance open access initiatives, especially in developing countries.

DOI: 10.4018/978-1-5225-5840-8.ch001

INTRODUCTION

The deployment of an appropriate model for information dissemination and use to ensure information produced are easily and freely accessed by potential users has attracted much debate among information professionals, scholars and stakeholders. Ogunmodede, Apata and Nwokeoma (2017) noted that access to and utilization of information such as research publications is vital for modern development. According to Olurode (2017), there is a dire need in recent times for the call for the use and application of research findings and publication to enhance development and reduce human sufferings especially in developing countries such as Nigeria. Different models have been introduced and deployed by various information producers/users such as Arthur-Fee for publication- where author pay for publications and users obtain easy and free access to published articles; and/or user-fee for access- where authors do not pay for publication but such information are provided for users at a particular fee, thereby restricting users' access; among others.

Even within the open access model, there are different types of sub models: "gold, green, and hybrid models". A gold journal is an open access journal which makes published contents available for free on the publisher's website for readers/ users. In this type of journal, there is a delayed open access, where articles become free for readers on the publisher's website after some time (usually 12 months) after initial publication (Kieńć, 2015). A green journal is a journal which publishes non-free content, but allows its authors to republish their articles in open access repositories. Thus, while such article on the publisher's website is pay-walled, the author can place the same text somewhere on the Internet using avenues such as Google scholar, Academia, Research Gate, or on a blog, among others. The Hybrid journals are generally pay walled and offer the possibility for authors to open individual articles by paying an extra fee otherwise their articles would be placed on subscription before user can access them. Despite all these models, there seem to be dilapidating bridges between publishers and authors, publishers and users, etc. thus, the need for efficient model as provided by this study to fill these bridges.

These models and sub models have attracted debates in the information industry (Hall, 2008; Suber, 2012) especially in developing economies where poverty is very high and the market system for such information industry is distorted and affected by so many factors such as poverty, inflation, unemployment, illiteracy, lack of a knowledge based society, among others. Since the major objective for publishing research findings and information is to ensure that such findings are effectively and easily accessed and used by potential users, it is expedient that users are given access to such works. This has given birth to the use of open access models to achieve an efficient information society nevertheless some publishers do use other models to ensure their continuity in the industry. According to Hall (2008), open access offers solution to many of the problems currently confronting scholars as a result of the decline in state funding for higher education and increasingly market-and profit-driven nature of the academic publishing industry. The possibility of making research findings and publications open access and available at very low or no cost to the public on a global scale have been hotly debated within scientific, technical and medical circles (Hall, 2008). Peterson, Emmett & Greenberg (2013) have stated that communication of research findings is the life blood of the academic society. In other words, it can be reaffirmed that dissemination of research findings and scholarly works is the life blood of the information society which include tertiary institutions.

Open access, open archives and its affect on research findings and information accessibility have attracted the attention of stakeholders such as the authors, publishers, government, organizations and other bodies. Therefore, from global perspective, governments have canvassed for the right to knowledge and information (Hall, 2008). Also, many universities have also provided opportunities for their academic staff to publish their research electronically via local repositories and to access other stores held by institutions participating in open archives initiative (OAL) and the scholarly publishing and academic resources coalition (SPARC) thus, by pass commercial publishers of increasingly expensive journals (Hall, 2008). However, Nwagwu (2013) noted that with the increase in awareness, efforts and initiatives of open access by governments and stakeholders in developed countries, those in developing countries do not understand the concept of open access issue very well. This has challenged the opportunity to provide a common and unified open access model that could be deployed and used to enhance and ensure efficient distribution of information redistribution and use. This has led to poor access to published papers and information especially in developing countries such as Nigeria (Nwagwu, 2013) and also where open access is to be displayed, poor quality of publications are provided for accessibility (Omiunu, 2014). This in the long run has thwarted the major objectives and activities of open access initiative. According to Nwagwu (2013), many journal publishers operating open access model consist of unknown people who may be inexperience in the field of the articles they claim to publish and have poor editorial quality of published papers, despite that they collect money from authors such as the author fees or article processing charge. These journal publishers are known as predatory publishers and the journals known as predatory journals.

Many of the predatory publishers are corrupt and exist only to make money from the author processing charges that are billed to authors upon acceptance of their scientific manuscripts (Lambers, 2014). In addition, Kearney (2015) and Xia, Harmon, Connolly, Donnelly, Anderson and Howard (2014) stated that scholars from developing countries are said to be victims of predatory journal publishers. The poor editorial quality and other menace of predatory journals make Beall to continuously provide updated lists. According to "Beall's List" (2015), there are 914 predatory publishers. The impetus of this could only be felt when one considers their impact on the academia in the next few years because most of these findings would lead many scientists and researchers astray, due to poor quality and falsification of research results. Also, because of the free access, students and faculty members, these predatory journal articles are mostly used in the academic environment. It is not a gainsaying to affirm that most of the academic projects, dissertations and theses are all full of predatory journal articles. This could affect development as provided by Mohammed (2011) and also affect the use of existing quality journals and thus liquidate the journal publishing industry and thus lead to increase proliferation of more predatory journals if not curtailed. In addition, this could affect and threaten the existence of libraries in the academic environment whose sole objective is to ensure that users have access to quality information resources and sources.

A major challenge that brought out these predatory journals is the high cost of publishing with high quality journals such as Elsevier, Sage, ScienceDirect, among others. For example, as at the time of this study, the 5th publisher request for an article processing cost (APC) of $1200.00 CAD and eligible author can apply for some discount; Academic Knowledge and Research Publishing request for article processing cost (APC) of $200 US dollars for publication fee for each manuscript; Academic Research Publishing Group charges between $50 - $100 per articles depending on the journal an author is submitting to; academy journals charges an APC of $200 per article; Management and Administrative Sciences Review charges APC of $100 and $200; the International Review of Management and Business Research (IRMBR) charges APC of $200 and $300 for both (Online and Print) version; among others. To authors who are from developing countries, these cost are too high, and to circumvent these high cost, authors send articles to and published in predatory journals due to their low cost. Another important reason is that the expectations of high quality journals are high and most often, authors from developing countries may not meet up with the publishing standards and ethics thus to make sure they contribute their quota in the information and research industry, they publish articles in predatory journals. It has been affirmed that institutions/faculties/departments and other stakeholders can contribute to a better information society *(Elsevier.com, 2015)*.

Although, Kieńć (2015) noted that institutions of authors can assist in the provision of funding to reduce the burden of the high publishing cost on authors where need be however, high quality journals can thus provide policy that could help inculcate authors from developing countries into the system. In addition, it deems fit to state that, most often, it is as if high quality journals favour authors with high reputation while those with no or low reputation are not welcomed. To this end, these sets of authors, instead of been discouraged out of the information and research community tend to publish with predatory journals or other journals that could accommodate them into the system. To this end, Harnad et al. (2004) affirmed that most of the journal are not affordable to users and institutions and that this is a further problem: as a consequence of the fact that most of their would-be users at most universities cannot access most of the 2.5 million articles published yearly (because their universities cannot afford the journal access-tolls), a significant portion of the potential research impact of those inaccessible articles is being lost.

An article's research impact is the degree to which its findings are read, used, applied, built-upon and cited by researchers in their own further research and applications. Research impact is a measure of the progress and productivity of research. That is the reason why researchers' careers (their salaries, promotions, tenure, funding, prestige, prizes) depend on their impact; it is also why their universities (which co-benefit from the research funding, progress and prestige) as well as their research funding agencies (which are answerable for the way they spend tax-payers' money) reward research impact (Harnad et al., 2004). However, this is not been practiced in developing countries such as Nigeria. Research impact is measured in number of articles published and this has also given room for the wide acceptance of predatory journal publishing and articles.

Suffice it to note that majority or these institutions hosts most of the authors of these articles they are subscribing for. Therefore, it is very important to come to a consensus where they contribute to the publication of the articles with authors and have free access to the published contents or they are exempted but will pay for access to such published articles. For example, some publishers such as Elsevier would obtain a publication fee for articles to be in open access else it will be placed on subscription where access and use will be restricted thus, such articles do not meet pareto optimality in the information society. In the long run, such articles may end up not been used or reused at all before they are discarded. In addition, academics, scholars, institutions, publishers, and libraries, among others have the commitment to value quality of research, accompany with it the responsibility to extend the circulation and disseminating of such works as far as possible, and ideally to all who are, or may be interested in it and all who might profit by it (Willinsky, 2006), thus the need for collaboration and thus pareto optimality approach to ensure publication and use of quality researches and studies, quality journals, and quality journal articles within the information society.

A major Gap in Willinsky (2006) and other authors such as Hall (2008) and Kieńć (2015) that this study seeks to fill, is that they never show how this collaboration could be possible. It is one thing to embark on and be a part of a research either through the donation of fund, or as a co-author, or to contribute to the success of the article, it is another thing to be able to have access to such article when published. Hall (2008) maintained that, there is a major concern as to whether open access business model can be sustained especially with regards to standard of ''quality''.

However, to some, open access is seen as a means of democratizing knowledge and research finding by making not just journal, books, and databases but also the computing technologies such as internet, that are required to develop and support them, to make them available to individuals who cannot afford to invest in such resources- this is what I termed pareto optimality in this study.

The fundamental principles backing pareto optimality is hinged upon welfare economics (welfarism) and is divided into two parts. First, if every relevant good such as information is traded in a market, at a publicly known price and if households (which in this context are users community such as institutions, students, faculties, departments, among others) and firms (which in this context are information producers such as publishers of journal articles, libraries, institutions, among others) are perfectly competitive (in this case, users and publishers contribute to the premium (worth of the information), then such market outcome is pareto optimal. However, if either the firm (producers of information) or the users of information only determine the premium and worth of such information, there is an imperfect market and such market cannot be pareto optimality. This is why the publishing of journal articles should adopt the supply and demand approaches to best achieve pareto optimality in the information society especially for research publications.

Second, if households (users) preferences and firms (producers) production set are convex (that is are different), there is a complete set of markets with publicly known price where prices of information are stochastic, because every agent acts as a price taker and decision maker, then such market does not operate at pareto optimality. However, to obtain pareto optimality in such market, appropriate lump-sum of wealth/resources which include money, technology and information resources are transferred and re-distributed evenly. These transfer and re-distribution are mostly directed towards those who may not have the resources to partake in the information society in such market system such as users and authors in the information market especially in the developing economies.

Pareto optimality uses society's initial resources and technological possibilities efficiently (especially in the advent and increasing use of technologies such as the laptops, i-pads, smartphones, internets, among others) in that there is no alternative way to organize the production and distribution of information that makes other users better off without making other users worse off (Mas-Colell, Whinston and Green, 1995). Pareto optimality does at the very least say that there is no waste in resource distribution and use and that resource distribution and use are not skewed to favoring some users than other users – it provides an equilibrium market in the distribution and use of commodity such as information achieving an efficient information society. Thus, the justification of the deployment of the pareto optimality model through a qualitative study to provide a model to enhance open access for journal publishers with emphasis on predatory journal publishers towards enhancing quality journals and journal articles in the information society.

A QUASI LINEAR INFORMATION SOCIETY

Bringing in the concept of quasi-linear information society, users' preferences of information are quasi-linear when the boundaries of the information utility of the various sets of information provided and available are linear, and all points at these boundaries are associated with the information that are made available for a particular user and differ from those of other users or group of users due to the distribution of other information which could either be a substitute or complementary information product to such information. *Information utility,* in the context of information science refers to the satisfaction obtained by a user in meeting his/her information needs in the use of information. This implies that the satisfaction obtained in using particular information by users differ among them thus taking a stochastic form because it changes from one user to another. The word 'stochastic' implies that such utility varies from one individual to another and that it is not constant.

According to Mas-Colell et al (1995), the *quasi linear society* is one which the agents have quasi-linear preferences. In this, a user utility function takes a quasi-linear form:

$$U_i(x, \theta_i) = V_i (K \theta_i) + (m_i + t_i)$$

where U_i is the consumers' utility function of x commodities (this time information).

$Xi \subset R^L$ - Implies the consumption sets of commodities given the constraints posed by the environment on consumers.

$$Xi = R_+^L = \{ X \subset R^L: Xi \geq O \text{ for } L = 1......n\}$$

$\theta_i (x)$ = consumers utility from a public good such as information/published articles.

Note that in public good, x does not have an i subscript like private goods. This is because the consumption of the public good at any point and time by one consumer does not affect the availability to and the consumption of such good by another consumer or to be more accurate consumer of information.

m_i - refers to as agent I's endowment to the numerae (resource such as money, technology, etc).

However, in public goods such as information, m_i is been normalized to = '0' for all 'I'- with the assumption that the i-agents have no outside source of finance.

This could imply donors, sponsors, etc. of research and research activities and sometimes authors because most researches and their activities are self sponsored except for a very few.

t_i *- refers to the transfer of numerae (money, etc) from author, institutions, among others.*

In addition, R_+^L *is the consumption set of consumers of L goods (which could be knowledge, information and information resources).*

The vector $x = (k, t_{1,} \ldots\ldots, t_i)$ *where k is an element of a finite set K and* $t_i R$ *is a transfer of a numeric commodity ("money") to agent i.*

So the agent i's utility function takes the quasi-linear form. Also, both m_i *and* t_i *are done to ensure pareto optimality in the information society.*

Also, $W_L \geq 0$ *and*

$$Y_j \subset R^L - Yj = Y_{ij} \ldots\ldots\ldots Y_{nj}$$

$Yj \subset R^L$ *is the set of all production vectors that constitute feasibility plans for the firm and is known as the production set. So I will say that* $Yj \subset R^L$ *are the production set of the information producers in the information society. Each firm J (publisher) is characterized by a technology and/or production set* $Yj \subset R^L$*.*

Furthermore, W_L *is the endowment of the producer (information producer) and must be greater than zero for such producer to be able to finance the publishing activities.*

Thus, there should be a collaboration of all these resources (from the stakeholders of information society) to enhance the distribution/dissemination and use of research articles.

THEORETICAL UNDERPINNING

The study adapted the Pareto Optimality or efficiency model of Mas-Colell et al (1995). Using substitution and elimination method, concepts of 'information' and 'information use' are substituted for the concepts used by Mas-Colell et al (1995), thus eliminating previous concepts. Therefore, considering an information economy consisting of *'i'* potential users *(i = 1, 2, 3, … n)* and *j* producers of information *(j = 1,2,3, … n)* and *L* information commodities *(L = 1, 2, 3…n)*, a potential user would make his/her preferences through rigorous and meticulous search (Omiunu, 2014) to meet his/her information needs. Considering the high elasticity of information available on the internet brought about by the ICT in the information industry, the high level of stochasticity in searching for information and users' preferences (usually in either the free access or restricted access) of $X_i s$ $(x_1, x_2, x_3, \ldots x_n)$, the users sets, $X_i \subset R^L$ would be presented by the utility function U_i.

From Mas-Colell et al (1995), $X_i \subset R^L$ are the consumption bundles an individual user can conceivably use given the physical constraints imposed on his/her environment.

Use of information set is given by:

$$X_i = R^L_+ = \{X \varepsilon\ R^L_+ : x_i \geq 0 \text{ for } L = 1, \ldots, n\}$$

R^L are the consumption set of information by a user given the constraints faced by such user.

One special feature of the set R^L_+ is that it is convex. The concept "convex" means that in the set of R^L, let's say it contains two vectors X and X^1, it also contains the entire segment connecting them. In addition, the use of the information set by one user does not affect its use by other users.

Also, $X_i \subset R^L$ represents the utility function of the users bundle $x_i (x_1, x_2, \ldots . x_n)$, and the total amount of each information commodity initially available in the information society producing firm is denoted by $w_L \geq 0$ *for* $L = 1, \ldots, n$ (Figure 1). It is also possible that the use of production technology by a firm can transform the initial information level into more information through use and re-use. Each firm which comprised of publishers, libraries, institutions among others has the production possibilities given as $Y_j \subset R^L$ *for* $Y_j = Y_{1j}, Y_{2j}, \ldots . Y_{nj,}$ which includes industries *1,…, n*. This will increase the total amount of information available in the information society due to use and re-use thus achieving information explosion as we have in recent time. At this period, producers must be careful especially in the information economy because of the high rate of increase in information output due to research and development and the deployment and use of the internet and web 2.0 and other technologies otherwise most information produced would not contribute to the development of the society educational sector and the economy.

RESEARCH METHODOLOGY

The study adopted a qualitative research method and respondents of this study were individuals from higher institutions and organization which include private organization in Nigeria. A three-stage sampling technique was used. The first involves a purposive selection of Oyo State from the 36 states in Nigeria due to the convenience in obtaining data and information from the respondents. Second, it involves a random selection of three institutions (names withheld due to security reasons). Also, one research institute and two organisations were purposively selected for the study. In addition, a convenient sampling technique was used to select participants for the study: fifteen from the higher institutions; two from a federal organisation and three from two other organisations in Nigeria all based in Oyo State, Nigeria. This gives a total of twenty respondents used for this study.

An interview guide was used to collect information from the selected respondents. However, before slated for an interview, the aim of the study was made known to the potential respondents and an inform consent was obtained from each respondent after which the interview process was conducted. It was interesting to note that the respondents appreciated the study that they were willing to be part of it. The responses from the interview processes were recorded and transcribed and information obtained and transcribed were arranged into themes whence analysis was made. The transcribed interview is provided in the appendix. The thematic process was adopted to analyse information obtained from the respondents with respect to the objective of the study and discussion were provided.

RESULTS AND DISCUSSION OF FINDINGS

The findings of the study revealed that most respondents do not agree to the APC system for articles to be published by publishers. From the responses (Table 1 in the Appendix), one can affirm that authors do not agree to the payment of APC or publishing cost in either small or big amount. However, in some cases, where such cannot be avoided, lecturers in either universities or other institutions of learning stated that it would be an encouragement for them if their institutions/faculties/ departments and the publishers assist in the contribution to such author fees to making dissemination of scholarly works free and of high quality. Although, they did not provide a detail and percentage of the contribution from these stakeholders, however, they would appreciate their contribution. The findings of this study support the work of Mas-Colell, Whinston and Green (1995) that to achieve pareto optimality, society's (which include publishers, authors, institutions, organization, governments, among others) initial resources and technological possibilities are efficiently used (especially in the advent and increasing use of technologies such as the laptops, i-pads, smartphones, internets, among others) in the sense that there is no alternative way to organize the production and distribution of information that make some users better off without making other users worse off. Thus, every member is involved and every member enjoys the benefits.

Also, findings of this study revealed that publishers should not see publishing articles for authors as a means of business, but they should see it as a means to contribute to the achievement of better information society. This would help eliminate the errors and jargons been published by publishers in the information society. This supports the findings of Nwagwu (2013), Omiunu (2014) and Beall's (2015) that some journals publishers publish poor editorial quality articles or papers. In addition, this sustains the findings of Nwagwu (2013) that majority of stakeholders in the information society have tend to take lightly the issue of open access and thus undercut the activities of agencies to initiate a unified open access model to enhance and ensure efficient distribution (which in this paper is referred to as pareto optimality) of information redistribution and use and have led to poor quality of and poor access to published papers and information especially in developing countries thus, the inability to achieve an efficient information society. The findings of this study also boost the work of Omiunu (2014) that most of these published papers online are of low quality and have many errors which includes grammatical errors, poor use of research terminologies and data analysis methods, among others. Furthermore, the findings of this study bolster the work of Clark and Phillips (2014) that a publisher must be involved in the use of resource which could include money, time, energy, among others in the publishing process. This means that a publisher also have some level of risk to incur in the business of publishing. In addition, the findings of this study reinforce those of Mas-Colell et al. (1995) that it deem fit to bring in, the resource endowments of producers (this time publishers) and those belonging to the other groups in the production chain such as the institutions, faculties, departments, among others to enhance the success of the information society and open access initiatives.

Howbeit, respondents from private organisations insist that the individuals or authors from higher institutions and other research institutions can afford the publication fees pose on the publication of articles and that it would not be good if the publishers wave the publication cost for them. The reasons for this are that, author gets the honour for publishing and these published works are used to promote them at the long run. In addition, publishers on the other hand use this publication fees to run the costs of their businesses. Thus, the publishers depend on the authors' publication fees to publish their works and run their business while the authors depend on their published papers through the publishers to advance their academic pursuit. The findings of this study reveals that, the bargaining power of the author (s) and the publishers come to play in this case since the market structure of information goods demands the efforts of the stakeholders to be efficient because of its market nature (this may not hold for high quality journals). Furthermore, the worth of the paper or article such author wants to publish is also important. Some papers may be so valuable that it may increase the impact factor of the journal, such papers should not be handled carelessly except otherwise. In some occasions, authors from less developed countries may be treated with preference to reduce or eliminate the payment of publication costs thus leading to free publication of article. In this way, all the stakeholders can unite together to create a better information society at the global, nation and/or local level.

Putting these together, it could be affirmed that at least authors in higher institutions of learning should be involved in the payment of publication fee because they also earn a honor from such published articles. From the result, few respondents accepted the APC posed by journals on authors. It was revealed that when one pays APC to high quality journals, it does three things to ones career. One, they help to rate ones work so that such individual has higher value of recognition and chances for career development and promotion. Two, they open one to a wide range of stakeholders that would advertise and make such person well known. Third, one is also paying to get global attention because in most occasions, when people see that a certain paper is published with these high quality journals, it attracts their attention to the author. This could cover for the cost of APC when paid to such high quality journals especially the five, four, and three star journals. In addition, institutions, faculties, departments, and other stakeholders should be involved for three reasons. First, they host the author and this also would either bring honour or shame to the institution, faculty and department. Second, their contribution would enhance a better information society. Third, there is need to motivate scholarly potentials in the academic sector which have the slogan, "Publish or perish". Thus, the need for the pareto optimality model for an efficient information society.

CONCLUSION AND RECOMMENDATIONS

In conclusion, the justification for the use of pareto-optimality model to ensure information dissemination and use is based on the fact that all stakeholders of information society should jointly contribute towards attaining efficient information society. In addition, both author(s) and institution of authors take glory when authors work(s) is/are used. Publishers are also commended if a published paper is good and if such papers have errors, such may taint the image of the publishers- this is why articles in journals are subjected to a peer review. This is why Beall (2010) provide the list of predatory journals. To this end, to ensure users' free access to such information, all stakeholders in the information economy should shoulder the responsibilities of information production, distribution and use. Thus, the diagram below could best explain the proposed model.

From the resource collaboration model for effective production and use of quality research output, various stakeholders ensure that articles to be published are done in quality journals based on policies and standards of the said institution before resources are provided for collaboration. After articles are been published in journals, it is then sent to the various stakeholders such as to the authors and the libraries of institutions, faculties and departments. In addition, authors, publishers and libraries can place those articles on repositories such as websites, databases, among others. Furthermore, institutions should also establish policies that could ensure thc use of quality journals and non-use of poor quality journals. Moreover, users can now access such quality journals via the libraries, authors and publishers websites and repositories, among others. Furthermore, users could also access those articles through the authors where need be without accessing their websites which occur in some cases where potential users may ask for such articles be sent through email for their use.

Thus, it is recommended that a unified global policies, to this end be formulated and introduced into various institutions which would be acceptable to all stakeholders of the information society such as academic and research institutions/organisations and the governing bodies and councils of these various institutions, federal and state government and other stakeholders such as faculties and departments of higher institutions which include universities, polytechnic, colleges of education, among others. This is needed to ensure the collaborative effort to share and re-deploy resources towards the enhancement of a better information society thus enabling an open access and efficient dissemination and utilization of information and/or research articles - thus achieving a pareto optimality in the information Society. In addition, stakeholders from both developed and developing countries would

Figure 1. The Pareto Optimality Model to ensure quality scientific outputs

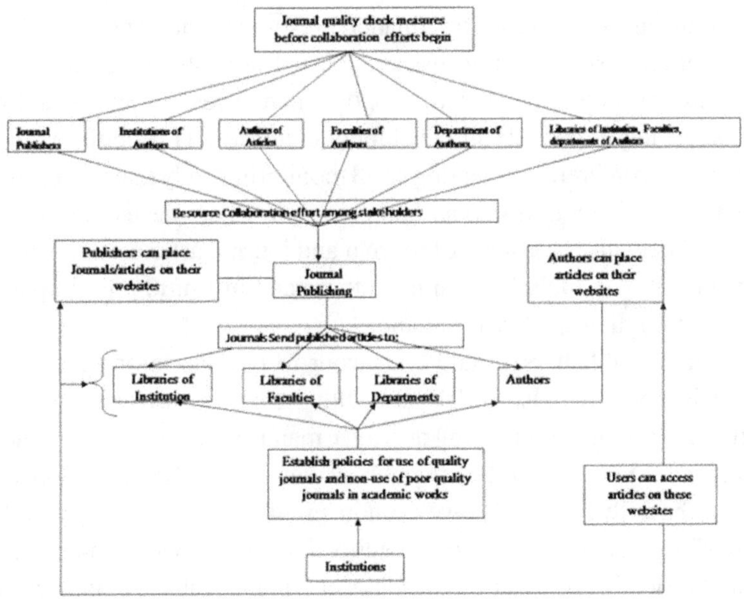

also benefits from these policies. There should also be a standard organization or body that would control quality of journal at the local and global level and every journal publishers must be dully registered and also before registration, this body or organization would have scrutinize published articles of the journals and would continue in the scrutiny from time to time to checkmate deviation from the original quality observed. Also, developing countries should learn from Canada, the United States and UK in the initiative by also introducing bodies at the local, state and regional level to curtail and checkmate poor quality of journal and journal articles and also enhance open access model by deploying the pareto optimality model. This would need the collaborative effort of all the stakeholders in the information society as provided by the pareto optimality model.

Also, journal publishers should support open access journal by providing a realistic APCs to authors and also providing a policy that would allow authors to place their published articles on various repositories either by authors or by institutions of authors. Departments, faculties and institutions of authors are also needed to support open access by providing a realistic policy to assist in author scholarly activities such as research and publishing of articles. It is expedient at this point to draw attention to the need for such policy to be durable and sustainable. Journal publishers should endeavour to provide the needed editorial quality which is part of the peer review policy to author to enhance the quality of journals and journal articles. This would help increase the likelihood for use and subscription by either individuals or institutions. Also, it is important that journal publishers consider deploying the hybrid model in some instances where needed so as to help cover cost of publication. This will help to also cater for authors that have great scholarly contribution but have low financial resources and cannot pay for APC or other publication costs where necessary. Journal publishers can also collaborate by harnessing resources together to support open access initiative and build the information society especially in developing countries. This could be in terms of collaboration for conferences, creating an all monitoring body that will ensure control measures in the information society and prosecute where necessary any offenders that by-pass the quality measures of journal and journal articles at the global level. This punishment may include warning authors and institution not to publish with such journal until their quality is enhanced.

Also, journal publishers should endeavour to provide informative services to authors, institutions, and also collaborate with them to ensure and provide detailed information and training on ensuring quality in manuscript development and how this can be attained. There should be ethical consideration in manuscript development and this must be dully followed however, non-English speaking countries should not be left out of this as they may need an editor for such service. To this end, policy that would be flexible to meet the needs of the non-speaking countries should be considered. This would reduce the editorial review stress and thus enhance quality in the long run. In addition, since excellence and quality of journal is an important phenomenon in the publishing industry, it is expedient for journal publishers to raise standards for and introduce policy which encompass quality.

The sustainability of journal and journal publishers in the publishing industry should be put into consideration by the stakeholders in the industry. To this end, it is expedient that there should be collaboration among stakeholders to harness resources together so as to enhance quality assurance in the system. Moreover, journal publishers should give reasonable APC or publishing charges that would not constitute burden to authors especially those in developing countries due to lack of or limited resources. To this end, consideration should be given to authors from developing countries by reduction or total waver of APC and/or publishing costs for authors from developing countries. Also, The pareto optimality model can also be deployed by high quality journals to enhance open access for published works and institutions of authors can be part in the support for the payment of such APC if such journal publishers is a high quality journal however, this could be deployed differently by different institution because what constitute high quality in one institution may be overlooked by other institutions.

REFERENCES

Beall's List. (2015). Retrieved from http://scholarlyoa.com/publishers/

Elsevier.com. (2015). Retrieved from http://www.elsevier.com

Hall, G. (2008). *Digitize This Book! Digitize This Book! The Politics of New Media, or Why We Need Open Access Now*. Minneapolis, MN: University of Minnesota Press. Retrieved from http://www.academia.edu/11922788/Digitize_This_Book_

Harnad, S., Brody, T., Vallieres, F., Carr, L., Hitchcock, S., Gingras, Y., ... Hilf, E. R. (2004). The Access/Impact Problem and the Green and Gold Roads to Open Access. *Serials Review*, *30*(4), 310–314. doi:10.1080/00987913.2004.10764930

Kearney, M. H. (2015). Predatory Publishing: What Authors Need to Know. *Research in Nursing & Health*, *38*(1), 1–3. doi:10.1002/nur.21640 PMID:25545343

Kieńć, W. (2015). *Green oa-vs-Gold-oa- Which one to choose*. Retrieved from http://openscience.com/green-oa-vs-gold-oa-which-one-to-choose

Lambers, H. (2014). *Why do authors publish in "predatory open access journals"?* Retrieved from http://www.researchgate.net/post/Why_do_authors_publish_in_predatory_open_access_journals

Mas-Colell, A., Whinston, M. D., & Green, J. R. (1995). *Micro Economic Theory*. New York: Oxford University Press, Inc.

Mohammed, M. A. (2011). *Technology and Infrastructural Development: What the Future holds for the Book Industry in Nigeria?* Paper presented at the 9th and 10thNigeria International Book Fair, National Book Fairs and NPA General Meeting.

Nwagwu W.E. (2013). Open Access Initiatives in Africa- Structure, Incentives and Disincentives. *The Journal of Academic Librarianship, 39*, 3-10. doi:10.1016/j.acalib.2012.11.024

Ogunmodede, T. A., Apata, M. E., & Nwokeoma, N. M. (2017). Effect of Information Utilization on Decision-Making by Senior Managers: A Case Study. *International Journal of Library Science, 15*(2). Retrieved from http://www.ceser.in/ceserp/index.php/ijls/article/view/4813

Olurode L. (2017, March 30). Don seeks use of research findings. *The Nigeria Nation Newspaper*.

Omiunu, O. G. (2014). Conceptualizing Information Need: A Phenomenological Study. *Journal of Library and Information Science, 2*(2), 29–54.

Omiunu O.G. (2014). Towards enhancing research qualities in African Universities and sustainable development: A phenomenological study. *International Research of Human and Social Sciences, 1*(4), 100-123.

Peterson, A. T., Emmett, A., & Greenberg, M. I. (2013). Open Access and the Author-Pays Problem: Assuring Access for Readers and Authors in a Global Community of Scholars. *Journal of Librarianship and Scholarly Communication, 1*(3), eP1064. doi:10.7710/2162-3309.1064

Suber, P. (2012). *Open Access*. Massachusetts Institute of Technology. Retrieved from https://mitpress.mit.edu/sites/default/files/9780262517638_Open_Access_PDF_Version.pdf

Willinsky, J. (2006). *The Access Principle: The Case for Open Access to Research and Scholarship*. Cambridge, MA: MIT Press.

Xia, J., Harmon, J. L., Connolly, K. G., Donnelly, R. M., Anderson, M. R., & Howard, H. A. (2014). Who publishes in "predatory" journals?" *Journal of the Association for Information Science and Technology*. doi:10.1002/asi.23265

APPENDIX

Table 1. Responses to the Interview

R.Q: Would you agree with the Article processing Fees for authors pose by journal publishers?	Initial Coding	Focus Coding
"..., how should one pay to publish his/her work, when the publishers have other ways to make profit from the published works. For example, many libraries subscribe to them and pay for access to publications. The only way libraries would not subscribe to them is when their works are of poor quality because no library may want to subscribe to such kind of poor quality journals with poor editorial works and poor research errors. In most occasions, such kind of works are not deployed or used. As for me, I cannot use or site predatory journals in my papers. Moreover, for any journal to be collecting APC from authors, it shows that such journal is not sure of their product and knows that there may be no other way to market or maintain their product other than collecting APC or publication fees from authors. So to such publishers, they know that no library would patronize them"	Not Pay APC; Poor Quality of article	Does not Support APC
"..., when an author agrees to pay APC or whatever it may be called to publish his/her work, it shows that such author is not sure of him/herself and of the work. If you as an author knows that your work is good and that there are no jargons in it and can meet international standard, you won't see the need to publish with such journals asking for such money. Also, as an author, you must have spent some resource to make such paper a success like your effort, money in collecting data (that is if such researcher went to the field at all), time, among others. To me, I think authors who pay APC or publication fees are simply causing more harms in the information society. If you want to sell an idea or a product and you are paying for it, then something is wrong with either you or your product/idea or something is wrong with both you and your product. In addition, I can say maybe such an individual is just getting him or herself into such business or is making way advertise him or herself into the system."	Not in support for APC	Does not Support APC
"..., the high fee placed on the publication of articles is discouraging. For example, some publishers take up to 200 US dollars and when you change this to Nigerian currency, which depends on the cost of dollar to Nigerian currency, you have 40,000 naira at approximately 200 Naira per dollar at present. This is discouraging and can affect the motivation to achieve a better information society. For some publishers, authors pay as much as 500 US dollars and even between 1000- 2000 dollars and even more. Paying 2000 dollars which is equivalent to 400,000 naira at 200 naira per dollar would be a neck breaking scenario. When all the stakeholders in the information society contribute together, this would make publishing less burdensome and published articles free to users thus ensuring better dissemination. The publishers should also see to it that these author fees charges are much and thus contribute also to the information society"	High APC is discouraging to author Stakeholder should collaborate to ease the financial burden of APC on authors	Support APC but should be reduced High APC discourages authors to write
"..., publishers should not see publishing articles for authors as a means of business, but they should contribute to the achievement of better information society. This would eliminate the jargons been published by publishers in the information society"	Support APC High APC is Making journal publishing a business Reduces quality of works	Support APC but should be minimal
"..., observing many published papers on the internet, there are so many errors in them. These papers go international because one major advantage of written works is that they reach far beyond the writer may possibly reach. Also, the publishers fail to understand that these published papers may either sell them or destroy them. To them, publishing journal articles is one of these businesses. Author pay money and they publish the articles and are made available. Some of these journals, with time disappear and are not found again. Thus, making such article useless because even the website of the publishers go into extinction with them"	Support but should be minimal and quality journals	Support APC but minimal with a quality journal
"..., I think there should be room for other authors working in low endowed organizations. If such identities of authors can be traced (because authors may want to hide their identities if they discover that APC for them can be waved), and known by such publishers there should be a place for them in the information society however if their idea and knowledge are good and of high premium to the information society. Also, publishers should note that such authors from less endowed organisations may have less resource to be able to pay such APC of publishing fees. Then, there is room for consensus between such author and the publisher to come to an agreement on how much to pay or whether such payment can be totally waived"	Support APC but should be waived for the less endowed scholars	Support APC but minimal and could be waived
In my own view, I am not really against it, but I think authors from developing countries should be put into consideration for even the high quality journals because most of us use almost our whole salary to publish in trying to meet the demands of job, of publishing and the institutions one is working with. It will be better if considerations is given to authors from developing countries because of the limited resources within our disposal and this will also help us and motivate us to direct some of this resources to self and career development.	Support APC but with consideration to authors from developing countries	Support APC but with consideration to authors from developing countries

continued on following page

Table 1. Continued

R.Q: Would you agree with the Article processing Fees for authors pose by journal publishers?	Initial Coding	Focus Coding
Starting a journal publishing business, like other business is not an easy thing and it needs financial, managerial, organisational, and other capabilities to make it work. We cannot dispute the fact that these publishers need finance to run their businesses and maintain the sites, pay staff (if actually they have), motivate their editorial board (if actually they have), among others. However, life in Nigeria cannot be compared with in developed countries and this has made the APC or Author fee a burden for authors in developing countries. I may have to suggest that it could be better if this APC is reviewed to suit authors from developing countries since we are all working towards the betterment of the information society and knowledge dissemination and use.	Support APC but with consideration to authors from developing countries	Support APC but with consideration to authors from developing countries
I may have to be straight forward here, APC charging on author for manuscript publication has been something that is given us academics concern especially those in developing countries whose institution don't care on how you do about your career. In developed countries, there are supports for authors, lecturers for research and conference grants, etc are also made available. Here in Nigeria, we carry the burden by ourselves. But there is nothing we can actually do to reduce this however, with this kind of study, we believe it can speak for authors from developing countries and also provide strategies that would make our institutions to also provide these social supports for its staff.	Support APC but institutions in developing countries should support their staff	Support APC but institutions in developing countries should support their staff
My own view on these types of journal publishers is really about the quality they publish. When observed, one would see that all they are after is the money obtained or collected from authors. For example, when they tell you to pay that APC and ones you cannot pay it, they refuse to respond to you and your mails again. All they will be emphasising is that you pay the money. The quality of their products is very low and bad as compared to other journals. More importantly, Beall and other organisations have listed many of these predatory journals due to their quality and he even shared his experience with them and they bad quality they produce and that they don't provide editorial quality for journal articles. Also, I believe that most of the authors that published with them do not have the quality papers to meet with the demands of high quality journals however, because they must meet the demand of academics and that they must publish, they just have to publish somewhere. Also, I think that this gave room for these predatory journals in the academics. In addition, often when you visit the websites of these journals publishers, you will hardly find their address or their location, you will likely be unable to trace them. Even in some occasion, one may find that their websites are not available.	Support APC but necessary editorial process should be done to make quality work published.	Support APC but necessary editorial process should be done to make quality work published.
In my own case, my institution doesn't take predatory journals. When you present papers for your promotion, the will reject the papers that are published with predatory journals. They don't accept published papers that are not from top journals such as Elsevier, Sage, Taylor and Francis, among others. However, some predatory journals could be accepted due to the fact that they have passed the test of quality such as include those published by institutions and in most occasions, they give them lesser marks than papers published with the high quality journals. Most often, when reading the articles published in such predatory journals, you will find enough logical, grammatical, and statistical errors that are not professionally friendly. This can be disgusting to the academics.	Support APC but necessary editorial process should be done to make quality work published.	Support APC but necessary editorial process should be done to make quality work published.
…, actually most of the high quality journals also collect APC, but they usually give options for authors to choose whether they would prefer open access or subscription based. One thing, I have learnt from these high quality journal is that most times, they would like you to choose subscription based because when you as the author choose open access, it limits their business profits but when you choose subscription, and your paper is good, it opens them to a range of consumers who would need the work which they must subscribe to such journals to purchase such articles. Also, when you pay APC to high quality journals, it does three things for your career. One, they help to rate your work so that you have higher value of recognition and chances for your career development and promotion. Two, they open you to a wide range of stakeholders that would advertise you and make you well known. Third, you are also paying to get global attention because in most occasions, when people see that a certain paper is published with these high quality journals, it attracts their attention to you. This could cover for the cost of APC when paid to such high quality journals especially the five, four, and three star journals.	Support APC but for high quality journals	Support APC but for high quality journals

Chapter 2
Economics of Resource Sharing via Library Consortia

Arnold Mwanzu
International Centre of Insect Physiology and Ecology (ICIPE), Kenya

ABSTRACT

The chapter seeks to discuss the role played by library consortia in resource sharing among libraries, media organizations, and archives. It will outline the existing models that are functioning effectively especially in the developing countries and discuss the best practices. The target audience being libraries, archives, and media. While unravelling the economics of resources sharing among the information players, the chapter will address the challenges and opportunities in supporting research, teaching, and learning. The value of the book chapter is that it will give an insight into the development of library consortia and their significance as opportunities to provide equal access to research in libraries, archives, and media. The chapter will also provide a comprehensive comparison between library consortia in developing countries and developed countries highlighting how resource sharing in developing countries has helped to bridge the gap of information access, thereby showing progressive development.

INTRODUCTION

The advent of library consortia in the modern era is touted as a proactive and reactive response to the risk of libraries being rendered irrelevant in the ever-growing information industry. To accommodate all information user audiences, Libraries have undergone a dynamic shift from old-fashioned shelves of books to virtual information access enablers. The timely revolution has seen libraries come

DOI: 10.4018/978-1-5225-5840-8.ch002

together to cost share the acquisition of electronic resources and in turn strategically place Libraries in a position to maintain a competitive edge. Resource sharing via consortia is a mode of library operation whereby part of the functions of a library are shared among several libraries with the aim of maximizing the availability of materials and services at an affordable minimum expense. The different objectives of library consortia include collective acquisition of electronic resources, capacity building and continuous professional development of human capital, collective policy and standard formulation etc. It may also involve resource sharing for instance of bibliographic databases, creation and use of a union catalogue, sharing digitization equipment, expertise and services. Resource sharing via a library and information service network calls for automation of services, efficient communication and effective cooperation.

Muhammed (2012), considers resource sharing to denote a working arrangement where two or more libraries make their collection available to their respective users as well as enabling collective sharing of respective functions. Kent & Galvin (1977), define a resource as a thing/ person/ action to which one turns to and in time of need. Sharing on the other hand refers to apportioning, rationing or contributing something that is owned to benefit others. In the library, archives, media and information services context resource sharing has been alluded to sharing of; information, personnel, equipment, expertise and services.

Most libraries are well aware of the current predicament of competition in the information industry and that they cannot entirely satisfy their users with the information resources they have. With these, library networking has stepped up to bring about innovative ideas that can overcome the situation. According to UNESCO (1985), the networking and resource sharing functions of a consortium are: Cooperative acquisition; assignment of specialization in material acquisition; Co-oriented subscription; Exchange of duplicate holding; Cooperative cataloguing; Inter-library loan; Reciprocal borrowing privileges; and Reference and/ or referral service. UNESCO also classifies the following as activities of resource sharing: Union catalogue of books and periodicals; Indexing and abstracting services; List of new arrivals on accessions/ acquisitions list; Bibliography development; Network newsletters; Directories and inventories; Manuals; Translation service; Users interest survey; Joint research projects; In-service personnel training; Workshops and meetings; Marketing of network services; reprographic services etc.

Today, majority of the libraries and archives predominantly in the less developed and developing countries are considering and preferring cooperative acquisition to overcome the challenge of insufficient and diminishing budgets. Library consortia are the best solutions for establishing a formal structure regarding resource sharing. This must be backed up with formal agreements and memoranda of understanding for each participant library to ensure commitment and compliance. Cooperative collection development of participant libraries and archives can easily lead to acquisition of many relevant collections for member institution as compared to individual institution collection development. Also, important to note is that access to resources is increasingly considered more important than collection building. The consortia models that exist are meant to facilitate wider access to electronic resources at affordable costs and with the best terms of licensing.

There is no doubt that information technology has in the recent past made significant progress especially in the library and information domain. Through technology the current information handling procedures have become appropriate for supporting and encouraging the sharing of resources among libraries and information centers. The pace at which technology is advancing shows no signs of waning therefore libraries and information centers find it worthwhile to explore networking possibilities made practicable by the advent of consortia. There has been notable renewed interest in cooperation of libraries for communal benefits, conspicuously at national and international levels. Both big and small libraries survive the competitive information era by accelerating cooperation with other information providers so as to maximize their resources and services. The 'progress through partnership' with other libraries and information centers helps to deal with the ever-increasing costs of information resources and tremendous growth of literature. Collaborative advocacy and marketing via consortia helps to achieve optimal utilization of subscribed information resources. Consortia can work together to explore technological solutions and meet needs of users thus resulting in user satisfaction.

Library consortia are networks which exist primarily to mitigate the challenge of the diminishing library budgets and to lessen the operational cost of libraries, archives and documentation centers. Libraries both in developed and developing countries do not certainly get allocated the required or requested budget percentage as per the existing standards and policies. More often, libraries fall victim during budget cuts and reallocation because they are less regarded in terms of priority. Resource sharing aims to provide convenient access to information, in many forms and wherever they are located, at probable minimum costs. Resource sharing via library networks is premeditated to achieve goals such as: Electronic union service and maximized user satisfaction; established links with other automated library systems and services; operational union catalogue and joint circulation through interlibrary loan services; Shared abstracting, indexing and federated search services etc.

The economics of resource sharing is envisaged in many ways such as inter library loan to avoid double acquisition; co-operative cataloguing (Union catalogue) to ensure a common retrieval source; co-operative archiving and dissemination via national repositories; communal reprographic service; common documentation center and union list of serials and bibliographies etc. According to Bhargava (1986), with resource sharing networks Library users ought to eventually have access to more materials or quality service at less cost, increased service at level cost, or much more service at less cost. It is well noted that the best practices in library consortia involve sharing of services and human expertise; sharing the responsibility of acquiring and processing information materials; Increasing the availability and accessibility of resources to ensure and enhance maximum utilization.

Several factors have made resource sharing a necessity. This include: the increased growth of publications in the past decade, the rapid increase of cost of information sources, improvements that offer newer approaches of information processing, retrieval and dissemination; and overpricing trends by publishers. Library co-operation and collaboration is a concept and form of resource sharing that existed long ago. This was when the desire and need for resource sharing was comprehended by libraries. Apart from venturing into inter-library practice, libraries and information centers also thought of resource sharing in other aspects, such as co-operative selection, acquisition, cataloguing, classification, etc. Inter-library loan has been practiced as one of the most popular resource sharing activity amongst libraries. This type of loan in an outmoded library was severely affected by poor information communication and barriers such as indifference of the lending libraries, long distances, impassable roads, language barrier, time etc.

However, an automated inter-library loan system overcomes these barriers and limitations. In resource sharing member libraries are required to partner and work together the following areas: Developing the collection on shared terms and developing services for exploiting. During collective resource sharing it is vital to eliminate double acquisition of resources by participating libraries. This is where when one library or information center has acquired a resource, the others should aim to acquire others and not the ones already acquired. When developing shared resources member institutions ought to focus on acquisition and rationalization.

LIBRARY AND INFORMATION SERVICE CONSORTIUM

A library and information service consortium is a network of information providers which advocates for collaborative efforts for information exchange, collective subscription, cooperation, resource sharing and networking. According to Kaula (1986) resource sharing is not a new concept in the field of libraries and is similar to the conventional 'library co-operation' that has been in use all along among those who had been working in libraries or had anything to do with the development of libraries. Resource sharing is a new coinage which sounds more attractive and makes more sense in these times of budget cuts and inflation.

Library consortia can also be described as a collaborative activity of a group of libraries and information centers towards information resource sharing. Its development has improved at local, national and international levels. OCLC is considered the leading international library cooperative, helping libraries to serve people by providing economical and affordable access to knowledge and information through innovation and collaboration. Some of its notable products and services include the OCLC Worldcat, EZProxy off campus access etc. Other major consortia recognized for their successes are Swedish consortium model, Virginia's VIVA, Georgia's Galileo, Ohio's OHIOLINK, etc.

Characteristic of Library Consortia

Library consortia are characterized with the following objectives:

1. To collect as many quality and peer reviewed information materials published at national and international levels because of the limited library budgets.
2. To eliminate the common and different problems faced by the libraries and information centers in providing specific services and to meet the needs of the many users due to tremendous growth of population all over the world.
3. To cope up with the newly generated knowledge published in different forms such as printed documents and electronic media on various disciplines, multidisciplinary and new subject areas.
4. To secure financial sustainability to be able to acquire all information resources that are otherwise too expensive for individual member institutions.
5. To build synergy and empower member institutions to have capacity to advocate and maximize the utilization of subscribed and acquired information resources.

Responsibilities/Functions for Information Resource Sharing

In resource sharing many tasks and responsibilities are done centrally either at the secretariat level or by volunteered staff within the member libraries and information centers. The main responsibilities and functions of resource sharing are:

- Joint collection development among the member libraries and Cooperative processing of information resources acquired through the consortium.
- Compilation of bibliographical and/or full-text database of the holdings of the member libraries, both print and non-print.
- Sharing of information resources, both traditional and digital, of member libraries through network or document delivery service as the case may be.
- Allowing reciprocal borrowing by the members of all libraries of the consortium.

- Digitization of valuable and rare collections of member libraries available in printed format and providing access to such materials to the members of all the libraries of the consortium.
- Supporting member libraries for setting up institutional repositories, e-print archives, electronic theses collection, etc.
- Creation of virtual digital libraries covering all the e-information resources available in member libraries by networking of those libraries.
- Developing common interface to catalogues, databases and e-collection by creating portals.
- Creating interoperability among the member systems, databases and services.
- Balanced collection development and negotiation of group pricing.
- Establish a standardized resource sharing system and prepare the union catalogue among participating libraries and create databases of resources among participating libraries.
- Use of web resource for each other and document / Electronic media delivery service.
- Strengthen communication system.
- Sharing professional expertise and conduct training programme.
- Library co-operation and co-ordination with contractual obligations for each participant.

Library Networks Share Resources for the Following Needs

Being economical by collectively contributing to acquire resources helps individual institutions to save a lot of money and get more resources than they would have gotten individually. Library networks share resources because of various reasons.

- Dwindling Library budgets.
- Demand for expertise and rare documents.
- Space constraint.
- Explosion of literature in every field of knowledge.
- Array of documents in different subjects, languages and formats.
- Development of new subjects and subject specialization.
- Increased needs of information seekers.
- Multiplicity of user groups and their ensuing information needs.
- Increased access to information and library services at existing cost; The pressure of competition in the information market is enhancing and compelling information providers.
- To reduce the cost of collection development.
- To provides more, better, faster and cheaper services for less money.

- To counter the challenge of finding it hard to maintain subscriptions to even core journals due to ever increasing cost of the journal subscriptions.
- To address the shrinking fiscal resources, sudden price hikes in scientific, technical and social science journals and eBooks.
- To be able to meet information needs from the fast-changing trends and developments in the area of information communication technology.
- To improving the quality and standard of research in universities and research centers by improving the access base of literature.
- To exploit the option of electronic journals and eBooks which is comparatively cheaper than print versions.
- To reduce tasks of acquisition staff and focus their expertise in other responsibilities.
- To be able to enhance human capital and re-engineer their services and operations in such a way that they meet user-expectations better.
- To rationalize the utilization of funds in parent organizations.
- To exploit qualitative resource sharing for effective document delivery.
- To address the growth in number of users, particularly in academic and research institutions and fulfil the law of librarianship – every user his/her own book/information material.
- To address the increase in user demand for quality services.
- To conform with the emerging changes in the publishing industry since a lot of publishing is now done in digital form.
- Access to information resources at reduced costs.
- Increased cost of resources by publishers and aggregators vis-à-vis the Quantity.
- Demand for identified, comprehensive and prompt information services.

Advantages of Resource Sharing

Resource sharing through a consortium fulfills the fourth law of library science.

- It is very economical in terms of saving the library space.
- Standardization in classification and cataloguing is possible with a union catalogue.
- It avoids duplication of documents and work.
- It reduces individual acquisition of library materials and promotes sharing collections.
- It provides researchers with a wide range of information resources.
- It avoids duplicate purchases and ensures collection of unique material.
- It establishes and maintains efficient communication systems.

- It develops an information marketing mechanism through collaboration and control of the quality of collections thus enhancing maximum utilization.

Impediments to Resource Sharing via Consortia

- Lack of commitment and consistency in paying member fees for subscriptions.
- Difficulty in establishing mutual agreements.
- Urgent requirements are by a hair's breadth met.
- Lack of goodwill by publishers during negotiations of agreements and fees for resources.

The absence of effective information infrastructure in countries in the sub-Saharan Africa and parts of Asia affects resource sharing among libraries. According to Odini (1991), the major constraints are lack of firm national policies of libraries resulting to poor rating of information services among the national priorities. Consequently, library budgets are correspondingly low, which makes it difficult for libraries to provide their dues under collaborative resource acquisition due to gross underfunding and annual decreases in budgetary allocations. Lack of basic facilities and infrastructure for swift communication establishes a solemn impediment to effective planning of library development in general or of a resource sharing project.

Lack of adequate funds has been identified as the greatest impediment to resource sharing. This is because a networking arrangement of libraries is bound to fail if funds are not made available (Nwalo, 2002). He further notes that most failed projects on the adoption of collaborative resource sharing activities are because of money constraints. Nurturing partnerships and collaboration among libraries fails because important steps are not taken while some libraries and information centers lack faith in the ideas and suggestions fronted. Blakes (2006), states that resource sharing activities have a significant role in African countries. However, most libraries face many constraints in their efforts for sharing resources. The factors affecting consortia are mismanagement of resources, inflation which has heightened and negligence of libraries and information centers. Financial support for most libraries in Africa has also diminished. This unfortunate situation drastically affects all aspects of library and information services.

Odini (1991), argues that lack of steady national policy on libraries in African countries contributes to ineffective resource sharing. He adds that some libraries lack the data on current user needs and information resource gaps thus constituting a serious obstacle to effective planning both for individual library or information center development or for resource sharing programs. Another constraint is poor infrastructure for rapid communication with members and suppliers, for instance:

inconsistent electricity supply, poor internet and telecommunication. However, this has changed as telecommunication has largely improved in some countries.

LIBRARY CONSORTIA MODELS

Library consortia models are generally based on collaboration, affiliation, participation and funding sources. They are various examples of consortia models such as: the open consortium which is very flexible for members as they can join and leave as they please; the centrally funded model where consortia exclusively depend on the parent institutions; and the shared-budget model which allows the participating libraries to take the lead and manage the consortium. The most common consortium model is the shared budget model. Some examples of consortia that use this model include the Kenya Libraries and Information services consortium (KLISC), the Zimbabwe Universities Library Consortium (ZULC), the Consortium of Academic and Research Libraries in Ghana (CARLIGH), the consortium of Uganda University Libraries (CUUL), Indian Institute of Management Libraries Consortium (IIM) and Forum for Resource Sharing and Astronomy (FORSA) of India.

Closed Group Consortium

The closed group consortium operates under the confines of a defined group. Such a consortium forms either by collaboration or affiliation and its operation procedures, rules and administration is quite simple and relaxed; the publisher initiatives consortia whose members get unfathomable discount prices when buying resources. The Emerald Full-Text Library by the Emerald Publishing Group is a publisher initiative consortium.

To reinforce the networks of librarians, archivists, information managers, researchers and academics in developing countries, the International Network for the Availability of Scientific Publications (INASP) has been in the forefront to spearhead and encourage librarians in parts of Africa and Asia to establish national consortia. INASP have sponsored several workshops to spearhead the establishment and operationalization of library consortia in these regions. They have done this by engaging in three to six-year partnership projects in countries such as Zimbabwe, Uganda, Ghana, Ethiopia, Botswana, Tanzania and Kenya that enhance capacity building and empowerment. The Consortium of Uganda University Libraries (CUUL) was established in 2001 during a forum that addressed issues of library cooperation for effective provision of information in Uganda and beyond. The consortium was established with rationales for existence and cooperation such as resource sharing, resource mobilization, training and marketing of member libraries (Kinengyere,

2007). According to Kinengyere (2007), one of the challenges being addressed by CUUL is the sustainability of e-journal subscriptions at the end of donor funding. He notes that in November 2005, the consortium agreed on the mechanism of cost sharing the electronic resources which was to commence in 2006. He points out that out of the 43 registered Programme for the Enhancement of Research Information institutions-(PERI) institutions in Uganda, only 11 (25%) responded to the electronic resources sustainability initiative in time for the 2007 subscriptions and this trend has prevailed for some while. Despite consortium initiatives, objectives have not been fully achieved and this has been attributed to the lack of funds, lack of timely payments, lack of commitment from its membership, and mistrust on its leadership.

The Electronic Information for Libraries Network (EIFl) is another organization that has focused efforts on negotiating affordable subscriptions to electronic journals for libraries in the education and research sectors. It has offered immense support to emerging national library consortia in developing countries which it has mapped as its member countries and continually advocates for the wide availability of electronic resources for library users in these developing countries. EIFl ensures access to electronic resources via consortia and becomes a natural partner for the open access movement through capacity building and knowledge sharing on open access across the eIFL community. The network also advocates and encourages greater visibility of locally produced content in its member countries through the establishment of institutional repositories within member institutions of the consortia. Some of the members of the eIFL community as per their website are Kenya, Uganda, Zambia, Zimbabwe, Bangladesh, South Africa, Sudan, Swaziland, Syria, Tajikistan, Ukraine, Uzbekistan among others.

Library consortia with their collective strength of many participating institutions, have attracted highly discounted rates of subscription with most favorable terms of agreement. Consortia are largely regarded as tools, which aid in exploiting the opportunities of quality research in commercial electronic databases as well as in effecting savings. Library consortia are helping the researchers, faculty and the students to retrieve the information and save their time. They aid libraries and information centers to procure more electronic resources in the library with limited library budgets and this is what libraries require to remain relevant.

A library consortium that offers its member institutions joint collection development and priority access to shared services such as interlibrary loan ends up saving their would-be expenses. This is contrary to commercial document delivery, traditional interlibrary loan, and direct journal subscriptions to publishers. Economic sustainability of a consortium is key to ensuring continuous access of quality resources by member institutions. There are two potential sources of financial savings for consortium member institutions. One is when consortium delivery can be achieved at a lower cost than alternate sources of document delivery and interlibrary loan, then member libraries or archives will save costs involved on interlibrary loan. The second option is when member libraries and archives identify journal subscriptions individually and instead of acquiring directly from aggregators and publishers, they request the consortia to negotiate and acquire for them. In this way access is more efficiently provided by sharing a subscription with the consortium rather than individual subscription by members and the money spent in acquisition is reduced by more than half. Consortium document delivery and collaborative collection development is considered very economical.

C5 Model for the Consortium Management

According to Srinivasa Rao (2017), libraries embrace consortia models to plan and perform functions effectively using SWOT analysis. In his study, he proposes an 'information necklace model' to determine the relationship among stakeholders of a consortium. In his recommendations and findings, he proposes a unique 'C5 model' (clients, connectivity, content, copyright and cost) for the consortium based on its essence and usefulness in the present-day framework of libraries. Each component of 'C5 model' of the consortium of libraries was evaluated using a Strength Weakness Opportunities Threats (SWOT) analysis method. In this information necklace model, information is used to connect publishers, consortia, libraries and clients. According to the author, the components of the C5 model are clients, connectivity, content, copyright and cost.

Resource Sharing at KLISC

KLISC (Kenya Library and Information Services Consortium) was established in 2003 with the main objective of collective subscription to electronic resources to cope with the increasing cost of information resources. Subsequently, it was agreed that the Consortium would draw its membership from University Libraries, Research institutions and Public/National Libraries. It started off by having its Secretariat based at the University of Nairobi library until 2016 when it moved its offices to Kenyatta University which is also a member of the consortium. KLISC's aim is to promote the interests of libraries and information services and bring them together for common good and benefit of stakeholders spread in all the institutions as well as the government and public at large. The consortium adopted the vision "To be a leading library consortium with unlimited access to knowledge and information" which reflects the consortium's commitment to maintain, monitor, promote, and exploit knowledge management for learning, teaching, innovation, research, community service, and national development.

The consortium has benefited its members of about 100 libraries by ensuring access to quality peer reviewed resources at very low costs as compared to individual subscription to the resources. By establishing partnerships with organizations like INASP and Eifl, KLISC was able to get negotiated and subsidized rates of subscriptions from international publishers. The economics of resource sharing have also been encouraged by capacity building workshops that have been organized for members of the consortium so as to empower them to have negotiating and licensing skills to approach publishers as a consortium and get even lower costs for new and existing subscriptions.

Resource sharing via consortium also ensures that publishers do not exploit individual libraries and archives by charging them exorbitant fees higher than the market rate. This is because through building international networks and partnerships, consortia can benchmark regionally and globally to find out the acceptable fees and the rates being given to other consortia or institutions.

Shared-Budget Consortia Model

Using the shared-budget consortia model KLISC develops membership tiers for subscription depending on the number of users in the specific institutions. This ensures that all the big institutions like university libraries and national libraries with more than 10,000 users get to pay a much higher amount than the research libraries and special libraries with less than 500 users. Ultimately all the member institutions get the same resources that have been subscribed at very subsidized rates through a shared budget. Libraries, archives and information centers that are in KLISC save a lot of money and access high quality resources at subsidized rates as compared to if they were to acquire individually. A case in point is where a certain academic Library in Kenya had in a previous year subscribed to a publisher resource at about 20,000 USD, but later on they came to find out that they could join the consortium and pay the same 20,000 USD and have access to the same publisher resource they had initially subscribed to directly together with eighteen other different high-quality publisher resources. This means that the amount they used to get one resource could be used to get multiple resources so long as they engage in collaborative collection development and resource sharing via consortia.

Resource sharing via consortia demands shared vision, mission, values, and commitment, together with a good political situation, additional funding and proactive participation by all the stakeholders. KLISC is driven by the mission of providing leadership and building synergy in knowledge and information resources sharing through capacity building, advocacy, networking and collaborations. They aim to be the leading library consortium with unlimited access to knowledge and information and envisage that by 2030, the consortium will be recognized internationally as the leading library network for providing knowledge and information for sustainable development. For them to achieve this they developed a strategy to guide their plans. Commitment and passion for the consortium is also very significant in order for member institutions to benefit from it. The leadership and administration of KLISC comprises of heads of libraries and information centers and identified librarians with innovative ideas. The organizational structure has an executive committee of nine elected members who must be leaders in their institutions and influencers of decisions. These members are involved in all the executive decisions of the consortium including managing the contributions of the members and liaising with publishers for subscription on behalf of member institutions. The executive committee further appoints working committee members to help in operationalizing the strategic plan. A licensing and negotiation working committee for instance is tasked to negotiate with publishers, aggregators and vendors for possible deals, then they recommend to the executive committee the resources that should be bought.

Consortium members come from different parent institutions with different structures and rules. Administration of a consortium is not an easy task especially when it comes to collecting annual subscription and membership fees from member institutions. Some institutions delay in remitting their payments hence inconveniencing all members. Consortia subscriptions are the most common cost-effective channels of acquisition of materials and resource sharing. With the globalization of all spheres of life, it is paramount that the trend will continue. The unity of consortia, with collective strength of member institutions, easily attracts highly discounted rates of subscription with most favorable terms of agreement. This is because when publishers and suppliers discover that they cannot penetrate to individual institutions without going through the national consortium, they are bound to flex their terms and exaggerated fees. This works to the advantage of member institutions as negotiation is done on their behalf by the consortium leadership.

Good Infrastructure

The availability of good infrastructure is essential in ensuring maximum utilization of shared resources among member institutions. Consortia play a big role in providing high quality resources for research and learning at affordable costs. However, most of the developing countries lack reliable internet connectivity to enable efficient access to information resources. In Cameroon, the Cameroon Interuniversity Network exists to provide universities with modern infrastructure. It is an initiative of the Cameroonian authorities of higher education. In Kenya, the Kenya Education Network (KENET) was established to provide a high speed, reliable, and sustainable IP network for interconnectivity among educational institutions. In Malawi, the Malawi Academic and Research Network (MAREN) is an initiative meant to provide high bandwidth to major academic institution. Senegal also established the UCAD information technology network to connect Universities and schools. All these initiatives are an indication of how consortia and networks are being established to promote learning and research in Africa. Internet connectivity has improved quite significantly through national collaborative initiatives.

Development of Consortia in Sub Sahara Region

As of 2016 many national consortia have positioned themselves as the main agencies providing access to electronic resources in their countries. These consortia have been relying on support from organizations like INSAP, Eifl, SIDA etc. for sustainability and negotiated deals with publishers. However, slowly some of them are becoming independent and pursuing their objectives while more detached. The success of national consortia in the sub Saharan Africa region is largely credited to the support and mentorship of INASP and Eifl. This is because this organizations engaged in five to ten-year partnerships with the African sub-Sahara countries and aimed to empower and develop capacity for libraries and information centers to be able to stand on their own they have sponsored numerous capacity building workshops and seminars and encouraged participation by consortium members. These efforts have seen the emergence of great consortium ideas such as building a strong financial reserve through investments and sourcing for donor funds to help in acquiring quality but expensive electronic resources.

INASP for instance has successfully organized regional consortia forums since 2013 in Africa. These forums bring together leaders of national consortia to be empowered and given training on effective licensing and negotiation skills so as to be able to deal with international publishers. During the 2017 INASP regional consortium conference for Africa, that was organized in Nairobi Kenya, consortium leaders from the Kenya Library and Information Services Consortium (KLISC), Consortium for Uganda University Libraries (CUUL), Consortium of Academic and Research Libraries in Ghana (CARLIGH) and the Zimbabwe University Libraries Consortium (ZULC) converged to share experiences and best practices. This forum helped the different consortia to learn from each other on the economics of resource sharing and the participants were even able to pick new ideas that they later implemented in their specific consortia. Networking between consortia is quite significant since members learn from each other. In the wake of publishers charging exorbitant fees, networking among consortia can be a good means of finding out the market rates so as to avoid being given overpriced quotations.

REFERENCES

Adams, R. (2017). Library Consortia: Models for Collaboration and Sustainability. *The Electronic Library, 35*(5), 1067–1068. doi:10.1108/EL-07-2017-0147

Bhargava, G. D. (1986). Library resource sharing network, an evaluation. In Planning in library resource sharing. Lucknow: Print House.

Blakes, E. F. (2006). *ICT Availability and Resource Sharing in some Academic Libraries in Nigeria*. Paper presented at the NLA Conference, Abuja.

Eaton, N. L. (1995). Resource sharing: The public university library's imperative. *Journal of Library Administration, 21*(1-2), 27–38. doi:10.1300/J111V21N01_03

EIFL. (2014). *Frequently Asked Questions - Consortium Management*. Available at http://www.eifl.net/faq/consortium-management

Getz, M. (1991). Document delivery. *The Bottom Line (New York, N.Y.), 5*(4), 40–44. doi:10.1108/eb025354

Hightower, C., & Soete, G. J. (1995). The consortium as learning organization: Twelve steps to success in collaborative collections projects. *Journal of Academic Librarianship, 21*(2), 87–91. doi:10.1016/0099-1333(95)90119-1

Hirshon, A. (1995). Library strategic alliances and the digital library in the 1990's. The OhioLINK Experiment. *Journal of Academic Librarianship, 21*(5), 383–386. doi:10.1016/0099-1333(95)90065-9

Kaula, P. N. (1986). Towards resource sharing in libraries. In Planning in library resource sharing. Lucknow: Print House.

Kent, A., & Galvin, T. (1979). *The Structure and Governance of Library Networks*. New York: Marcel Dekker.

Kingma, B. R. (1996). *The economics of access versus ownership to scholarly information: The costs and benefits of access to scholarly articles via interlibrary loan and journal subscriptions*. Binghamton, NY: Haworth Press.

Kingma, B. R., & Eppard, P. (1992). Journal price escalation and the market for information: The librarian's solution. *College & Research Libraries, 53*(6), 523–535. doi:10.5860/crl_53_06_523

Lowry, C. B. (1990). Resource sharing or cost shifting? The unequal burden of cooperative cataloging and ILL. *College & Research Libraries, 51*(1), 11–19. doi:10.5860/crl_51_01_11

Muhamed, R.A. (2012). The Roles of Library and Information Resource Sharing in the emerging Information Society. *Journal of Information and Knowledge Management, 2*(7), 79-85.

Muthu, M. (2013). *Resource Sharing in Libraries: A Vital Role of Consortia.* Academic Press.

Nwalo, K. I. N. (2002). *Fundamentals of Library Practice: A Manual on Library Routines*. Ibadan: Stirling-Horden Publishers.

Nwalo, K. I. N. (2006). Collaboration in the provision and utilization of IT facilities for library and information science education in Nigeria. Information Technology in Library and Information Science Education in Nigeria.

Odini, C. (1991). Problems and Prospects of Resource Sharing in Developing Countries. *African Journal of Library, Archives sand Information Science, 1*(2), 93-108.

Rao. (2017). C5 model for the consortium management: SWOT analysis. *Library Management, 38*(4-5). doi: 10.1108/LM-09-2016-0073

UNESCO. (1985). *Information networking in population education*. Bangkok: Unesco.

Chapter 3
Status of Electronic Thesis and Dissertations (ETDs) in India

Rupak Chakravarty
Panjab University, India

ABSTRACT

INFLIBNET (information library network) has gradually emerged as the backbone of the higher education sector of India. The remarkable initiatives taken by the INFLIBNET strive for strengthening and supporting information needs of the students, scholars, teachers, scientists, and peers. Scholars all around the world would be thankful to the INFLIBNET for their marvelous and ambitious project in the direction of bringing millions of theses and dissertation under the umbrella of OA. With 166,675 full-text ETD items and growing, it qualifies to be called a massive digital library (MDL). This chapter discusses the salient features, significance, and implications of the Shodhganga. It also discusses Shodhgangotri, a database consisting of approved research proposal submitted by the research scholars. The chapter concludes with discussion on the evaluation report of the Shodhganga website with the web-analyzer software Nibbler.

INTRODUCTION

The term "Electronic Theses and Dissertations" (ETD) is used primarily to differentiate between analogue theses and dissertations (paper, microfilm) and their digital counterparts (digital objects). However, "ETDs" may also be digitized or born digital. (Hartsock & Alemneh, 2018). Of all the ETD initiatives operating in the world, Networked Digital Library of Theses and Dissertations (NDLTD), established in 1996, is one of the largest such repositories with the global presence.

DOI: 10.4018/978-1-5225-5840-8.ch003

Its members include universities around the world, as well as partner organizations, including - Adobe, the American Library Association (ALA), the Association of Research Libraries (ARL), the Coalition for Networked Information (CNI), the Joint Information Services Committee (JISC), Online Computer Library Center (OCLC), Proquest/UMI, and Theses Canada. This partnership is based on the common goal of unlocking the benefits of shared knowledge for all. NDLTD celebrated its 20th Anniversary on August 2, 2017.

Another initiative which is equally doing great work in promoting Open Access scholarly communication in the field of ETD is Open Access Theses and Dissertations (OATD). It provides access to over 3.5 million ETDs (as of August 2017, indexes 3,987,722 ETDs) which are free to download and excludes closed-access and embargoed ETDs. It aims to be the best possible resource for finding open access graduate theses and dissertations published around the world. The ETD metadata comes from over 1100 colleges, universities, and research institutions.

REVIEW OF LITERATURE

Institutional repositories are a concept gaining movement today. India is moving ahead in this direction and major education and research institutes have already created their own institutional repositories. In analysis and findings, a detailed report of the analysis of data collection and its subsequent interpretations are given (Lihitkar & Lihitkar, 2014). Besides UGC-recognised universities, other private/ deemed universities, IITs, NITs and IISERs should also be welcomed for voluntarily deposit their theses in the Shodhganga central repository, and one of the fastest ways to make progress is to let students upload their works directly (Panda, 2016)

A growing realization has emerged among those working on ETDs in Iran that it is critically important that libraries remain not just involved, but centrally positioned in the development of the national information infrastructure. The future of E-theses and of archiving and searching, in general, depends on institutions being able to deliver top quality services, with a high degree of interoperability. Systems must continue to be developed and they must be able to handle many different types of digital objects. As we prepare students for scholarship in the twenty-first century, Iran 1400, for example, it is imperative that librarians consider how to manage these important new forms of writing. (Ardalan & Feyzbaksh, 2011). Electronic theses and dissertations (ETDs) provide opportunities to enhance and expand student research in terms of access, content and impact. While printed theses and dissertations are most often restricted to a smaller readership and limited to simple text and images, authors of ETDs may include video clips, audio files, colour, and embedded software within the research documents published electronically. Because ETDs are published and accessed from Web sites, there is a great reduction in the time required for graduate students to collect information, and subsequently, compile and report their own original research. This results in dramatic improvements in graduate education and reduces institutional barriers to resource sharing. This chapter provides background information and an overview of the ETD movement as well as core resources and related readings for administrators, graduate faculty and librarians involved in ETD program development (ETDs: From the Beginning, 2011). ETDs provides the students and the researchers to express their interpretations and research findings through colour imagery, audio, video, and interactive media. ETDs enhance the visibility of students and their supervisors, significantly leading to improved job prospects/ placement for students. Students are not required to spend a lot of money in printing multiple copies of theses, and institutional libraries are saved from the never-ending problem of space crunch on account of storage of multiple copies. ETDs can be accessed and downloaded as and when required without any geographical, time and copyright barrier thus an effective way of sharing original research both across and beyond the academy. By comparison, most printed theses and dissertations are seldom used (Fyffe & Welburn, 2008) There is a need to adequately represent ETDs to describe the content and efficient access. This can be achieved by the use of effective indexing terms – both authorized terms from controlled vocabularies and free-text keywords. There is a need to distinguish functional representation from mere descriptions of a topic (Alemneh & Phillips, 2016)

Theses and dissertations are considered an important part of information resources in any institution. They are often the only source of research work. Unfortunately, access to these valuable unpublished resources is often restricted to parent institution only. The authors found that ETD repositories are addressing this problem by making institutional knowledge available online and thereby not only increasing its visibility and use but also making them contribute to the impact and ranking of their institutions. Asian countries are beginning to embrace the idea of digitizing, archiving and making their theses and dissertations available online. The study found that more than half of all IRs listed in the directory of OpenDOAR contain ETDs. ETD system is growing fast in some Asian countries. However, the number of universities having e-theses repositories is meagre considering a large number of quality academic and research institutions across Asian countries. ETD repositories not only benefit students and institutions by enhancing education and expanding research, but also by increasing a university's visibility and use and thereby contributing to the impact and ranking of its parent institutions (Ahmed, Alreyaee & Rahman, 2014). A major challenge facing research and scholarship in Africa is the poor dissemination of research findings embedded in theses and dissertations. Adoption of ETDs is low due to poor ICT infrastructure. For the region to be relevant and competitive in the new global information platform, African universities should try to translate theory into practice in the adoption of ETDs. This requires the serious commitment on the part of African governments and the university administrators. The successful implementation of ETDs in African universities will equally afford academic community of the region the opportunity of expanding the latitude of their professional growth through linkages with professional colleagues and other academics all over the world (Ezema & Igbo, 2016). Semantic interoperability is needed for lifecycle models of metadata and concerned with the long-term curation and preservation of ETDs (Potvin & Thompson, 2016).

The Mandate

The University Grants Commission of India (UGC India) is a statutory body set up by the Indian Union government under Ministry of Human Resource Development(MHRD), and is charged with coordination, determination and maintenance of standards of higher education. It provides recognition to universities in India, and disburses funds to such recognised universities and colleges. Electronic

Figure 1. Status of open access repository in India
Source: www.openaccessmap.org)

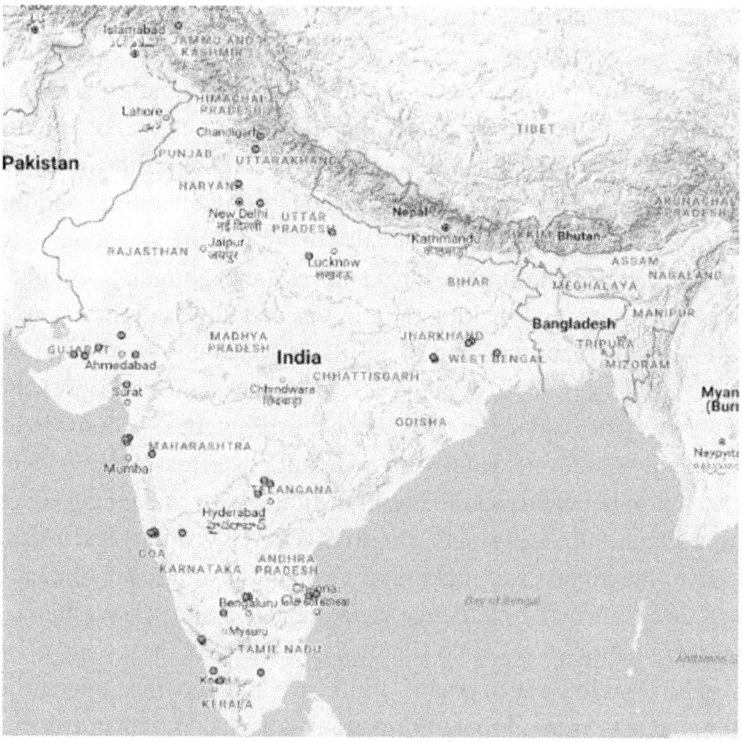

Theses and Dissertations are primary sources of research materials that originate from doctoral theses/dissertations submitted to the universities for the award of Ph.D. As per UGC Notification (Minimum Standards & Procedure for Award of M.Phil./PhD Degree, Regulation, 2016) it is mandatory to submit an electronic version of theses and dissertations by the researchers in universities into a national repository with an aim to facilitate open access to Indian theses and dissertations to the academic community world-wide. Generally, put under the category of grey literature, access to electronic theses and dissertations remain closed as only limited users can access the hard copies of the same via their libraries. The problem becomes worse if a scholar needs to consult theses belonging other institutions. Thus, knowledge produced after years of hard work remained undiscovered, unused, uncaptured. In India, most of the libraries used to have restricted access to these and are non-issuable items. With the coming of ETD repository, most of the concerns and difficulties were solved.

The centrally-maintained digital repository, not only ensure easy access and archiving of Indian doctoral theses but also help in raising the standard and quality of research. It helps in addressing the serious issue of duplication of research. It also helps in dealing with the poor quality resulting from the "poor visibility" and the "unseen" factor in research output. As per the Regulation, the responsibility of hosting, maintaining and making the digital repository of Indian Electronic Theses and Dissertation (called "Shodhganga"), accessible to all institutions and universities, is assigned to the Information and Library Network Centre (INFLIBNET). Universities are expected to submit electronic version of theses in Shodhganga on regular basis. If a university is not able to facilitate online submission of theses into the national ETD repository, Shodhganga, the university may accept e-version of theses on CD ROM / DVD ROM and send it to the INFLIBNET for offline submission. Designated University Coordinator needs to authenticate and certify that the student has submitted the complete, correct and same version of the thesis that is submitted in print.

Shodhganga: A Reservoir of Indian Theses

INFLIBNET has developed a low-cost affordable integrated library automation system (ILMS) known as SOUL for Indian libraries. It hosts the national union catalogue, IndCat. Apart from hosting open access (OA) journals, it is responsible for maintaining the national level consortium known as e-ShodhSindhu providing access to premium scholarly journals. For colleges, it has made available consortium known as NLIST (National Library and Information services Infrastructure for Scholarly Content). For students, it has launched another very useful Open Educational Resources (OER) project called ePGPathshala.Theses and dissertations document the new knowledge that is being created out of continuous and consistent endeavour of scholars. They are considered to be the rich, valuable and unique source of information, often put under the category of grey literature as they are not available through common publication channels linked with the publishing industry. In case they are not available for furthering research, the hard work involved in their creation is mere wastage of huge resources, both human and financial. In print format, they may remain an untapped and under-utilized asset, leading to unnecessary duplication and repetition. The electronic version of theses and dissertations (ETDs) serve and satisfy the intended goals and purposes quite successfully.

The INFLIBNET Centre, promotes setting-up of institutional and ETD repositories in member universities using OAI-PMH complaint software. A number of member universities have already set-up their institutional and ETD repositories using either DSpace or other OAI-PMH compliant Institutional Repository software. It would be possible for universities having sufficient network and computing infrastructure to maintain their own ETD repositories wherein their research scholars could deposit e-versions of their theses and dissertations. In such a case, Shodhganga serves as backup archives. The Central ETD Repository (Shodhganga) does the metadata harvesting from all such geographically distributed university ETD repositories. This serves as the backbone of research infrastructure by facilitating unified access to theses and dissertations through its harvesting server. Universities hosting ETDs on their own repository must evolve suitable IPR policy pertaining to the doctoral theses.

ETD Repository Software

The Shodhganga@INFLIBNET is set-up using an open source digital repository software called DSpace developed by MIT (Massachusetts Institute of Technology) in partnership between Hewlett- Packard (HP). The DSpace uses internationally recognized protocols and interoperability standards. Shodhganga provides a platform for research scholars to deposit their Ph.D. theses and make it available to the entire scholarly community in open access.

Important Features

- Shodhganga has 166675 fulltext ETD items.
- Universities that sign MoU with the INFLIBNET Centre and mandate submission of electronic version of their theses and dissertation to Shodhganga may get financial assistance from the UGC for digitizing their back-files of theses.

Figure 2. Top Ten ETD contributors (as of 17 September 2017)

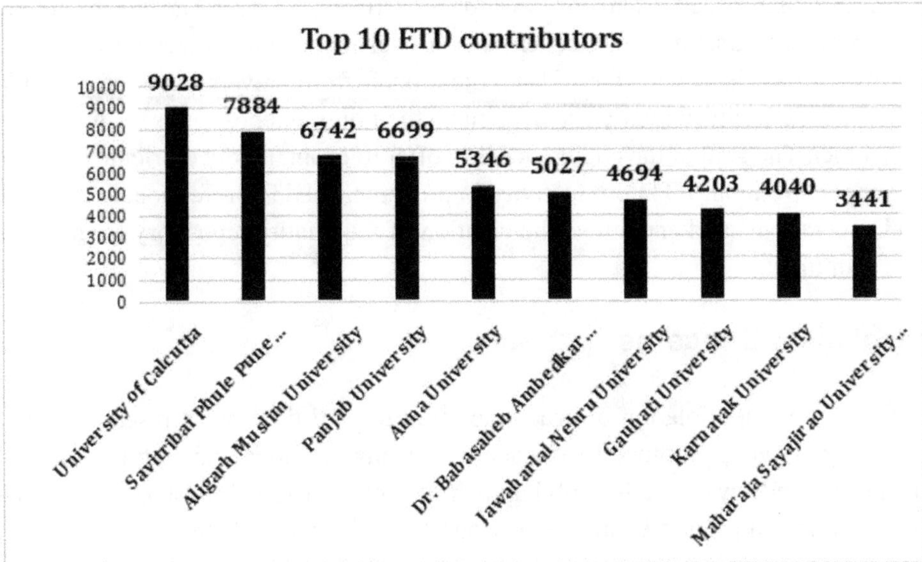

- Besides, UGC may also provide financial assistance to the INFLIBNET Centre for the subscription to software tools that detect plagiarized portion of theses and dissertations.
- Access to software designed to detect plagiarism will be provided to universities that sign MoU with the INFLIBNET Centre for Shodhganga.
- The repository has the ability to capture, index, store, disseminate and preserve ETDs (Electronic Theses and Dissertations) submitted by the researchers.
- DSpace supports "Open Archives Initiative's Protocol for Metadata Harvesting" (OAI-PMH)
- Uses a qualified version of the Dublin Core schema for its metadata.
- Facilitate ease of navigation.
- Option for simple search and advanced search are available on the home page along with browsing facility through universities and departments.
- INFLIBNET is also developing a semantic web-based interface to facilitate subject-based browsing, navigation, search and retrieval of content available in the repository.

iETD 2017 National Conference

This national conference on iETD 2017 is fourth in the series. The first national conference was organized in JNU, New Delhi on March 22nd-23rd, 2012. The second and third national conference was organised at INFLIBNET Centre, Gandhinagar from 22nd-23rd January, 2015 and on 5-7 October, 2016 respectively. The fourth national conference would serve as an excellent educational opportunity to librarians, research scholars, supervisors and other ETD professionals from universities to create/build policy on ETD/anti-plagiarism and maintain their digital repositories by interacting each other. The goal of the conference is to offer relevant, practice-oriented content to support National ETD productivity improvement, ETD professionals, advance ETD operations, and encourage the creation of the quality repository for national ETDs in India.

Plagiarism Concerns

Plagiarism is the violation of academic integrity and dilution of research ethics. Claiming the wrong authorship of academic writings and ideas amounts to academic dishonesty and any research involving such "recycled writings" must be discouraged by enforcing appropriate rules at various levels along with the mechanism for detecting followed by punitive action as defined in the rules.

Plagiarism in ETDs results in the poor quality of research with duplication. There exist contrasts towards the perception when it comes to the question - whether open access to theses will deter plagiarism or will it facilitate plagiarism. Though those believing it will encourage plagiarism are less. In India, universities signing MoU with INFLIBNET for submitting ETDs to the Shodhganga repository maintained by it, are provided free access to the plagiarism detection software URKUND.

Significance

- Increased visibility of theses and dissertations through open access repositories.
- Deterrent to plagiarism.
- Attract collaborative research on topics of mutual interests.
- Avoid duplication of research.
- Motivation for creation of new knowledge.
- National research output can be measured (Theses & Dissertations).
- Alerting and analytical services deploying data mining and other technology tools to be launched in future.

ROLES AND RESPONSIBILITIES

Successful execution of the national ETD repository "Shodhganga" necessitates that all the three stake holders involved in the process of content generation, hosting and extending access should adhere to well-defined roles and responsibilities.

Roles and Responsibilities of INFLIBNET Centre

Pre-Submission

1. Facilitates online as well as off-line submission into the central repository (Shodhganga) officially through University's Research Cell or voluntarily by students themselves and methods to get the thesis authenticated.
2. Online registration of research scholars.
3. Authentication by supervisors/designated University Coordinator to authenticate the submission.
4. Financial assistance to eligible universities for digitization of back volumes of theses.
5. Provide system configuration and specifications for procurement of computer hardware and related equipment for setting up of IRs for ETDs in universities.
6. Provide training.
7. Provide access URKUND, anti-plagiarism software, to detection of plagiarism.

Post-Submission

1. Ascertain post submission authentication online through supervisor / designated University Coordinator.
2. Set-up Web-based interface to facilitate research cell/university coordinators to create departments/ centres/colleges, etc.

Roles and Responsibilities of Universities

1. Universities signatory to "Shodhganga" should mandate submission ETDs into Shodhganga.
2. Abide by copyright laws and IPR for their theses. They much evolve mechanisms and implement them strictly to check plagiarism in theses submitted to their universities.
3. Extend computer and network infrastructure and requisite software to facilitate online submission of theses and dissertations by researchers into Shodhganga and requisite manpower for support and guidance.

4. Digitize its old hard copies of previously submitted of theses and dissertations.
5. Obtain declaration/consent from the students assigning non-exclusive rights to archive and distribute their doctoral work through Shodhganga as well as through university's IR in full-text.
6. Approve standards file formats for ETD submission. These formats may include -Open Office document format, MS Office document format, Tex, LaTex, etc.
7. Awareness regarding the conversion of various file formats into PDF may be provided to the researchers by the Research Cell or in the library or university.
8. Organize formal training programmes to educate students on various aspects of electronic submission of theses and dissertations including its advantages, creation, submission, conversion from native format to PDF, etc.
9. Set-up and maintain their institutional repository (IR) for hosting ETDs. A copy should be made available to "Shodhganga"
10. A dedicated website explaining policy, procedures & training for electronic submission of theses and dissertations.
11. Provide link to the Shodhganga website from University website or Library website.

Responsibilities of Students/Research Scholars

Pre-Submission

1. Use Standard Application Software for composing the thesis.
2. Use Standard Template for compilation of a thesis incorporating all essential elements.
3. Use Standard Citation Style for rendering bibliographic references as well as web resources. (e.g. APA/Chicago).
4. A researcher can Register on Shodhganga Web Site for submission as well as for editing of submitted record and files.
5. Convert all Files into PDF before uploading them into ETD repository.

Submission /Post-Submission

1. Registered researchers would be required to create metadata for records which they may be edited if required.
2. Assign keywords/descriptors to thesis using standard subject headings.
3. Uploading full-text of E-Thesis into the ETD repository.
4. Scholars must get their thesis authenticated by guide/university coordinator.

Metadata Standards and File Naming Convention

The submission process is simple involving one-page (one-form) submission with almost all mandatory fields. While some of the fields can be selected from drop down box and another field should be filled with care. Metadata has to be assigned to each thesis in order to maintain quality, standards and uniqueness in all theses.

Sample naming conventions are shown in Table 1.

The standardised naming convention facilitates easy identification of the relevant parts of a thesis by its file name that is common across all theses. Users can quickly look at the table of content and other introductory information without having to wait for the entire thesis to download.

Data Format@Shodhganga, INFLIBNET Centre

PDF is the preferred document format for submission of thesis in the Shodhganga. It retains all format codes, graphic images and retains page integrity. In addition, PDF files can be indexed and searched by keywords. Apart from being an open standard, it maintains the integrity of the document. It can be converted to PostScript format, which can be used for electronic delivery and printed directly. Other open standard document formats such as HTML, XML, Tex, LaTeX can also be used. Open Image

Table 1. Naming Convention used for each PDF file

01_title.pdf	Title Page
02_certificate.pdf	Certificate
03_abstract.pdf	Abstract
04_declaration.pdf	Declaration
05_acknowledgement.pdf	Acknowledgement
06_contents.pdf	Content/Index page
07_list_of_tables.pdf	List of Tables
08_list_of_figures.pdf	List of Figures
09_abbreviations.pdf	Abbreviations
10_chapter1.pdf	First Chapter
11_chapter2.pdf	Second Chapter
12_chapter......	Chapter...
13_conclusion	Conclusion
14_summary	Summary
15_bibliography	Bibliography

File Formats like Portable Network Graphics (PNG) and Joint Photographic Experts Group (JPEG) are recommended for uploading images, such as scanned copy of certificates, supplementary material, etc.

Restricted Access

All theses and dissertations submitted to Shodhganga are available in full-text in open access to the academic community world-wide. However, it is possible to impose restrictions on access as a special case, if so desired, by the university/ research scholar.

Memorandum of Understanding (MoU)

Universities are required to sign a MoU with the INFLIBNET Centre to participate in the Shodhganga project. This MoU spells out the responsibilities of Universities and INFLIBNET Centre related to Shodhganga. Total number of MoUs signed is 323 out of which 295 are contributing e-Theses including 13 CFTIs (Centrally Funded Technical Institutions).

RESEARCH PROPOSAL

It may take 3 years or more to complete a Ph.D. thesis. During these three years, another scholar may start working on the same topic leading to the duplication of research. To avoid such duplication and to get a better, quick and comprehensive status of research trend, the project Shodhgangotri was started by the INFLIBNET. It consists of completed research proposal which is an intermediary step and founding stone of the completion of thesis. As of writing this chapter, it consists of 3900 research proposal on various topics.

Shodhgangotri

Shodhgangotri is a new initiative that compliments “ShodhGanga”. While “ShodhGanga” is a repository of full-text theses submitted to universities in India, Shodhgangotri hosts synopsis of research topic submitted to the universities in India by research scholars for registering themselves for the Ph.D programme.

Under this initiative, research scholars/research supervisors are supposed to deposit electronic version of approved synopsis submitted by research scholars to the universities for registering themselves for the Ph.D programme. The repository will provide deeper insight on the trends and directions of research being conducted in Indian universities while providing appropriate mechanisms to check duplication of research. The repository claims that the synopses submitted in this repository would later be mapped to full-text theses in "ShodhGanga", but as of writing this chapter such mapping has not been implemented. The much-needed mapping will facilitate better tracking. Once the full-text thesis is submitted for a synopsis, a link to the full-text theses would be provided from ShodhGangotri to "ShodhGanga"

Users can register and login as ShodhGangotri User, University Coordinator and Administrator. The screenshot of the user registration UI is given in Figure 3.

Figure 3. Registration and Submission Interface

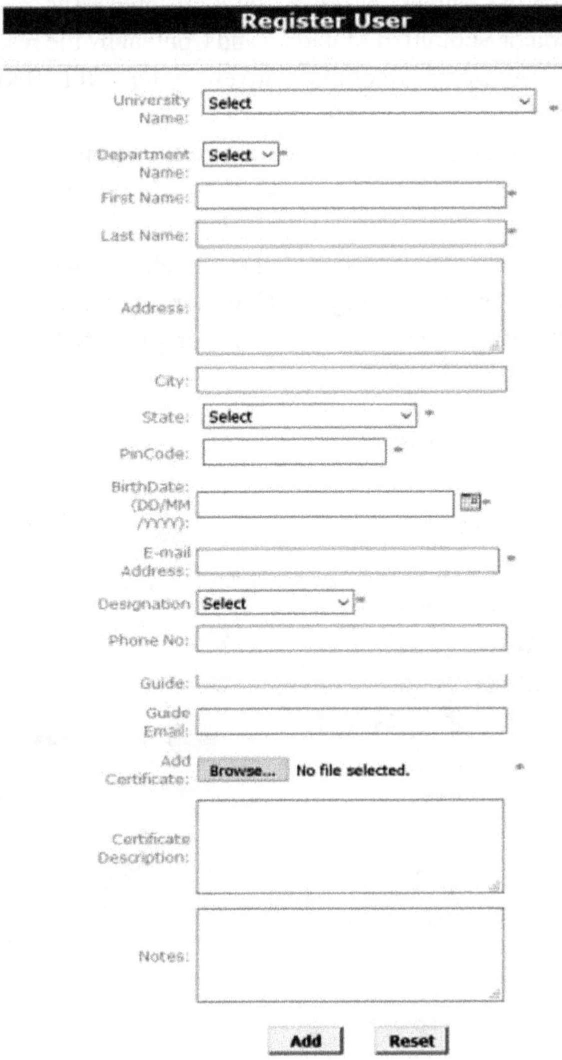

Submission Process

ETD online submission of approved synopsis to Shodhgangotri can be done by researchers/supervisor or university coordinator. However, individual researchers can submit their approved synopsis either online or off-line (through E-mail or CD / DVD) on voluntary basis. Workflow for submission of electronic version of synopsis consists of the following six steps:

Step 1: Registration/Login by the research scholar/research supervisor/authorized representative of the University.
Step 2: Validation of Account by INFLIBNET.
Step 3: Submission of Content / Metadata by Registered User.
Step 4: Verification of Submitted Metadata and Content by the research supervisor or university representative or alternatively by the INFLIBNET Staff.
Step 5: Publish on ShodhGangotri Repository.
Step 6: Intimation to stakeholders by Sending Notification to Researcher / Guide and the University.

ShoghGangotri provides both basic searches as well as advanced search interface. Advanced search can be done by keyword, Author, Title, Subject, Language, etc. Multi-field search can be done using Boolean operators AND, OR, NOT.

Figure 4. Advanced search interface

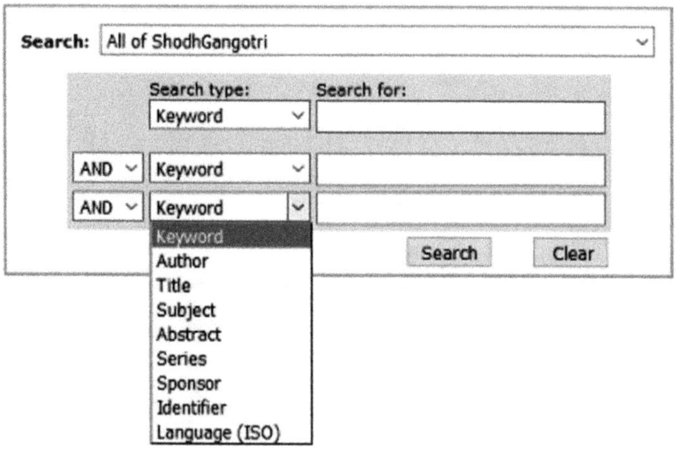

SHODHGANGA WEBSITE QUALITY EVALUATION

Any information retrieval system needs to be evaluated as its purpose gets defeated if users find it hard to retrieve desired information from it. Websites have become the vital source of information. Organizations prefer to disseminate information online than in any other form. Websites are the de-facto mode of mass communication. When it comes to research output, it becomes essential that the websites meant for dissemination of research being produced at the national level, must be high quality. They must fulfil the requirements of the target audience (peers & scholars) quite comprehensively. Keeping this in view, the Shodhganga website has been evaluated using Nibbler (a web app).

Nibbler provides a score out of 10 in Accessibility, Experience, Marketing and Technology. It also provides an overall score of the website as an average of the scores in the aforementioned areas. Accessibility is determined by the definition relied on this paper in the context; how a website is accessible to disabled users and the users who rely on other devices such as mobile phones to access the website. Nibbler uses six tests to determine a websites accessibility; mobile, code quality, internal links, headings, page titles, and the URL format. The Shodhganga website

Figure 5. Shodhganga website evaluation score
Website tested: Shoghganga
URL: http://shodhganga.inflibnet.ac.in/
Date of testing: 26 August, 2017
Number of webpages tested: 5

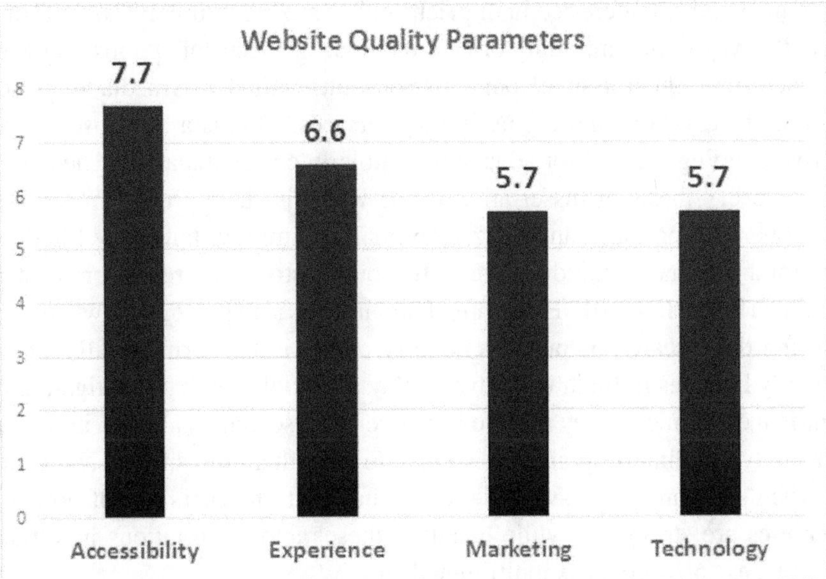

has scored well (7.7) in terms of accessibility which stands for dissemination of research output manifested in the form of ETDs. User Experience (UX) encompasses all aspects of the end-user's interaction with the company, its services, and its products. It includes usability, ease of use, and pleasure provided in the interaction between the website visitor and the products. Shodhganga website was able to score 6.6 which indicates, the User experience design (UXD or UED) needs to improve in order to enhance user satisfaction and affinity.

In the marketing segment, the Shodhganga website was found to be average (5.7) indicating need of adopting social media for its branding and promotion. On technology part, it has scored the same (5.7). This is evident as subject search is not up to the mark as a user has to struggle a lot to obtain precise subject specific results. Also, there exists ample scope for customization of the user interface (UI). Overall it scored 6.2 out of ten which not so discouraging but demands fresh intervention.

CONCLUSION

In time to come, ETDs would become more commonplace, grant-giving agencies and accreditation bodies like All India Council for Technical Education (AICTE), National Assessment and Accreditation Council (NAAC) and University Grants Commission, would evaluate and rank innovative universities by taking note of their initiatives such as ETDs and IRs. This would certainly prove to be an impetus for HEIs of India to pro- actively enrich the Shodhganga repository by contributing more and more ETDs. This Initiative benefiting millions of learners, teachers, scholars, researchers, and the many others interested in this rich genre. Into the future, ETDs can continue to lead the way to the unfolding of new methods of electronic publishing, sharing of datasets, reproducible scholarship, use of multimedia/hypermedia technologies, curation, preservation, and digital library services. This is a low-cost and highly effective ongoing method for advancing scholarly communication. The day is not far when every thesis or dissertation in the world is shared in the most effective way, as openly as possible, and utilized optimally to improve humanity. Shodhganga stands for the reservoir of Indian intellectual output stored in a repository hosted and maintained by the INFLIBNET Centre. Plagiarism is a major concern when it comes to hosting the research output of a country online in the form of full-text ETDs. University libraries in India will have to play a crucial role in the mitigation of the plagiarism epidemic as they need to sensitize the researchers along with providing the capacity building programmes in order to train them in handling and using the plagiarism software made available to the university teachers. As of now, Indian universities are struggling while handling theses and dissertations in vernacular languages, as software lacks multilingual support.

For its innovative and ambitious project Shodhganga was conferred The NDLTD Leadership Award 2017 (instituted since 2004) at the National Conference iETD 2017 (26-27 September, 2017) on the theme: "Re-Envisaging iETDs: Roles and Responsibilities" which was organised by INFLIBNET, India. However, efforts are required to enhance the website quality to meet the information needs of the users irrespective of their diverse information seeking behaviour.

REFERENCES

Ahmed, A., Alreyaee, S., & Rahman, A. (2014). Theses and dissertations in institutional repositories: An Asian perspective. *New Library World*, *115*(9-10), 438–451. doi:10.1108/NLW-04-2014-0035

Alemneh, D., & Phillips, M. (2016). Indexing quality and effectiveness: An exploratory analysis of electronic theses and dissertations representation. *Proceedings of the Association for Information Science and Technology*, *53*(1), 1–4. doi:10.1002/pra2.2016.14505301111

Ardalan, R., & Feyzbaksh, O. (2011). What are universities doing here? Migrating traditional dissertations into ETDs in Iran. *Library Hi Tech News*, *28*(9), 7–11. doi:10.1108/07419051111195573

Chapter 1 ETDs: From the Beginning. (2008). *Technical Services Quarterly*, *25*(sup1), 1–10. 10.1080/07317130802127819

Ezema, I. J., & Igbo, H. U. (2016). Electronic theses and dissertations and the promotion of scholarship in African universities: Prospects and challenges. *The International Information & Library Review*, *48*(1), 21–30. doi:10.1080/10572317.2016.1146038

Fyffe, R., & Welburn, W. (2008). ETDs, scholarly communication, and campus collaboration: Opportunities for libraries. *College & Research Libraries News*, *69*(3), 152–155. doi:10.5860/crln.69.3.7952

Hartsock, R., & Alemneh, D. G. (2018). Electronic Theses and Dissertations (ETDs). In M. Khosrow-Pour (Ed.), Encyclopedia of Information Science and Technology, Fourth Edition (pp. 6748-6755). Hershey, PA: IGI Global. doi:10.4018/978-1-5225-2255-3.ch584

INFLIBNET. (2017a). *ShodhGangotri: Repository of Indian Research in Progress: Home*. Retrieved from http://shodh.inflibnet.ac.in/

INFLIBNET. (2017b). *Shodhganga: a reservoir of Indian theses @ INFLIBNET.* Retrieved from http://shodhganga.inflibnet.ac.in/

Lamprecht, E. (2017). *The Difference Between UX and UI Design - A Layman's Guide.* Retrieved from https://careerfoundry.com/en/blog/ux-design/the- difference-between-ux-and-ui-design-a-layman's-guide/

Norman, D., & Nielsen, J. (n.d.). *The Definition of User Experience (UX).* Retrieved from https://www.nngroup.com/articles/definition-user-experience/

Open Access Theses and Dissertations. (n.d.). *OATD – Open Access Theses and Dissertations.* Retrieved September 17, 2017, from https://oatd.org/

Panda, S. K. (2016). Shodhganga – a national level open access ETD repository of Indian electronic theses: Current status and discussions. *Library Hi Tech News, 33*(1), 23–26. doi:10.1108/LHTN-09-2015-0062

Perrin, J. M., Winkler, H. M., & Yang, L. (2015). Digital preservation challenges with an ETD collection - A case study at texas tech university. *Journal of Academic Librarianship, 41*(1), 98–104. doi:10.1016/j.acalib.2014.11.002

Potvin, S., & Thompson, S. (2016). An analysis of evolving metadata influences, standards, and practices in electronic theses and dissertations. *Library Resources & Technical Services, 60*(2), 99–114. doi:10.5860/lrts.60n2.99

Sarkar, P., & Mukhopadhyay, P. (2016). Full-text etd retrieval in library discovery system: Designing a framework. *Annals of Library and Information Studies, 63*(4), 274–288. Retrieved from www.scopus.com

Shalini Ramdas Lihitkar, R. S. (2014). Electronic theses and dissertations (ETDs) in India: A comparative study. *Library Hi Tech News, 31*(2), 9–14. doi:10.1108/LHTN-10-2013-0061

The Networked Digital Library of Theses and Dissertations (NDLTD). (2017, August 2). *Mission, Goals, and History.* Retrieved August 28, 2017, from www.ndltd.org/about

Website report for shodhganga.inflibnet.ac.in. (2017). Retrieved from http://nibbler.silktide.com/en_US/reports/shodhganga.inflibnet.ac.in

Chapter 4
Governance of Liquid Communications in the Botswana Public Sector:
Neither Restricted by Time nor Space

Tshepho Mosweu
University of Botswana, Botswana & University of South Africa, South Africa

Mpho Ngoepe
University of South Africa, South Africa

ABSTRACT

Botswana government uses ICT to deliver services and communicate with the public to increase access and usage of services. One of the platforms for such communications is social media which generates liquid communication. Liquid communication is defined as a type of communication that can easily go back and forth between participants involved which is neither restricted by time nor space. This can be shared and re-tweeted many times beyond the control of the creating agency, resulting in challenges regarding its management. The question that arises is, How do government agencies ensure governance of such records? Using literature review, this chapter explores governance of liquid communications by Botswana government. The study established that there are no guidelines for managing liquid communications. The chapter recommends that Botswana government should design a governance framework to guide ministries in the management of liquid communication. Failure to regulate this environment would result in trouble for the country such as loss of memory.

DOI: 10.4018/978-1-5225-5840-8.ch004

INTRODUCTION

The increasing use of information and communication technologies (ICTs), especially the internet, in government operations around the African continent as driven by public sector reform, has given impetus to the generation of electronic records (e-records) (Wamukoya & Mutula 2005). Just like their paper counterparts, e-records support the day-to-day operations of government services and interactions with citizens, private and public-sector partners. The availability of ICTs and their inherent advantages in communication has now accelerated the use of social media by organisations to create and disseminate information, making it easier to reach a wider spectrum of users. Different scholars have defined social media in different ways. It has been defined by Gartner (2016) as an online environment in which content is created, consumed, promoted, distributed, discovered or shared for purposes primarily related to communities and social activities, rather than functional, task-oriented objectives. The United States (US) Navy (2012) describes social media as a variety of communication media and platforms, including social networks, blogs, mobile applications and others. According to Boyd and Ellison (2007) this social networking service is an online service, platform or website that focuses on building and reflecting social networks among people who share interests and activities. As observed by Begum (2015), social media has become an integral part of people's lives. For example, in the United States of America, the National Archives and Records Administration (2013) reported that 70% of agencies used social media. In agreement with this assertion, Latham (2014) observed that studies of government use of social media showed that using social media as a communication tool can enable governments to reach new audiences, establish communities of practice, provide services and deliver important and effective messages to the community. The United States' Department of Energy (2010) consequently advises that if one tweets, blogs, or uses other social media to conduct official business, the resultant records should be managed in accordance with records management principles.

Interaction with citizens and the public through social media creates what is called liquid communication. This kind of communication continuously changes as and when shared as in the case with Facebook and re-tweeted in Twitter. Duranti (2014) describes liquid communication as an ongoing communication and movement of material from one circle of people to another, crossing the public-private lines through social media. For example, with Facebook, users post or share information to recipients in the network and interaction takes place as recipients make comments where the one who initially posted can respond and the communication goes on and on continually. The same post can be edited and shared several times, resulting in liquid communication. The concept of liquidity, according to Choi, Im and Yo (2013:3) was introduced around 2000 by Bauman to explain how our society has become busier and more fragmented. He used the word "solid" to symbolize postmodernity, to indicate "solid" concepts, such as traditional values, customary rights, civic obligations, and individual family duties. Bauman (1999) stated that "fluids … liquids, unlike solids, cannot easily hold their shape. Fluids, so to speak, neither fix space nor bind time. While solids have clear spatial dimensions … fluids do not keep to any shape for long and are constantly ready … it is the flow of time that counts, more than the space they happen to occupy: that space, after all, they fill but 'for a moment'" (Choi 2013:3). In the field of archives and records management Smit, Glaudemans and Jonker (2017) argue that paradigms and concepts that formed the basis of recordkeeping in the analogue world have lost their central place and attempts to create a new paradigm on archives in the digital information society have not yet been convincing as reflected in the liquid times, which the archival profession is also going through.

Social networks have become a platform for liquid communication through which real business transactions take place. When referring to social media communication, Begum (2015) observes that with the number of users of social networks growing exponentially, the need for managing and preserving the resultant communication (records) has gained prime importance. However, the challenge with liquid communication is that this information can be shared many times beyond the control of the creating organisation, resulting in confusion regarding its management and preservation. Despite challenges related to the preservation of liquid communication, the records created still have to be governed in line with records management principles to ensure that they are available for use as and when required. For the purpose of this chapter, liquid communication refers to records generated by the government on social media for customer service, access to information and direct community involvement needs. The chapter looks at the governance of liquid communication in the Botswana public sector. The interpretation by Ngoepe and Saurombe (2016) of what records entail in terms of Botswana archival legislation reveals that the legislation is intended to cover as many forms of records as possible in as many types of media as possible. In legal terms, wide coverage is mostly encouraged so that other aspects may not be subjected to non-protection owing to their falling outside the ambit of the legislation.

BACKGROUND

The use of ICTs to deliver public services in Botswana is part of the government's electronic government (e-government) programme. Millar (2004) contends that governments in both the developing and developed world computerise their core functions and use ICTs to improve access to their services. Not to be left behind, the government of Botswana hatched public sector reforms in order to improve service delivery. These included the formulation of the National Vision 2016 (Government of Botswana 1997) and the National ICT Policy (Government of Botswana 2007), known as the Maitlamo Policy, which advocates for the use of ICTs in the delivery of services to the public. This policy promotes e-government through which technology, particularly web-based applications, will be utilised to enhance access to and delivery of government information and services to citizens, business partners, employees, other agencies and government entities.

Apart from the National Vision 2016 and the Maitlamo Policy, the government of Botswana developed an e-government Strategy that serves as a framework for all e-government initiatives. The Maitlamo Policy provides a policy framework for the overall use of ICTs in the public sector (Government of Botswana 2007) while the e-government Strategy specifically guides the implementation of e-government initiatives. The strategy outlines interrelated projects that are meant to collectively move all appropriate government services online, significantly improve public sector service delivery and accelerate the uptake and usage of ICT across all segments of the society (Government of Botswana 2012). Moloi and Mutula (2007) opine that the ICT infrastructure in Botswana was fairly developed to support e-government and the bureaucracy appreciated e-government initiatives.

The Botswana Government Communication and Information System (BGCIS) was established through Presidential Directive CAB: 30/2006 and is mandated to ensure that the government communicates appropriate information to the public in a timely, authoritative, coherent, coordinated and proactive manner, and responds promptly to public concerns, queries and criticism. It manages and coordinates government communication by promoting effective and interactive communications between government and the public, promoting a positive communication environment and improving the quality of government information and communication. One of the ways the BGCIS uses to fulfil its mission is the use of social media to communicate with the public. The Botswana government Facebook page, titled "BWGOVERNMENT', provides updates about government programmes and policies, as well as any information that the government needs to impart to the nation (Masilo & Seabo 2015:124). The government of Botswana mainly uses Facebook and twitter (as reflected in Table 1).

USE OF SOCIAL MEDIA BY GOVERNMENT AGENCIES IN BOTSWANA

The government of Botswana has embraced social media in its interaction and regularly communicates with citizens through social networking sites, especially Facebook

Table 1. Statistics showing Botswana Government social media accounts

Statistics for Botswana Government social media accounts (BWGovernment)		
Platform	Launch Date	Engagements
Facebook	September 2011	340 300 likes (08.02.18)
Twitter	June 2011	156 000 followers (08.02.18)

Source: Botswana Government social media pages

and Twitter. A study done by Batane (2013) on internet access and use among young people in Botswana has revealed that entertainment and communication comprised about 75% of young people's internet time. This means that most of the communication by the Botswana government reaches many young people in Botswana. The use of social media such as Facebook and Twitter has become common with citizens of Botswana. Social networking sites such as Facebook, Twitter, Google+, Pinterest, Instagram and LinkedIn have risen in popularity in Botswana like elsewhere in the world. Statistics by World Stats have shown that the most used social network in Botswana is Facebook, with a usage of about 92.88%. Pinterest ranks second with 3.05% usage, followed by Twitter with 3.02% usage, Google+ ranks fourth with 0.37% and the remaining social networks hold 0.68% using mobile internet. Figure 1 presents the types of social media platforms used in Botswana.

Figure 1. Showing types of social media platforms and percentage social media usage by young people in Botswana
Source: World Statistics

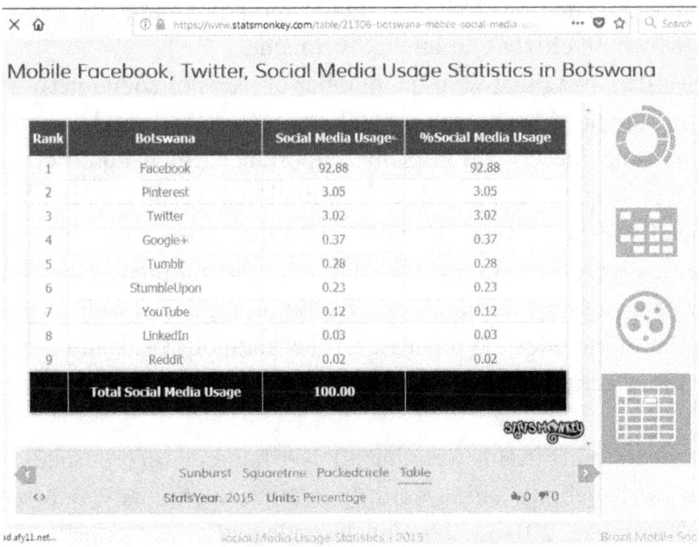

Mobile Facebook, Twitter, Social Media Usage Statistics in Botswana

Rank	Botswana	Social Media Usage	%Social Media Usage
1	Facebook	92.88	92.88
2	Pinterest	3.05	3.05
3	Twitter	3.02	3.02
4	Google+	0.37	0.37
5	Tumblr	0.28	0.28
6	StumbleUpon	0.23	0.23
7	YouTube	0.12	0.12
8	LinkedIn	0.03	0.03
9	Reddit	0.02	0.02
	Total Social Media Usage	100.00	

Sunburst Squaretree Packedcircle Table

StatsYear: 2015 Units: Percentage

A number of government departments in Botswana now use social media to interact with citizens as part of the delivery of public services. Table 2 summarises and analyses publicly available social media pages by Botswana government ministries. These are central government offices and the data does not include local government authorities and departments falling under the ministries. Some of the ministries do not have social media pages but their departments do. Data as presented in Table 2 depicts the ministries that have social media pages that are either Facebook or Twitter.

Ramsay (2009), the Coordinator of Botswana Government Communication and Information System (BGCIS) has indicated that online communications had resulted in a massive increase in the demand for public information. As noted by Batane (2013), the government of Botswana is committed to increasing access to technology (information?) by different sectors of the population. Challenges are inevitable Jansen and Duranti (2013) argue that the use of social media, which creates liquid communication, brings about challenges that relate to issues of ownership, jurisdiction and privacy regarding internet-based records. The said challenges need to be resolved especially in government or public bodies since technology does not stand still to wait for legal and regulatory systems to catch up. Neal & McDevitt Intellectual Property and Marketing Attorneys (2010) outlines the following as some of the legal issues that an organisation may face as it integrates social media into its business practices; disclosure of confidential information, unauthorized use of trademarks, unauthorized use of copyright-protected works, defamation issues, electronic discovery, dynamic information, human resources issues, securities, privacy/publicity and endorsements. These legal issues need to be taken into consideration when using social media to conduct government business, including sharing public information, lest they hinder the enjoyment of benefits of social media usage by both citizens and the government.

Begum (2015) avers that with the number of users of social networks growing exponentially, the need for managing and preserving the liquid communication in a network has become crucial in prime importance. Such liquid communication records have to be subjected to proper information governance in order for it to be duly managed and preserved. Gartner (2016) describes information governance as the specification of decision rights and an accountability framework to ensure appropriate behaviour in the valuation, creation, storage, use, archiving and deletion of information. It includes the processes, roles and policies, standards and metrics that ensure the effective and efficient use of information in enabling an organisation to achieve its goals.

Internet accessibility in Botswana has allowed hundreds of thousands of Botswana residents to use Facebook and, according to Nielsen company, quoted by *Sunday Standard* Newspaper (2016). Botswana's participation rates on Facebook placed

Table 2. Showing Botswana Government Ministries which had social media pages (July 2017)

Ministry	Social Media Use	
	Facebook	Twitter
Administration of Justice (AOJ)	×	×
Attorney General's Chambers (AGC)	✔	✔
Government to Government	✔	✔
Independent Electoral Commission (IEC)	✔	✔
Industrial Court (IC)	×	×
Ministry of Agriculture (MOA)	×	×
Ministry of Defense Justice and Security(MDJS)	×	×
Ministry of Education and Skills Development	✔	✔
Ministry of Environment, Wildlife and Tourism (MEWT)	✔	×
Ministry of Finance and Development Planning(MFDP)	×	×
Ministry of Foreign Affairs and International Cooperation (MoFAIC)	✔	×
Ministry of Health (MOH)	✔	✔
Ministry of Infrastructure, Science and Technology (MIST)	×	×
Ministry of Labour & Home Affairs (MLHA)	✔	×
Ministry of Lands and Housing	✔	×
Ministry of Local Government (MLG)	✔	×
Ministry of Minerals, Energy and Water Resources (MMEWR)	✔	×
Ministry of Trade and Industry (MTI)	✔	×
Ministry of Transport and Communications(MTC)	×	×
Ministry of Youth, Sport and Culture	✔	✔
Office Of The Auditor General (OAG)	✔	×
Office of the Ombudsman(OMB)	×	×
State President	✔	×
The Parliament Office (PO)	×	×

Botswana far ahead of all sub-Saharan African countries. The Facebook profile was derived from three variables: awareness, penetration and usage. In terms of awareness, Botswana ties with Namibia with both countries having a slight edge over their neighbour, South Africa. In terms of penetration, Botswana beats both its neighbours easily, with South Africa coming in a distant second. In terms of usage, Botswana also ties with Namibia (Sunday Standard 2016)

IMPLICATIONS OF NOT MANAGING LIQUID COMMUNICATION GENERATED THROUGH SOCIAL MEDIA

Liquid communication or records generated through the use of social media need to be managed in accordance with accepted records management principles. For example, Begum (2015) contends that social media technologies have already taken on an important role among the means of communication between the users and the government agencies in such a way that they have to preserve the important communications between the users and the agencies for future access. If electronic records created are not managed properly, issues of their security, privacy, preservation and general management arise (Hohman 2011). The following issues have to be taken into consideration to ensure proper governance of liquid communication.

Preservation of Social Media Records

Some social media platforms have developed tools to assist users with capturing content for retention purposes, so it may be necessary to purchase third-party tools or develop in-house applications to electronically capture social media records (Ohio Electronic Records Committee 2014). Just like their paper equivalents, liquid communication generated through the use of social media should be captured and preserved if they possess continuing value. Di Bianca (2014) argues that data residing on social media platforms is subject to the same duty to preserve as other types of electronically stored information. As noted by Ngoepe and Saurombe (2016), liquid communication is also considered as records in terms of Botswana archival legislation.

According to Duranti (2014), preservation includes the whole of the principles, policies and strategies that control the activities designed to ensure materials' (data, documents or records) physical and technological stabilisation and protection of intellectual content. It has been acknowledged that it is challenging to ensure long-term preservation of liquid communication generated through social media (Duranti 2014; Begum 2015; Franks & Driskill 2014). Despite the format, records should be organised and preserved for easy access for as long as needed. Some social media sites provide tools to extract information in open formats, while other sites do not. As a result, agencies must consider how frequently information needs to be captured, the stability of the social media site, and the functionality of the tools used to extract the information (Ohio Electronic Records Committee 2014:5). This therefore means that the Botswana Government should have policies and strategies in place designed specifically to ensure long-term preservation of liquid communication. DiBianca (2014) argues that regardless of the method employed, preservation of social media evidence is critically important and the consequences of failing to preserve it could be significant. The Library and Archives Canada

(2013:17) reports that in the United States of America, the Minnesota Historical Society (MHS) faced exponential growth in storage required for the preservation of digital collections consisting of images, audio, video, text, and other formats. It is now evident that other technologies have improved and enabled better preservation measures for digital records. Library and Archives Canada (2017: 4) reports that the National Archives of Australia has built a state-of-the-art storage facility that contains a conservation laboratory, digital archives for records, cold storage areas and 114 kilometres of shelving which is expected to provide enough new space to accommodate the National Archives collections until 2030.

Legislative and Policy Framework

Public sector records management is subject to provisions in laws and regulations. The Botswana National Archives and Records Services (BNARS), as a government department mandated by the National Archives and Records Services Act to manage all records created in government agencies, should also ensure good governance of liquid communications generated through the use of social media. There is still a need for Botswana to make the necessary changes in the country's current legislation. Until 2014, there was no legislative framework to facilitate and enable the provision of e-services in Botswana, whereby laws prohibited rather than promoted the use of ICT to provide services (Keetshabe 2015). As an example, Keetshabe (2015) points out that the legislation did not provide for recognition of electronic signatures, authenticity of electronic documents and admissibility of electronic evidence as records in the courts. Most laws have records management implications, but the main ones required especially in the context of social media usage, such as data protection and privacy laws are yet to be adopted. There is also a need to amend existing ones such as the National Archives and Records Services Act of 1978, Cybercrime and Computer Related Crimes Act of 2007, Electronic Communications and Transactions Act of 2014 and the Electronic Records (Evidence) Act, 2004, to accommodate the governance of liquid communication generated through social media. As one of the concerns for government agencies using social media is the possibility of termination of service and the loss of information that the agency is obligated to maintain, agencies, along with legal counsel and information technology professionals, should read and negotiate, where applicable, the "terms of service" agreement to incorporate language for the proper retention and disposition of records in accordance with the country's legislation (Ohio Electronic Records Committee 2014:4)

As acknowledged by the BGCIS coordinator, the ideal is that communications should become an integral part of policy development whereby communications plans can be formulated across the cycle of policy development, delivery and refinement (Ramsay 2009). A study by Ngoepe and Keakopa (2011) found that the Botswana National Archives and Records Services did not have infrastructure to ingest electronic records in their custody for permanent preservation. According to the National Archives and Records Services Act of 1978 as amended in 2007, a record:

includes any electronic records, manuscript, newspaper, picture, painting, document, register, printed material, book, map, plan, drawing, photograph, negative and positive pictures, photocopy, microfilm, cinematograph film, video tape, magnetic tape, gramophone record or other transcription of language, picture or music, recorded by any means capable of reproduction and regardless of physical form and characteristics.

As this definition of a record in this act is not content specific, a record may be in any format, including those generated through the use of social media. According to Ngoepe and Saurombe (2016:29), this wide coverage shows that the legislation intended to cover as many forms of records as possible in as many types of media as possible. In legal terms, wide coverage is mostly encouraged so that other aspects may not be subjected to non-protection owing to their falling outside the ambit of the legislation. The advent of technology especially that of the use of social media, is critical for the proper understanding of preservation of records going into the future. The creation, use and preservation of liquid communication can be considered intrinsic to records management and thus liquid communication need to be managed accordingly and in accordance with applicable legislative instruments.

Social Media and Trust in Government

In recent years, researchers have recognised the relatively unexplored area of study related to the use of social media by government and its correlation to citizen trust (Franks & Driskill 2014). A study done by Khan and Rahim (2016:5) identified citizens characteristics, government factors, risk factor and social media characteristics as antecedents of trust in adoption of Government social media.With liquid communication generated through social media, as Duranti (2014) argues, the nature of trust relationships is rife with risks, weaknesses and fault-lines inherent in the management of records and their storage in rapidly changing technologies where authorship, ownership and jurisdiction may be questioned. As a result, the trustworthiness of liquid communication generated through the use of social media in terms of their reliability and authenticity as evidence before the law courts should be investigated. This is even paramount in this era of post-truth and fake news where it has become easier to create and share information beyond the creator's control.

The question now becomes how do we maintain the authoritative role of records as evidence in the digital era?

The issue of social media and trust in government have been extensively explored in a research project titled 'The Social Media and Trust in Government' under the research agenda of InterPARES Trust (InterPARES 2016). The goal was to develop case studies that analyzed citizen experience with government social media tools and use, with respect to issues of trust, including concepts of openness, transparency, accountability, and authenticity. (InterPARES 2016:6). The study explored the types of social media initiatives undertaken by government organizations in the United States and Canada to determine how they utilize social media to engage citizens and provide customer service, as well as how the public reacts to those initiatives (InterPARES 2016:6). In both countries, significant care was taken to implement controls around account creation, access and content. This promoted trust by citizens of social media use by government.

Security and Privacy Issues in Social Media Records

By its nature, liquid communications tend to be technically volatile, hence, it has security complications. Security of liquid communication generated through social media may increase the risk of unauthorised access, inadequate data protection measures, ownership and control. For example, Duranti (2014) lists the following as threats to records posted online, unauthorised access, hackers, documents can be stored anywhere and can be moved at any time-without the knowledge of the records creator, encryption might be breached, shared servers could intermingle information. Hohman (2011) observes the rapid and free flow of information between employees, colleagues and online social media tools presents serious risks to a business and to the protection of personal information. It is on that note that the Ohio Electronic Records Committee (2014:6) advices that government agencies should ensure the security of data and technical infrastructure by developing best practices such as the implementation of password security and additional controls to monitor web site content as posted or viewed.

This then means that the Botswana government should have policies and procedures in place that deal with the security of liquid communication generated through social media in government. It has been found that an information governance programme ensures a reasonable level of protection to records and information that are private, confidential, privileged, secret, classified, essential to business continuity, or that otherwise require protection (ARMA 2014). According to ISO 15489 (2016), to ensure authenticity of records, organisations should implement and document policies and procedures that control the creation, receipt, transmission, maintenance and disposition of records to ensure that records are authorised and identified and that records are protected against unauthorised addition, deletions, alteration, use and concealment.

RECOMMENDATIONS

Public records created through liquid communication need to be managed properly and the following measures are suggested. There is need to enact relevant legislation or adopt policies and procedures that ensure governance of liquid communication generated through social media. In the case of Botswana, legislation such as National Archives and Records Services Act, Cybercrime and Computer Related Crimes Act, Electronic Communications and Transactions act of 2014 and Electronic records (Evidence) Act (Government of Botswana 1978; 2007; 2014) need to be amended so that they become relevant and applicable to the preservation of liquid communication. There exists a need for a shared regulatory and procedural framework that promotes consistency and balance in terms of policies and practices regarding the handling of digital objects (Jansen & Duranti 2013). Unlike in the traditional way of managing records, governance of liquid communications generated through the use of social media may need the development of distinct infrastructure and appropriate legislative framework to regulate its sustainable use and preservation. Where these issues are not taken into account, the use of social media to enhance access, promote wider dialogue and gather data has the potential to create archives and records management problems.

As issues of trust in government in cyberspace arise, measures should be put in place to ensure that public records created through liquid communication are trusted by citizens. Thurston (2012) argues that for data to be trusted, it needs to be substantiated. For liquid communication generated through the social media to be trusted the following questions as outlined by Thurston (2012) should be addressed: "Can the records from which the data are derived be trusted?", "Are they complete?", "Are they authentic?", "How were they generated, by whom and in what conditions?", "Is there sufficient contextual information to enable them to be understood?" and "Are they being captured and held securely to allow comparisons over time?"

Another suggestion is to introduce some governance framework to guide the management of liquid communication generated through social media in Botswana. Gartner (2016) describes information governance as the specification of decision rights and an accountability framework to ensure appropriate behaviour in the valuation, creation, storage, use, archiving and deletion of information. It includes the processes, roles and policies, standards and metrics that ensure the effective and efficient use of information in enabling an organisation to achieve its goals. The ARMA Generally Accepted Recordkeeping Principles, also known as The Principles, are a good governance tool to manage liquid communications generated through the use of social media by the Botswana government. These eight principles are accountability, transparency, integrity, protection, compliance, availability, retention and disposition describe effective information governance (ARMA 2014). The use of The Principles could ensure information governance. The fact that there has to be a programme that ensures compliance with the applicable laws and other binding authorities, as well as with the organisation's policies, cannot be overemphasised.

CONCLUSION

This chapter has defined the concept of liquid communication. It has also identified government agencies in Botswana that utilise social media as part of the delivery of public services. The use of ICTs to conduct public affairs in Botswana is part of the wider government reform named e-government. Liquid communication generated though social media by the Botswana government should be properly managed, otherwise issues of trust, privacy and security of information arise. Apart from that, the preservation of resultant records comes into question. Will the records be available in the long term if they possess continuing value? This therefore means there is a need to institute some form of governance of liquid communication generated through social media by the Botswana government. This chapter draws on an ongoing study and a bigger project for University of South Africa (UNISA) and InterPARES, respectively, which sought to develop a governance framework for preservation of liquid communication generated through social media.

REFERENCES

ARMA. (2014). *Generally Accepted Recordkeeping Principles, Information Governance Maturity Model*. Retrieved February 20, 2017, from: https://www.arma.org/docs/bookstore/theprinciplesmaturitymodel.pdf?sfvrsn=2

Batane, T. (2013). Internet Access and Use among Young People in Botswana. *International Journal of Information and Education Technology (IJIET)*, *3*(1), 117–119. doi:10.7763/IJIET.2013.V3.246

Begum, R. A. (2015). *Preserving Social Media (A case study at LTU archives)* (Master's Thesis). Luleå University of Technology, Department of Computer Science, Electrical and Space Engineering. Retrieved April 4, 2018, from: http://www.diva-portal.org/smash/get/diva2:1031685/FULLTEXT02

Botswana Government. (2012). *Botswana's National e-Government Strategy 2011-2016*. Retrieved March 31, 2018, from: http://workspace.unpan.org/sites/internet/documents/unpan048687.pdf

Boyd, D. M., & Ellison, N. B. (2007). Social network sites: Definition, history and scholarship. *Journal of Computer-Mediated Communication*, *13*(1), 210–230. doi:10.1111/j.1083-6101.2007.00393.x

Choi, K. S., Im, I., & Yoo, Y. (2013). *Liquid Communication: An Analysis of the Impact of Mobile Micro-blogging on Communication and Decision-Making*. Retrieved February 20, 2017, from: http://aisel.aisnet.org/cgi/viewcontent.cgi?article=1301&context=icis2013

Di Bianca, M. (2014). *Discovery and Preservation of Social Media Evidence*. Retrieved February 20, 2018, from: https://www.americanbar.org/content/dam/aba/publications/blt/2014/01/social-media-evidence-201401.authcheckdam.pdf

Duranti, L. (2014). *A clear sky forecast on a cloudy day: Making, Keeping and Preserving Records in a Public Cloud Environment*. Retrieved February 20, 2018, from: http://www.ffzg.unizg.hr/ada2014/wp-content/uploads/2014/07/08-Duranti-Making-Keeping-and-Preserving-Records-in-a-Public-Cloud-Environment.pdf

Duranti, L. (2015). Special Issue: Data, Records, and Archives in the Cloud. *Canadian Journal of Information and Library Science*, *39*(2), 91–96. doi:10.1353/ils.2015.0013

Franks, P., & Driskill, M. (2014). *Building Trust in Government through Social Media: An InterPARES Trust Research Project*. Retrieved May 16, 2018, from: https://interparestrust.org/assets/public/dissemination/FranksDriskill_ECSM2014_BuildingTrustInGovernmentThroughSocialMedia.pdf

Gartner, Inc. (2016). *Information Governance*. Retrieved February 20, 2017, from: https://www.gartner.com/it-glossary/information-governance

Government of Botswana. (1978). *National Archives and Records Services Act Cap 59:04*. Gaborone: Government Printer.

Government of Botswana. (1996). *Vision 2016*. Gaborone: Government Printer.

Government of Botswana. (2007). *National Information and Communications Technology Policy (Maitlamo Policy)*. Gaborone: Government Printer.

Government of Botswana. (2014). *Electronic Communications and Transactions Act*. Gaborone: Government Printer.

Hohman, C. (2011). *A records and information management guide to social media.* Retrieved May 13, 2018, from: http://www.incontextmag.com/articles/2011/a-records-and-information-management-guide-to-social-media.html

Internet World Stats. (2017). *Internet Statistics users for Africa (Africa Internet Usage, 2017 Population Stats and Facebook Subscribers).* Retrieved February 08, 2018, from: http://www.internetworldstats.com/stats1.htm

InterPARES Trust. (2016). *The Social Media and Trust in Government.* Retrieved June 24, 2018, from: https://interparestrust.org/trust

ISO 15489. (2016). *Information and Documentation – Records Management. Part 1. General.* International Standards Organisation.

Jansen, A., & Duranti, L. (2013). *The InterPARES Trust Project – Trust and Digital Records in an Increasingly Networked Society.* Retrieved April 10, 2018, from: https://interparestrust.org/assets/public/dissemination/203JansenDurantiTheInterPARESTrustProject.pdf

Keetshabe, A. M. (2012). *Development of ICT legal and regulatory framework in Botswana.* Retrieved February 02, 2018, from: https://www.gov.bw/globalassets/.../ict.../e---legislation---ict-pitso-2012-legal-framework.ppt

Khan, S., & Rahim, N. Z. A. (2016). *Factors Influencing Citizens Trust on Government Social media.* Retrieved October 25, 2018, from: http://ais.utm.my/paris2016/files/2016/11/3-Factors-Influencing-Citizens-Trust-on-Government-Social-Media.pdf

Latham, R. (2014). *Information Management Advice 57 Managing Social Media. Records Part 1: Overview.* Retrieved November 26, 2017, from: https://www.informationstrategy.tas.gov.au/Records-ManagementPrinciples/Document%20Library%20%20Tools/Advice%2057%20Managing%20Social%20Media%20Records%20Part%201%20-%20Overview.pdf

Library and Archives Canada. (2013). *Governance and Records Keeping around the word.* Retrieved February 08, 2018, from: https://www.bac-lac.gc.ca/eng/services/government-information-resources/information-management/Documents/february-2013.pdf

Library and Archives Canada. (2017). *Governance and Records Keeping around the world.* Retrieved August 2, 2017, from: http://www.bac-lac.gc.ca/eng/services/government-information-resources/information-management/Documents/May2017vol5-no8.pdf

Linke, A., & Zerfass, A. (2013). Social media governance: Regulatory frameworks for successful online communications. *Journal of Communication Management, 17*(3), 270–286. doi:10.1108/JCOM-09-2011-0050

Millar, L. (2004). Legal Status of E-Records. In *Problems of Authenticity in an Electronic Environment*. Academic Press. Retrieved April 23, 2017, from: http://www.wien2004.ica.org

National Archives and Records Administration. (2013). *Best Practices for the Capture of Social Media Records*. Retrieved April 20, 2017, from: https://www.archives.gov/files/records-mgmt/resources/socialmediacapture.pdf

Navy, U. S. (2012). *Navy Command Leadership Social Media Handbook*. Retrieved May 13, 2017, from: http://imagery.navy.mil/documents/Navy%20Social%20Media%20Handbook%20Fall%202012.pdf

Neal & McDevitt Intellectual Property and Marketing Attorneys. (2010). *Top 10 Legal Issues in Social Media*. Retrieved February 8, 2018, from: http://www.nealmcdevitt.com/assets/news/Top_10_Social_Media_Legal_Issues_FINAL.PDF

Ngoepe, M., & Keakopa, S. M. (2011). An assessment of the state of national archival and records systems in the ESARBICA region: A South Africa-Botswana comparison. *Records Management Journal, 21*(2), 145–160. doi:10.1108/09565691111152071

Ngoepe, M., & Saurombe, A. (2016). Provisions for managing and preserving records created in networked environments in the archival legislative frameworks of selected member states of the Southern African Development Community. *Archives and Manuscript, 44*(1), 24–41. doi:10.1080/01576895.2015.1136225

Ohio Electronic Records Committee. (2014). *Social Media: The Records Management Challenge*. Retrieved June 12, 2017, from: http://ohioerc.org/wp-content/uploads/2014/09/OhioERC-Guideline-Social-Media1.pdf

Ramsay, J. (2009). *Government Communications in the Information Age*. Retrieved February 20, 2018, from: http://www.sundaystandard.info/government-communications-information-age

Smit, F., Glaudemans, A., & Jonker, R. (Eds.). (2017). *Archives in Liquid Times*. Retrieved February 8, 2018, from: https://www.academia.edu/35423093/Archives_in_Liquid_Times

Sunday Standard Newspaper. (2016). *Botswana has highest rates of Facebook use in Africa*. Retrieved May 13, 2017 from http://www.sundaystandard.info/botswana-has-highest-rates-facebook-use-africa

Thurston, A. C. (2012). Trustworthy Records and Open Data. *The Journal of Community Informatics, 8*(2). Retrieved March 24, 2017, from: http://ci-journal.net/index.php/ciej/article/view/951/952

US Department of Energy. (2010). *Managing Social Media Records*. Retrieved March 24, 2017, from: http://energy.gov/sites/prod/files/cioprod/documents/Social_Media_Records_and_You_Sept_2010.pdf

Wamukoya, J., & Mutula, S. (2005). E-Records Management and Governance In East And Southern Africa. *Malaysian Journal of Library and Information Science, 10*(2), 67–83.

World of Statistics. (2015). *Mobile Facebook, Twitter, Social Media Usage Statistics in Botswana*. Retrieved May 13, 2017, from: https://www.statsmonkey.com/table/21306-botswana-mobile-social-media-usage-statistics-2015.php

KEY TERMS AND DEFINITIONS

Information Communication Technology: A coherent collection of processes, people, and technologies brought together to serve one or multiple business purposes.

Information Governance: Specifications of decision rights and accountability framework to ensure appropriate behavior in the valuation, creation, storage, use, archiving, and deletion of information.

Liquid Communication: The type of communication that can easily go back and forth between the participants involved.

Record: Documentary evidence, regardless of form or medium, created, received, maintained, and used by an organization or an individual in pursuance of legal obligations or in the transaction of business.

Social Media: An environment, in which content is created, consumed, promoted, distributed, discovered, or shared for purposes that are primarily related to communities and social activities, rather than functional, task-oriented objectives.

Chapter 5
Media as a Threat and Subordinate of Cultural Heritage in Zimbabwe

Lazarus Sauti
The Southern Times, Zimbabwe

ABSTRACT

The major focus of this chapter is to discover how the media can be a subordinate of cultural heritage and at the same time pose a threat to cultural heritage. It explores the link between media and cultural heritage. Attention is also on the use of the internet in the promotion of cultural heritage in Zimbabwe. Media use of internet permit cultural heritage of different groups to be uploaded, downloaded, and accessed by other people around the world, presenting opportunities for cultural exchange.

INTRODUCTION

Cultural heritage, which involves the complete multipart of unique spiritual, intellectual and emotional traits that epitomise society (Idang, 2015), is a collections-driven domain (Valtolina, 2016) and is based on institutions such as the media, libraries, archives and museums (Ekwelem, Okafor, & Ukwoma, 2011). These institutions, whose familiar denominator is that they are all foundations of accessing, storing and restoring information (Brawley-Barker, 2015), play a crucial role in safeguarding cultural heritage in any country (Bonn, Kendall, & McDonough, 2017). Cultural heritage, which is also an expression of the ways of living widened by a society and passed on from generation to generation (Nwegbu, Eze, & Asogwa, 2011), is often conveyed as either tangible or intangible (Lenzerini, 2011) and it takes in customs,

DOI: 10.4018/978-1-5225-5840-8.ch005

objects, values, places and artistic expressions (Fithian & Powell, 2009). The objective of this chapter is to unpack media as a threat and subordinate of cultural heritage in Zimbabwe. More so, the chapter underscores the connection of cultural heritage institutions – media, libraries, archives and museums, over and above exploring the notion and practice of digital curation and preservation.

UNPACKING CULTURAL HERITAGE

Although culture is an ordinary word, it is one of the most sneaky, litigious and ubiquitous concepts across disciplines. Many scholars have tried to unpack this term, but the truth is that it is difficult to define culture. In trying to unpack the concept of culture, Kwon & Kwon (2013), outlines it as a multifaceted whole and believes that it includes beliefs, art, law, morals, over and above customs.

Heritage, just like culture, is one term that is also used in some countries as a reference point of identity and unity. Every nation has a shared identity grounded in past events as well as elements which are considered noteworthy to it. This shared identity consists of natural and cultural environment (Nocca, 2017) and it is both tangible and intangible (Lenzerini, 2011). Tangible cultural heritage subsists in substance form and examples include buildings, sculpture, cultural landscapes, shrines and cemeteries while intangible cultural heritage takes account of rites, festive occasions, oral customs and social practices and expertise involved in making traditional crafts, performing arts, knowledge along with some practices concerning nature.

As for ecological heritage, it emanates from the environment and examples include caves, rivers, lakes, hills, mountains and cataracts conserved for the specific objectives of studying, admiring and enjoying the scenery which they provide while cultural heritages comprise important materials such as poems, stories, customs, fashions, songs, music, designs, and ceremonies of a place – significant expressions of a culture and/or monuments related to culture such as museums, religious buildings, ancient structures and sites.

Zimbabwe is a country gifted with a lot of cultural heritages sourced from its multicultural communities. These heritages are transmitted through the words of mouth. Village heads, kings, chiefs, aged/older men and women in the country serve as repositories and custodians of their oral traditions, which include proverbs, anecdotes, axioms, lullabies, poems, mysteries, charms and praise. Oral tradition is also proving to be useful instrument to librarians, archivists, media practitioners and archaeologists in locating and identifying cultural heritage sites for preservation.

Libraries, Archives, and Museums as Subordinates of Cultural Heritage

Huvila (2014) opines that libraries, archives and museums are often used for somewhat different purposes and are generally separated institutionally, but they are essentially similar in their objectives. They help to spread a broader appreciation for Zimbabwean culture simply by documenting and making available the knowledge, music, arts and beliefs of local communities. Furthermore, libraries, archives and museums use different types of media and technology such as CDs and slides for curating, preserving and passing on of cultural heritage (Stoner, 2009).

Curation is simply the process needed for principled and organised data creation, protection as well as management together with the capacity to add value to data (Freitas & Curry, 2016). The whole idea is about sustaining and adding value to a trusted body of digital information for current and future use. Freitas & Curry (2016) also say data curation activities permit data discovery and retrieval, maintain its quality, add value, and provide for reuse over time. They also highlight that curation includes archiving, management, retrieval and preservation – generally an act of responsible custody. Accordingly, preservation specialists in libraries, archives, and museums share a commitment to protect the 'stuff' of culture in all forms and formats, perhaps even including the built environment that houses the raw material of history and the evidence that feeds memories (Conway, 2010),.

Liew (2014) posits that cultural heritage institutions are also using social media to curate, preserve and create a culture of sharing and participation around their digital collections. Social media simply refers to many different web-based platforms, from social networking sites like Facebook to user-generated content sites such as YouTube (Kaplan & Haenlein, 2012). The Library of Congress, for example, collects tweets from Twitter whilst cultural heritage institutions in New Zealand are using various Web 2.0 applications to curate and preserve cultural heritage information.

Sharing cultural heritage contents through social media expands opportunities for the media, libraries, archives and museums to actively use and reuse these contents (Terras, 2011). Furthermore, sharing cultural heritage contents through social media platforms shapes and/or reshapes the practice of media and information sharing. As a matter of urgency, libraries, archives and museums in Zimbabwe and other African countries should embrace social media platforms to effectively collect the culture of the present day. The information collected should safely be regarded as true cultural depiction of the way of life of people in the country.

Media as a Threat of Cultural Heritage in Zimbabwe

Even though newspapers, television and radio stations in Zimbabwe are protecting and promoting cultural heritage, they are also failing to fully rouse the attention to and interest of Zimbabweans in indigenous arts and cultures. They are doing little as to the transformation of values and customs that embody the country as they are characterised by sensationalism, violence, crime, sectionalism, inaccurate presentation of issues, in addition to pollution of culture (Chikaan and Ahmad, 2011).

Zhen (2016) affixes that instead of developing cultural heritage in the country, mass media are relegating local culture, arts, technology and enterprises for Western culture mimicry. For Yanqiu (2014) mass media in Africa are dabbing African cultural heritage as being barbaric, obsolete and fetish. Media practitioners in Zimbabwe are thus bent to Western culture and globalisation trends of relegating, battering, damming and endangering anything indigenous. The government and other development players are worsening the situation by not supporting media institutions, libraries, archives and museums.

Daramola & Oyinade (2015) also say the most imperative and far reaching consequence of media and cultural heritage in Zimbabwe and other developing nations is the issue of the commercialisation of local cultures. Cultural goods such as music, dance and art are now sold in the market, just like food and beverages. This is undermining people's existing values and impacting heavily on people's sense of belonging – what they are, what they want and what they respect. True to this assertion, the implantation of pay media like DStv and Kwese in Zimbabwe is threatening local cultures as access to local cultural heritage is restricted for a greater part of the society, who does not have sufficient resources. This tendency, however, must be counteracted, especially by the public ownership media.

Mass media are also threatening religious values in Zimbabwe as traditional ways of worshiping are now portrayed as backward and evil (Osho, 2011). Radio stations like Star FM are promoting religious practices from the West at the expense of African traditional religion which deals with ritual practices, arts, symbols and cosmology of African people. For instance, the arrival of the Pentecostal movement in Zimbabwe has depopulated the traditional religious adherence in most, if not all, parts of the country. Thanks to Christianity, the country's rich cultural heritage is now looked upon not only as devilish, but outdated. Elders, for instance, are no longer respected. The youth are busy imitating foreign vices such as gangsterism, substance addiction, rape and semi-nudity which have dodgy effects on them.

Veisbergs (2012) asserts that language carries a culture. Sharing the same sentiments, Armenui (2014) adds that language is part of a country's identity. The use of local language is therefore of paramount importance to the preservation of culture in Zimbabwe (Chirimuuta, 2017). However, thanks to media imperialism, mass media in the county are promoting English at the expense of Shona, Ndebele, Ndau, Kalanga and other local languages. Broadcasting stations such as Radio Zimbabwe, Star FM and National FM, as well as newspapers like Kwayedza and Umthunywa are at least playing a crucial role in promoting local languages.

Mass Media as a Subordinate of Zimbabwe's Cultural Heritage

Newspapers, magazine, films, radio, books, television and the Internet downpour communities with messages that not only promote products, but also affect moods, actions, attitudes, thoughts and values (Potter, 2013). These platforms also play a crucial role not only in socialising people, but also in influencing the audience in a positive way. Newspapers such as The Herald, Sunday Mail, Kwayedza, Chronicle, Sunday News, Umthunywa, Manica Post, The Southern Times, Tell Zim, Masvingo Mirror, Newsday, Standard, Zimbabwe Independent, Dailynews, Dailynews on Sunday, Weekend Post, Financial Gazette and magazines like Ini newe provide information, education and convey cultural norms as subordinate of cultural heritage in Zimbabwe.

Matos (2012) also says mass media provide and enable access to cultural information. Without access to cultural information, it would be difficult for Zimbabweans to learn from their past successes and failures (Sauti, 2013). Zimbabwe Broadcasting Corporation Television (ZBC TV) and radio stations like ZiFM, Radio Zimbabwe, Khuluma FM, Diamond FM, Nyaminyami FM and National FM are providing culture-embedded programmes that are helping Zimbabweans to learn from their past. Furthermore, television programmes such as *Madzinza eZimbabwe*, *Tunga* and *Pedyo Kure*, as well as radio programmes like *Tsika nemagariro* are proving to be critical canals of cultural information for Zimbabweans. Also newspapers like *Kwayedza* and *Umthunywa* are popularising Shona, Ndebele and other local languages, exposing the country's rich cultural heritage to local, regional and international communities.

Books, newspapers and films in Zimbabwe are also subordinating cultural heritage by providing ideological guidance and orienting and implementing new social values and norms to citizens. Newspapers like The Voice and The Patriot, for example, are educating and transmitting cultural values through history. Past generations pick a lot of information from these and other media platforms. Radio stations in the country are also transmitting cultural values through arts and entertainment programmes where cultural artefacts such as food, dressing, music, and literature as well as art works of the country are featured.

Mass media as a subordinate of cultural heritage open up perspectives for the distribution of different cultural content (Sawyer, 2011). This means an increase in the cultural diversity of the media. Lekhanya (2013) avows that the media diffuse cultural values and ideas simultaneously. The digitalisation and convergence of mass media in Zimbabwe and other developing countries offer new possibilities for increasing cultural diversity. Zimbabwean films are also integrating internal and external values of culture and this, according to Topolsek and Orthaber (2011), leads to the increase of cultural diversity. Such diversity does not damage traditional culture, but strengthens it. Zimbabwean films such as *Tiriparwendo*, *Mawoko Matema*, *Mwanasikana* and *Tunga* promote Zimbabwean languages, marriage rites, burial and birth rites, traditional attires, greetings, music, folklore, religion, and other tangible cultural monuments, natural sites and cultural landscapes and promote cultural diversity in the country.

Sawyer (2011) also appreciates the role of social media in promoting cultural diffusion by stating that platforms such as Twitter, Facebook and WhatsApp are propagating visual activities as well as enhancing socio-cultural and national development. Though the uptake in still low in Zimbabwe, archivists, librarians and media practitioners are embracing new media technologies to protect and promote cultural heritage in Zimbabwe.

Mass Media, Globalisation and Zimbabwe's Cultural Heritage

Globalisation, the interconnectedness of world views, ideas and beliefs Litz (2011), lies at the heart of culture. At the same time, as asserted by Magu (2015), cultural practices lie at the heart of globalisation. This simply means that globalisation plays an important role in the promotion of cultural heritage. Consequently, mass media in Zimbabwe are utilising the Internet to upload, preserve and curate the country's cultural products. The Internet is also projecting the cultural identity of Zimbabwe by offering the greatest opportunities for cultural exchange as more people are relying on the Internet to access cultural information. Zimbabwean artists and filmmakers, for example, are using platforms such as YouTube in spreading the country's social, political, moral and religious values to other countries. Satellite television and other popular art forms are also cementing the Zimbabwean bond and national acquaintances that citizens aspire to forge ahead.

Sauti (2013), conversely, equates globalisation to a system with socio-economic cover equipped to destroy the remnants of African cultural and linguistic identity left by colonialism. He believes that globalisation is causing cultural imperialism in Zimbabwe and other developing nations. Sauti also asserts that whilst globalisation is helping in the promotion of Zimbabwean cultural heritage, it is also playing a leading role in relegating the country's indigenous knowledge systems. As a result, the country, which is a potpourri of rich and varied cultural values, is fast losing its cultural ideals, more than ever through the adoption of foreign cultures showcased through the mass media, especially television, newspapers and the Internet. For instance, most Zimbabweans, especially the youth are now focusing on the Internet and DStv for leisure and entertainment and gradually losing interest in their cultural values such as traditional songs and dances. They are not only consuming foreign content, but also borrowing heavily from other cultures. This borrowing, without doubt, affects cultural diversity.

However, Kaul (2012) disputes that mass media and globalisation are relegating Zimbabwe's cultural heritage and exposing Zimbabweans to Western culture by questioning the cultural imperialism theory. For Matos (2012), the cultural imperialism theory suggests that powerful Western nations dictate the media around the world and this imposes third world countries to Western views and therefore destroying their national cultures. The cultural imperialism theory also postulates that people do not have the free will to choose how they feel, act, think and live. Kaul is against this and believes that there are some aspects of Zimbabwean culture such as language, religious, ethnic, political affiliations and personal relationships that remain highly resistant to commodification.

RECOMMENDATIONS

To effectively promote and protect cultural heritage in Zimbabwe, the following recommendations are necessary.

- Repositioning media, archive, library and museum professionals in the new age. These professionals are fast becoming irrelevant in the digital era and this is a posing a serious threat to cultural heritage.
- Libraries, archives, museums and media institutions should partner with indigenous communities and look at broad issues involved in the curation and preservation of cultural heritage, as well as repackage cultural heritage to make it appealing to the international community.
- The media, libraries, archives, museums and other key stakeholders also need to extend information facilities simply by investing in multimedia communication and use it to promote cultural heritage in the country. More so, the government should offer aid to small multimedia companies in order to produce quality prototypes which develop home-produced contents.
- Cultural and heritage education should be communicated through mass media. Media campaigns should, thus, be intensified to bring about cultural behavioural change. This also means that there should also be an integration of electronic, print and digital media to sustain and preserve Zimbabwean culture.

- The government should build more community libraries and museums as well as license more community newspapers and radios as they empower communities to chart their developmental agenda through owning and determining programming content.
- As the biggest stakeholder, the government should promote people-centred development through locally available and accessible information platforms.

FUTURE RESEARCH DIRECTIONS

More research should be directed towards new media, especially in the services of cultural heritage. The objective should be to broaden this field of virtual heritage and explore the application of new media to cultural heritage from diverse viewpoints.

CONCLUSION

As evidenced in this chapter, the greatest resource of any country is its people, backed up by values, tradition and culture which they believe in. No country, irrespective of its size, population, resource or visible physical development, can call itself great or developed unless it takes care of its people as well as protect and promote its culture. The culture of a society is, therefore, important because it is the foundation for socio-economic transformation.

Zimbabwe is one country that is endowed with multiple cultural heritages and these heritages are preserved and curated in libraries, archives and museums, as well as communicated to Zimbabweans and other people through mass media such as the internet, radio, television, newspapers, magazines and books. These cultural institutions are acting as the subordinate of cultural heritage by safeguarding and promoting the preservation of culture in the country. On the other hand, some of these media are posing serious threats to cultural heritage by promoting Western cultures at the expense of local cultures, thanks to globalisation.

REFERENCES

Armenui, M. (2014). Languages policy, national identity and politics. *European Scientific Journal*, *2*, 273–277.

Bonn, M., Kendall, L., & McDonough, J. P. (2017). *Libraries, archives and the preservation of intangible cultural heritage: defining a research agenda*. Champaign, IL: University of Illinois.

Brawley-Barker, T. (2015, March). *Integrating library, archives, and museum collections in an open source information management system: A case study at Glenstone*. Paper presented at the ARLIS/NA Conference.

Chikaan, G. J., & Ahmad, I. J. (2011). *Mass communication for beginners.* Azaben Publishers.

Chirimuuta, C. (2017). *Empowering Zimbabweans through the use of indigenous languages in the media: A case of selected newspapers* (Unpublished doctoral dissertation). University of South Africa.

Conway, P. (2010). Preservation in the age of google: Digitization in the age of google: digitization, digital preservation, and dilemmas. *The Library Quarterly, 80*(1), 61–79. doi:10.1086/648463

Daramola, I., & Oyinade, B. (2015). Impact of cultural globalisation on Africa: The role of Western media. *International Journal of Education and Research, 3*(3), 31–46.

Ekwelem, V.O., Okafor, V.N., & Ukwoma, S.C. (2011). Preservation of cultural heritage: The strategic role of the library and information science professionals in south east Nigeria. *Library Philosophy and Practice, 562.*

Fithian, C., & Powell, A. (2009). *Cultural aspects of sustainable development.* Centre for Sustainable Development.

Freitas, A., & Curry, E. (2016). *Big data curation*. Galway: Insight Centre for Data Analytics. doi:10.1007/978-3-319-21569-3_6

Huvila, I. (2014). Archives, libraries and museums in the contemporary society: Perspectives of the professionals. *Proceedings of the Perspectives of the Professionals*, 45-64.

Idang, G. E. (2015). African cultures and values. *Phronimon, 16*(2), 97–111.

Kaplan, A. M., & Haenlein, M. (2012). Social media: Back to the roots and back to the future. *Journal of Systems and Information Technology, 14*(1), 101–104. doi:10.1108/13287261211232126

Kaul, V. (2012). Globalisation and crisis of cultural identity. *Journal of Research in International Business and Management*, *2*(3), 341–349.

Kwon, Y. J., & Kwon, K. N. (2013). Multifaceted appearance management as cultural practice. *Review of European Studies*, *5*(4), 19–29. doi:10.5539/res.v5n4p19

Lenzerini, F. (2011). Intangible cultural heritage: The living cultures of peoples. *European Journal of International Law*, *22*(1), 101–120. doi:10.1093/ejil/chr006

Liew, C. L. (2014). *Participatory cultural heritage: A tale of two institution's use of social media*. Wellington: University of Wellington.

Litz, D. (2011). Globalisation and the changing face of educational leadership: Current trends and emerging dilemmas. *International Education Studies*, *4*(3), 47–61. doi:10.5539/ies.v4n3p47

Magu, S. (2015). Reconceptualising cultural globalisation: Connecting the "cultural global" and the "cultural local". *Social Sciences*, *4*(3), 630–645. doi:10.3390ocsci4030630

Nocca, F. (2017). The role of cultural heritage in sustainable development: Multidimensional indicators as decision-making tool. *Sustainability, 9*(1882), 1-29.

Nwegbu, M.U., Eze, C.C., & Asogwa, B.E. (2011). Globalisation of cultural heritage: Issues, impacts, and inevitable challenges for Nigeria. *Library Philosophy and Practice, 674.*

Osho, S. A. (2011, July). *The uniqueness of African means of communication in contemporary world.* Paper presented at the seminar on cultural diplomacy in Africa and international conference on cultural diplomacy in Africa on strategies to confront the challenges of the 21st century: Does Africa have what is required, Berlin, Germany.

Potter, W. J. (2013). Synthesising a working definition of "mass" media. *Review of Communication Research*, *1*, 1–30.

Sauti, L. (2013, March 11). Document Zim culture. *The Herald*. Retrieved from http://www.herald.co.zw/document-zim-culture/

Sawyer, R. (2011). The impact of new social media on intercultural adaptation. *Senior Honors Projects, 242.*

Terras, M. (2011). The digital Wunderkammer: Flickr as a platform for amateur cultural and heritage content. *Library Trends*, *59*(4), 686–706. doi:10.1353/lib.2011.0022

Topolsek, D., & Orthaber, S. (2011). Understanding the importance of internal integration and its implications for intercultural business communication. *Research in Logistics and Production*, *1*(3), 187–201.

Valtolina, S. (2016). A storytelling-driven framework for cultural heritage dissemination. *Data Science and Engineering*, *1*(1), 114–123. doi:10.100741019-016-0007-z

Veisbergs, A. (2012). Semantic change in Latvian under the influence of English. *Baltic Journal of English. Language and Culture*, *2*, 103–121.

Yanqiu, Z. (2014, September). *Understanding China's media in Africa from the perspectives of constructive journalism.* Paper presented at the international conference on China and Africa media, communications and public diplomacy, Beijing, China.

KEY TERMS AND DEFINITIONS

Archive: A buildup of records of historical significance or the physical place these historical records are located.

Cultural Heritage: The legacy of indefinable aspects of a society that are inherited from past generations.

Cultural Imperialism: The tradition of endorsing a more influential culture over a least known one. It is a result of the imbalance in international flow of media products between developed and developing nations.

Culture: Attributes and familiarity of a particular group of people, encircling language, religious conviction, marriage, communal routines, songs, arts, and a million other things.

Curation: The process of collecting, classifying, analyzing, and presenting content related to a particular subject matter.

Globalization: The amplification of global social affairs which connect far-away regions in a way that local events are shaped by affairs taking place many kilometers away.

Heritage: The whole lot people gain from their predecessors. It is also an indispensable piece of the present as well as the future and it consists of habits or customs, languages, as well as physical structures of historical importance.

Library: An assortment of information sources made accessible to a group of people for reference purposes.

Mass Media: The primary means of providing information—whether spoken, written, or broadcast—about political, economic, social, technological, legal, environmental, and gender issues to the public. Examples of mass media include newspapers, magazines, books, advertising, radio, movies, television, and the internet.

Museum: A building and/or place where works of art and other objects of permanent value are kept and displayed.

Natural Heritage: All varieties of heritage that can be regarded as innate, real and came into being without the human response. Examples of natural heritage include plants, landscapes, rivers, forests, natural falls, caves, and animals.

Preservation: The fortification of literary and/or artistic goods to avoid loss of informational content.

Chapter 6
The Future of LIS and Media Training in the Global Era:
Challenges and Prospects

Walter Luvungu Musimbi
Moi University, Kenya

Purity Kavuri Mutuku
Kenya National Library Service, Kenya

ABSTRACT

There is growing concern among information science practitioners and librarians on their relevance in the constantly changing world of technology where their work is seemingly under threat. This has been caused by increase in technological advancement and processes that are automating the processes which basically entailed their work. This chapter thus seeks to provide these practitioners, particularly their trainers, with some insight into the future prospects and the place of LIS and media in the coming years by attempting to define roles and processes that they may play for them to remain as relevant as they have always been.

INTRODUCTION

We are now living in a digital era which is continuously experiencing technological transformation at a neck breaking speed. Every day, we wake up to new inventions in diverse fields that are technologically based and which are slowly but surely changing the course of traditional processes. Knowledge organization and management has experienced tremendous technological input that has resulted to digitization of

DOI: 10.4018/978-1-5225-5840-8.ch006

information. In the past few years, procedures for digitizing books at high speed and comparatively low cost have improved considerably with the result that it is now possible to digitize millions of books per year. This means that traditional library system where books were accessed physically from the library is gradually but surely diminishing as people, more so the elite are shifting focus from physical library to digital libraries. This may be attributed to the myriad advantages that the digital system has over the current conventional ones which include; multiple access, no physical barrier, round the clock availability, unlimited space, ease of access and retrieval as well as added value in terms of quality. This is the future of LIS and media and is one that cannot be wished away.

BACKGROUND

The future of LIS and media training is concerned with educational processes which involve the sharpening of skills, concepts, changing of attitude and gaining more knowledge to enhance the performance of employees and potential employees in the field of LIS and media with the aim of equipping them with requisite skills that will enhance their future operations and work (Reed, 2016). Initially trainees in this field were educated on the conventional way of handling information and knowledge in addition to basic computer skills. However, with the advent of technology especially digital communication soft wares, the conventional mode is at risk and no longer sufficient. Questions thus arise for trainers and trainees, do they move from conventional training models and shift to digital models? If so, what are the challenges? And what are the possible prospects amidst the challenges of this futuristic mode of training?

The above questions highlight substantial concerns in regard to the future practice of LIS and media training. For instance, in traditional libraries the ability to find works of interest is directly related to how well they were cataloged by the staff in that library while cataloging electronic works digitized from a library's existing facilities or any other avenues may be as simple as copying or moving a record from the print to the electronic form. In addition, people are now accessing books, cheaply and easily over the internet using myriads of tools and avenues such as Channels in communication applications like Telegram whereby someone asks for a particular book and is availed to him or her instantly in both digital print and audio format, or e-books site where all you need is to sign up and ask for a book you need and you get it impromptu.

Globally trainers and their trainees can no longer face the future with founded certainty bearing in mind the current wave of technological and digital changes which is constantly disrupting the norm in the practice of organization and management of knowledge (Mills, 2017). The role of these practitioners in the coming future is no longer definite. This is because currently their major role is acting as intermediary between knowledge/information and users who would wish to access and derive such information. Consequently, they are being trained on intermediary related processes such as storage, access and retrieval of information, a feature which is being continuously replaced by technology, specifically digital communication and access systems.

Library and Information Science

Libraries across the world present a diverse picture based on the perceptions that people have towards it, there are a variety of assumptions and in some cases facts as to how the existent of a library is perceived, some believe that the libraries is a safe house for researchers relentlessly pursuing various projects, others believe it is a facility intended for students who they occasionally see flock these precincts arming themselves with recorded information of previous scholars, while others believes it is a place where interested professionals go to keep up with the findings of their colleagues in different fields. As such the general global assumption whether it is of the striking and mindboggling *Dokk 1 in Aarhus, Denmark*, or the Humble *Nyilima Community Library* tucked in Western Kenya is that that library is a place meant for scholars and professionals. However the sole purpose of the existence of a library is for communication, the transfer of Knowledge from a host to a recipient, (Dean, 2002).

Libraries can thus be said to be agencies that store messages of the past and the present and render them easily retrievable and transferable over human communication networks. Librarianship however is not merely an academic discipline based upon the physical plant and equipment. There is another aspect to be considered and this is the professional element which is characterized by recognized professional training normally associated with institutions of higher learning and existence for an association for the development and control of the profession. As such it may be fairly accurate to regard library and information science not yet as much of a discipline in its own right, but as an approach closely linked to many disciplines such as media studies and journalism

Media

Media in its simplest form basically refers to the means of communication that reaches large number of people such as print, television and radio. These means which take different and diverse format yet seek to perform same roles of communicating are highly influential due to their ability to not only reach mass audience but also alter their way of thinking and subsequently action towards key societal issues. (Deirdre, 2015)

Media has been in existence ever since humans have been communicating. From script to print, from print to new media and recently from new media to digital media there has always been a constant and definite shift of media from an old version to a newer version and arguably a more powerful one (Fuchs, 2014). Though the different types of media are basically used in communication, a new medium has never been an addition to an old one, nor does it leave the old one in peace. A new media never ceases to oppress the older media until it fits new shapes and position for them.

For ages, print media has been the modus operandi when it comes to communication matters. Though new forms such as radio and television have been impactful especially in the political and social landscape, altering the lifestyle of people, print media or journalism has remained a significant and arguably unchallenged force until recently. Necessity has been a key factor of influence to the current state of media and the changing means and modes of dissemination of information.

People are now seeking information and they now want it packaged in multiple forms, better quality, limited barriers, and in a way that they can retrieve and access them with ease and timely. This is basically what informs constant and unceasing inventions in the world of media.

Social media has become a strong force to contend with, it is reshaping the practice of media and information sharing. Community journalism has never been stronger as it is right now and all indications suggest that it is a phenomenon that cannot be resisted all thanks to the platforms availed by the new medium of communication which has been largely fueled by internet and the ease of its access (Agozzino, 2012). The print medium though still largely operational in its primary format has been forced to reinvent itself and accommodate the digital wave. Currently most newspapers across the globe are now available in soft digital formats to be read over computerized systems such as desktops, laptops and smartphones. This is a clear show of the transformational influence of the new forms of media that are continuously being invented.

LIS and Media Training

We are now living in the digital age; librarians as well as communication experts are no longer at ease as myriad inventions in the field are being churned out at an alarming rate. Every day we wake up to newer inventions with added quality value such as smart phones, multiple communication and information soft wares, better filming devices and alternatives and so on (Murray, 2012). The LIS and media landscape in terms of communication is constantly shifting in scope and there is always something better, more powerful and more influential in the making. This is what LIS and media trainers globally have to grapple with.

If you want to keep up with media, you need to keep up with current trends in the media world. People are no longer satisfied just to enjoy print, video, or other forms of entertainment and information passively. In today's search-driven world, people are actively looking for control, community, and interactivity. That is the current guiding trend as people want to take part and exercise some sense of control in the manner in which they receive and use information. This is what has guided a majority of the media to go mobile because, *going mobile* encompasses the three mentioned scopes.

It is thus imperative that LIS and media trainers have to change from traditional models of training to accommodate the current necessity or demand from the consumers of the information shared by media and shift to adaptive learning models that will align the training not only with the current needs and trends but also with futuristic trends that must be accommodated for a particular media or course to remain relevant.

LIS and Media practice largely involves concept, skills and attitude; though the former two are equally important the determining factor in terms of success or failure of a particular medium of use in communication is the latter (Apurba, 2015). Trainers thus have to read the signs of time which largely suggests that the mass population is warming towards new media and digital media especially the youthful generation. Hence, for training to be in a position to positively impact to the students and practitioners, they must find a way in which their content not only adapts to the shifting trend but also seeks to control it by ensuring it is received with a positive attitude by its recipient.

LIS and Media institutions and trainers need to know that they do not exist in a vacuum. They are surrounded by myriads cases and entities of interest that exercise some considerable form of influence not only on the media itself but also on the trends dictated by technology. The field of information science, libraries to be specific is a key stakeholder in the media industry and one whose inputs must be deeply scrutinized and considered by media professionals for a harmonious coexistence and use of the different media and where necessary transition from an old to new media which is the current craze in the digital age that we now dwell in.

Trainers need to delve into finding out the role that the trainees can have in trying to limit the foreseen disadvantage in the future learning models which are digital such as User authentication, issues of copyright law, digital divide in terms of reaching the unreached, equity of access, interface design, quality of digital content and their roles in improving them as well as their role in taxonomy.

CURRENT ISSUES IN LIS AND MEDIA

Digitization of Books /Content

Digitization which is also referred to as digitalization in some quarters is basically the process of converting information into a digital (i.e. computer-readable) format, in which the information is organized into bits. (Terry, 2008) The result is the representation of an object, image, sound, document or signal by generating a series of numbers that describe a discrete set of its points or samples. The final product can thus be accessed via technological tools such as smartphones, tablets, laptops and desktops

With the advent of the internet, researchers are able to access and distribute knowledge much more easily than in the past. Most scientific journals are available online. More and more academic institutions require their staff to put their publications into digital repositories that are searchable online. Similar approaches are being explored for research data. (Alhaji, 2012) This can only mean that digitization is a wave that cannot be stopped and that which was meant to be. It is thus up to stakeholders in the library and media field to develop strategies that will ensure digitization will work for them and not against them

Digital Libraries are being created today for diverse communities and in different fields e.g. education, science, culture, development, health, governance and so on. With the availability of several free digital Library software packages at the recent time, the creation and sharing of information through the digital library collections has become an attractive and feasible proposition for library and information professionals around the world. African countries have gradually accepted digitization and are moving with speed to ensure that they have digital presence to be in a position to compete favorably with the outside world. Countries like Kenya through the Kenya National Library Service (Knls), the umbrella body of all the public libraries in Kenya have adopted digitization and have myriads of books available in digital format

Library automation has helped to provide easy access to collections through the use of computerized library catalogue such as On-line Public Access Catalog (OPAC). Digital libraries differ significantly from the traditional libraries because they allow users to gain an on-line access to and work with the electronic versions of full text documents and their associated images. Many digital libraries also provide an access to other multi-media content like audio and video.

Digitization has been largely accepted due to its numerous advantages over other formats which include but are not limited to: ability of more than one person to access the books at once, books access from anywhere and anytime, greater integration with business application, ability to transmit images with a structured workflow, ability to reuse existing resources limited by its format, such as large maps or materials stored on microfilms, obtaining safe and copy protected books, ability to increase productivity of an organization such a library and the application of classification indexing methods consistent for document retrieval, especially for hybrid records. (Peter, 2012)

Digitization also have proven to have some itchy disadvantages, piracy for instance is common in EBooks. If pirated the books lose their originality and generate no income for the author. It also lacks the excitement as some of the crucial parts of a book are missing in the pirated version. The digital books also have a shelf life as they can be lost due to any Trojan attacks on the device one is using or due to unintentional memory clear outs (Hyatt, 2014). In addition to eyestrain, reading from digital devices is sometimes uncomfortable as some reading screens are not visible and the reading flow has a tendency of being disrupted by other features of the device one is using.

Web and User Experience (UX) in the Library

Internet has enormous quantity of information with millions of web pages and thousands of newsgroups. We can get wide variety of information from the Internet ranging from simple web pages to interactive discussion groups. Considering this, we cannot ignore the fact that Internet is becoming one of the major information source and that it hosts a major part of information in its domain. Thus it has a status in the information source category and Internet plays a major role in providing information for various purposes. For any person seeking any information, the Internet can be a source, since it caters to various type of information from elementary to general type of information to more specific type of information (Apurba, 2015). The www has changed the landscape of library and information science in regards to user experience especially if contrasted to print media that has for ages been the primary mode of communication. The web has diversified not only the medium but the experience that readers now have.

Today's library services are incredibly complex. Long gone are the days when librarians were only questioning how to arrange their stock and have it circulate appropriately amongst their users. Now they also grapple with striking the right balance between print and electronic media, seamlessly serving both physical and remote users, actively embracing technology and research data, and delivering effective teaching and learning.

While consumer-oriented, social media technologies have become ever present and widely used, they continue to evolve and can be quite adaptable to use as discovery and dissemination tools (Reid, 2015). Though a physical library is well organized and have professionals to guide you through as well as quality control, there are myriad of advantages brought about by websites that make it appealing as opposed to physical libraries especially when it comes to cost and timelines. It is faster and cheaper to navigate through the webs as opposed to visiting a library.

Traditionally user experience in the library is attained through methods such as observation of user movement in the library, discussing with users how they are using the library and what works for them and what doesn't, directed storytelling, photo studies and unstructured interviews

By researching through using one or more of these methods, library managers are able to generate significant and large quantities of data which then need to be effectively collected and analyzed, but essentially there needs to be a coding process and the adoption of a critical standpoint. It is important not to lose sight of the fact that the aim of UX is to look at the service wholly from a user perspective.

With the advent of the web and its incorporation in library management, user experience is shifting and librarians can now do the follow up online via the library websites and social media platforms. Direct messaging using applications used by libraries such as Facebook and twitter as well as library system software's such as opaque are now giving the user experience a new face. However, none is replacing the other as improvement in user experience digitally over internet enabled tools is often interlinked with the improvement of user experience physically in libraries. LIS and Media trainers thus only need to ensure that they equip learners with useful knowledge to navigate through the two modes.

Metadata Creation

Metadata is data [information] that provides information about other data. Generally there are three distinct types of metadata, these are: descriptive metadata, structural metadata, and administrative metadata (Zeng, 2016)

- Descriptive metadata describes a resource for purposes such as discovery and identification. It can include elements such as title, abstract, author, and keywords.
- Structural metadata is metadata about containers of data and indicates how compound objects are put together, for example, how pages are ordered to form chapters. It describes the types, versions, relationships and other characteristics of digital materials.
- Administrative metadata provides information to help manage a resource, such as when and how it was created, file type and other technical information, and who can access it.

A metadata exists to help users find relevant information and discover resources. It helps to organize electronic resources, provide digital identification, and support the archiving and preservation of resources. Metadata assists users in resource discovery by allowing resources to be found by relevant criteria, identifying resources, bringing similar resources together, distinguishing dissimilar resources, and giving location information. basically metadata of telecommunication activities including Internet traffic is very widely collected by various national governmental organizations. This data is used for the purposes of traffic analysis and can be used for mass surveillance. (Radebaugh, 2014)

With the advent of digitization academic libraries are now developing units that collect and archive information. This is because they are now forced to do more than describe, organize, and provide access to traditional print material. They now have to come up with materials that can be accessed online without a person physically visiting the library. These informational sources are now made available using technological tools such as websites and social media channels such as telegram which is currently being used widely in circulating EBooks. Metadata creation has now shifted from traditional print to digital formats and the initial metadata processes traditionally used are being replaced with current trend in metadata creation

The growth of the web has been paralleled by the increasing importance of metadata both on and off-line. Metadata creation has become an important part of library and information science, which is demonstrated by the increasing number of jobs advertising positions for metadata/cataloging librarians. Metadata plays an important role in the Semantic Web and Web 2.0 which are both backed by more or less complex metadata schemas. (Selenay Aytac, 2013) While the web itself is only lightly organized, the Semantic Web takes a more rigorous approach to information organization. Transitioning to semantic web style RDF/XML metadata would allow librarians to connect their well described resources to the emerging resources of the Semantic Web and web 2.0. Because of the importance of the library in the public sphere, it is vital that library resources be interconnected with web resources as users most often begin their searches on the web rather than at the library. LIS and Media trainers and students thus need a proper understanding of the interconnections between information organization and information technology both on the web and in the library so as to guarantee them a place in the current libraries and libraries of the future.

Social Media

The advent of Internet technologies especially world wide web (WWW) facilitated people to use different social networking sites for different purposes. These SNS tools and services such as Facebook, WhatsApp, Twitter and Telegram enable users to connect, contribute, share and get feedbacks of their posts. Though the different tools and services differ with each other most have common features which aim to provide platforms to connect, contribute, collaborate post and get reflections for their inputs with little cost or with no cost at all. The most important feature of social networking sites is to facilitate users to make their social networks and build connections worldwide with ease. These are global tools and different people from different parts of the world have access to them and use them for different purpose. For instance, Kenya national library service (Knls) use platforms such as Facebook and twitter to interact with library users in Kenya and those seeking the services to answer queries directed to the library service, to advertise new services on offer and communicate important issues, which is a classic case of 17 of the sub-Saharan African countries who are members of the African Library & information Institutions & Associations (AfLIA), which is an independent international not-for-profit organization which pursues the interests of library and information associations, library and information services, librarians and information workers and the communities they serve in Africa. It was established in 2013 and registered as an international non-governmental organization (NGO) under the laws of Ghana in October 2014. (AfLIA, 2017)

Due to deeper impact and wide use of social media tools by the users, libraries across the globe have gradually adopted the tools and are now using them to advance their different needs. Worldwide the library and information science (LIS) professionals who are working in different libraries are connecting themselves and their libraries with the social media sphere and delivering different types of library services to the target users worldwide. The LIS professionals who are working in diverse libraries are exploring potentials of different social media tools and services regarding how these tools and services can be used for libraries effectively to disseminate library services to the users in social networking environment. (Anna, 2016)

PROPOSED TRAINING MODELS

Adaptive Online Learning

Adaptive learning is an educational method which uses computer algorithm to orchestrate the interaction with the learner and deliver customized resources and learning activities to address the unique needs of each learner. Computers adapt the presentation of educational material according to students' learning needs, as indicated by their responses to questions, tasks and experiences (Peter B., 2013).

Bearing in mind the diverse nature of LIS and Media students in terms of age, abilities time and needs, as some of the trainees may be employed or attached to other obligations this model can be used by trainers to equip individual learners with necessary skills and abilities customized to fit their needs in regard to LIS and

Media. Online training is more versatile and customizable than face to face training (Langat, 2016).

The trainers can use the following tips when making the courses for the trainees, (Pappas, 2017).

Integrate a Practical Micro Learning Online Training Library

Bite-sized online training libraries make online training quick and convenient. The learners have access to targeted online training tutorials, activities, video demos, and other online training resources during their moment of need. Each online training activity focuses on a specific topic or task. Thus, the learner is able to concentrate on individual skill and performance gaps. The secret is to include a good variety of online training tools that appeal to diverse learning preferences. For example, serious games for tactile learners who need a more hands-on approach or podcasts for audio learners who want to expand their knowledge base on the go.

Create Multiplatform-Friendly Online Training Content with a Responsive Design Tool

Modern learners are mobile. They use their smartphones and tablets to get most of their information. As such, flexible online training relies on responsive design. Responsive design tools enable you to create a master layout of the online training course that features breakpoints. The learners automatically receive the optimal version based on their device of choice. They can get the information they need from anywhere in the world at any time. This way they can be in a position to use their different tools such as phones and tablets to engage with the class content as well as with their tutors

Develop an Asynchronous eLearning Course Catalog

ELearning course catalogs often feature self-paced learning resources that learners can access whenever the need arises. They have the opportunity to pick-and-choose the online training courses that cater to their specific talents or areas for improvement. Another option is to provide employees with custom eLearning course catalogs based on their past performance. For example, an individual received low marks during Cataloguing module. In response, you can offer them a list of coursework that's custom-tailored to their needs, such as online training modules that focus on active hands on cataloguing skills.

Offer Social Media Support Resources

Social media give learners an outlet to share their thoughts and ideas. However, they can also get the support they need to make the most of their online training. Start a social media group or page where learners can ask questions and post links. Encourage them to visit your social media group to engage in lively discussions. The secret is to build a thriving online learning community that provides round-the-clock support. Learners have the chance to interact with peers and talk about issues that truly matter to them, such as compliance issues or tasks that are difficult to master.

Provide Personalized Online Training Paths

Ask the learners to take a pre-assessment before they begin the online training. Use the results to create a personalized online training path that centers on their strengths, weaknesses, and job responsibilities.

Allow trainees to Pick-and-Choose Their Online Training Activities

One of the most direct ways to create a more flexible online training program is to free up the navigation controls. Instead of following a linear format, allow them to choose their own online training activities and modules. Develop a clickable eLearning course map whereby they can access each online training activity when they're ready.

Empower Trainees With Self-Assessments

Learners usually dread eLearning assessments. Some may even feel like it causes unnecessary stress or pressure. However, self-assessments can be empowering, especially if employees are in control of the situation. Provide employees with a self-assessment database that features a broad range of categories or learning objectives. They have the chance to choose when they take the exams and how they follow-up after the fact.

Going Mobile

The library experience of today is greatly different from that of even 15 years ago, and mobile technology is the leading contributor to these changes. In response, public and college libraries are using mobile technology to increasingly enhance the user experience. By embracing the many growing capabilities of mobile technologies, libraries provide better service to their users in many different ways. (USCMarshall, 2017)

Trainers now need to find a way of incorporating the growing trend of mobile optimization which involves creating one app for all devices, where a website or web application responds to a user's screen size. For libraries, this means OPACs (Online Public Access Catalogs) are usable and viewable on any device, including tablets and smartphones. This will mean that they have to engage in technicalities of provision of such services and thus going mobile cannot be swept under the carpet. Mobile optimization allows users to read downloaded books across their devices. Trainers need to equip their trainees with knowledge into such operations as it is only by doing so that they will have a chance of remaining relevant in the current wave

As the percentage of users who access the Internet from mobile devices grows, libraries are working to catch up and optimize their services for mobile technology. Many libraries in western countries as well as African countries are warming up to mobile library catalogues and smartphone applications. This tells that in the future they are going to be part and parcel of the library if not the defining features of a modern library. Where library patrons used to visit the library to search for, borrow, renew, or reserve a book, they can now do so from the comfort of their own home, bus seat, or office. Some library mobile apps have other exciting capabilities as well, like the option to book meeting rooms, though such apps are widely used in western countries as opposed to Africa. This means that trainers in LIS and Media need to grant the mobile technology additional focus in their coursework to ensure that the trainees they churn out have an understanding of the role they are going to play in the near future.

In 2011, the University of Utah's Marriott Library launched a QR code project where users could take a photo of a posted QR code and receive valuable information like library maps, upcoming events, and new book releases from the library. QR codes for libraries encourage users to find out more information about events and programming, leading to better and more easily accessible library instruction. This means that experts and trainers in LIS and Media need to explore on how they can train their students to implement mobile library instructions. This is a fete that can only be achieved if the same trainers go mobile and transfer this technique to hands on experience in class and in the course work that they use to deliver their training

In tackling queries that arise from library users who require library service, going mobile cab be a great strategy in delivering quality services. With mobile phones availability and ease of use, public libraries, private libraries, universities and colleges offering library services are adopting a service whereby one can send a query or ask a question directly to a librarian using a particular number which is registered to that library. The message is received by the personnel of the library who act on it and get back to the person who has sent a query or asked about a particular service. A good example of a library offering such a service is Cornell University where patrons/students can dial a particular number and inquire about a particular service that they would wish to have. This means that LIS and media trainers need to explore this phenomenon an incorporate it into their trainings

While many worry or believe that libraries will become obsolete due to mobile technology, libraries and librarians are using technology to improve the college and public library experience. As mobile technology continues to grow and change, so should the libraries and the services that they offer. This can only be achieved if trainers accept the current changes and strive to incorporate them into their teachings. As matters stand, there's no much choice left for them to consider as regard to whether to go mobile or not, if they take too long to adopt such an experience changing phenomenon that cannot be swept under the carpet, it won't be long before their resistance is blown away.

THE FUTURE OF LIS

Library and information science in the world has come a long way. Since the early 1930s when the term library science appeared (Ranganathan, 1931)) devised five laws of library science that advocated for

1. Books are for use
2. Every reader his/her her book
3. Every book its reader
4. Save the time of the user
5. The library is a growing organism.

(Deirdre, 2015) New approach advocated for research using quantitative methods and ideas in the social science with the aim of using librarianship to address society's information needs. The research approach was mostly confined to practical problems in the administration of libraries whereas Ranganathans approach was philosophical and was tied more to the day today running of libraries.

In the more recent years the advent of digital technology has greatly influenced the information science field causing radical changes. These changes have seen the role of the librarian changing form the traditional "book keeper" to more of information disseminator thus becoming more of a media professional.

CHALLENGES

Librarians are now faced with myriad of challenges in LIS and media due to the changes currently experienced in the field especially in terms of technology. One of these challenges is setting up access to content so that it's easier to find and use – Access routes and all the various vendor platforms are a really complex landscape for both readers and the librarians who need to make sense of it all. Librarians and trainers thus need to delve into the technicalities involved and establish an understanding of access points and routes for them to register knowledge in handling needs of their users

With advanced technology which keeps evolving with time trainers in LIS and media as well as librarians need to have an understanding of *how* content is used in their institution, and by whom. They should be able to understand usage beyond their counter. This becomes a challenge considering the constant change in technology and advancement in the same. It is not easy for them to catch up with all the trends in LIS and Media but this is a requirement if they are to remain relevant. They should thus keep in touch with the new tools being developed especially those aligned to social media.

Librarians are now faced with stiff competition from peers who seek to provide similar services using the current technology. Considering that people are gradually shifting from physical libraries to portable libraries where they can get unlimited access to services that they need such as a book they want to read or reviews of particular books the they would love to read. LIS and Media trainers are thus faced with greater competition than they have ever had before because individuals, institutions and companies have now joined the fray and are eating into the opportunities that were initially preserved for the library by taking advantages of the opportunities availed to them by internet and online platforms. For example, one can easily join a group of EBook providers via telegram and use the platform to request any of the millions of books available on the internet and individual devices of people and all they need is to download it once sent on either of the groups and they are good to go. This is a challenge that cannot be wished away by librarians and they have to contend with it and move with speed to contain it by providing better services with faster access and even better terms.

Libraries buy content and deliver it to the public or client. The success of a library has always been judged by the ability of the content they've bought to impact on a student or client. As of now, they are faced with questions such as how can the library prove that it helped to produce a better student, bring in grant funding, make a discovery, and secure a patent. Demonstrating the value proposition to those that hold the purse strings is really critical. This is now more challenging because the intermediary role that they have been playing between content and client is now being swallowed up by technological tools especially social media. As such it will be very difficult for libraries to explain why they need more funding from public coffers especially public libraries. So unless they adopt and take advantage of the opportunities availed by internet enabled tools to transform their services and digitize operations, they may end up experiencing hurting financial constraints

Another key challenge faced by the librarians is how they can best present the nuances of licensing models to their patrons and upper management since digital licensing models are complex and explaining these can be difficult to those who are not steeped in them considering that those in management may not have an understanding of library operations in terms of license and yet they may be accessing digital products for free from social media and other online platforms that offer them for free without explanations. They may thus have difficulties in explaining the need to obtaining licenses for the digital products considering they are not cheap

More than ever before, libraries need embedding their services fully in the researcher and student workflow which is not easy anyway. To do this successfully they also need to intimately understand the needs and behavior of their users and the point of interactions with the library service. The question librarians need to answer is how do you deliver relevant information at the point of need with a service which makes a real difference to people's daily lives? This may compel the libraries to do more than service provision and engage in lots of research which will bring about additional costs and possibly outsourcing of research experts

Librarians in most cases are now acting as knowledge consultants which go beyond the normal research skills training that they got. This automatically translates to necessity of further training for their personnel. This might include training on understanding copyright, how to write a grant proposal, how to get published in the best journals such as IGI Global, etc. this may prove a challenge especially for public libraries which in most cases are cash strapped and are operating with a stringent budget that cannot accommodate this continuously arising need

The library should be best placed within the institution to support the data curation and research management behaviors of the departments and the labs they support. Libraries should be in a position to fill in the roles of developing data management tools. If not these roles may be filled up by enterprising individuals, peer institutions and companies which may in the long run render the librarians useless as far as this bit is concerned. This is the challenge that the librarians should thus warm up to. This point further to the need of evolving their roles and capabilities as librarians in order to support the mixed economy of subscriptions plus Open Access and delivering on the expanding knowledge consultancy needs of their organizations. As a consequence, this requires a reconfiguring of librarian roles in a time of tighter resource.

It is at this time that librarians and stakeholders in LIS and Media should reconfigure library policies to accommodate the mixed economy and the new realities librarians are now faced with multiple policy questions that they need to maneuver through to remain relevant as well as sustainable. If they decide to buy eBooks should they also buy print and what should be the priority? How much should be apportioned to demand driven acquisition? Should they be buying textbooks at all? And so on. These are key issues and challenges of concern as pertaining to library policies. The management should think critically as digitization is no longer a wave that can be contained, neither is it one to freely swim in as it may swallow up their roles

PROSPECTS: CHANGING ROLE OF THE LIBRARIAN

The role of the librarian of the future would be involvement in the packaging of information and even in electronic publishing and some librarian may become hypertext engineers. The role of reference librarians is evolving and shifting from providing online service where modernization is required in the form of one –to- one tutorial or search sessions to that of performance manager consultant and advocate. As the information technology has brought in fundamental changes in libraries therefore, the role of information professionals is continuously changing. The nomenclature of librarians has changed to "Documentation Officer", "Knowledge Manager", Information Manager", "Information Scientist", "Information Specialists", "Information Officers" etc. The libraries are similarly named as "Resource Centers", "Information Centre" and "Knowledge Resource Centre" etc.

Consultant: Generally speaking, consultants do not provide clients with existing published information, rather they advise to solve problems. The library and information professional often acts as an adviser who recommends both the best sources of information and ways in which to access information. However, to be convincing, skills need to be developed to a high level in order to achieve the librarian as consultant role

Content Manager: Digital and virtual libraries are a natural outcome of the movement of digitization and inter-networking. Library and documentation centers have increasingly used the technologies of intranets, extranets and portals for specialized techniques of content management and deployment. Use of Info maps and knowledge mapping are additional competencies for creating visuals for knowledge maps, which makes search and retrieval much easier and enjoyable

Facilitator: Rapid growth of electronic documents and their availability in the web now creates exploration of information. Even so many printed versions of books, journals have shifted their platform to Internet, which includes freely available and paid publications also. In addition to more efficient and more effective searches by librarians, research has determined that a single librarian or information professional can save the equivalent amount of time of three, or four, or even five end-users (Selenay Aytac, 2013).

Knowledge Manager: Some of the qualities of a librarian to become a knowledge manager includes;

- Providing services to the user community.
- Sharing the information and understanding the user needs.
- Theoretical and practical experience in designing and implementing information systems.
- Analyzing the documents, classifying and storing them for easy retrieval.
- Knowledge of current advances in information systems and technologies and their application in libraries.
- Building the index, using standard vocabulary.
- Ability to effectively teach end-users, individually and in groups.

Advocate: LIS professionals act as lawyer when they deal with the issue relating to law such as copyright law, intellectual property right, etc. Librarian champion the cause of academic libraries through various advocacy programs to promote the library and resources. International Journal of Interdisciplinary and Multidisciplinary Studies (IJIMS), 2015, Vol 2, No.9,48-52. 52

Consortia Manager: The LIS professional for Consortium operations is responsible for coordinating and overseeing consortium operations, including strategic planning, systems development and project management. Related responsibilities include facilitating communication among the participating libraries.

Guide/Teacher: Most often LIS professionals are acts as a teacher to ensure that patron know how to access relevant sources of information. The shifted role of the teacher-librarian has evolved from "keeper of the books" to "information resource specialist." Teacher-librarians play a vital role in educating users to become information managers and lifetime learners.

Intermediary: Librarian is a person who functions between the end-user and an online bibliographic retrieval system to assist in database selection, establish telecommunication connections, formulate useful queries in correct syntax and evaluate the relevance of information retrieved. Mediated searching is provided on request in most academic libraries by a public services librarian specially trained in online searching.

Web Designer: The use rate of Internet is increasing at a galloping stride. The Internet can now be accessed almost anywhere by numerous means and thus allowing users to connect to the Internet not only from the library. The traditional skill of a librarian in locating, evaluating and organizing the information would be of immense use in the creation, development and content filling of a Web site for the organization and library.

Researcher: LIS professionals have played a crucial role in research process. They are highly skilled in the research process. A well viewed interface always attracts the users and increasingly relevant to the way people access and use digital technologies.

CONCLUSION

Digitization is here with us and virtually every field of knowledge is experiencing the magnitude of its impact, it cannot be wished away. The above showcases the necessity and need for trainers and trainees to continuously pursue LIS and media related courses without the fear of their relevance in the field being swept away by advancement in digital technology. This is regardless of the obvious challenges that they face in the current trends because there is still a magnitude of roles that they can play in the future of LIS and Media which we are stepping into, and one in which they cannot manage to be spectators, neither by force nor by choice.

REFERENCES

AfLIA. (2017, October 21). *Public Libraries Network on Facebook*. Retrieved from AfLIA: aflia.net/

Agozzino, A. (2012). Building a Personal Relationship Throuigh Social Media. *Ohio Communication Journal*, 181-204.

Alhaji, I. U. (2012). *Digitization of library resources and the formation of digital libraries: A practical approach.* Lagos: Usman.

Anna, K. (2016). Use of Social Networking Sites Tools and Services by LIS Professionals for. *DESIDOC Journal of Library and Information Technology*, 284–290.

Apurba, M. (2015). *Impact of Internet on LIS Education & Role of Future Librarians*. Assam: Gauhatti University.

Dean, J. (2002). *Planning Library Education Programmes* (E. Evans, Ed.). London, Worcester, Trinity Press.

Deirdre, B. (2015, August 27). *Public Relations Foundation*. Retrieved from Lynda.com: https://www.lynda.com

Fuchs, C. (2014). *Social Media: A Critical Introduction*. London: Sage. doi:10.4135/9781446270066.n2

Hyatt, M. (2014, June 26). *Paper or Screen? Exploring the Pros and Cons of the Ebook*. Retrieved from Rightly Designed: htttps://rightlydesigned.com/ebooks

Langat, A. (2016). Adaptive Learning for Online Courses. *Digital Learning Conference* (pp. 193-227). Eldoret: Moi University Press.

Mills, E., Campana, K., & Goldsmith, A. (2017). Libraries as Learning Labs in a Digital Age. *Journal of Education for Library and Information Science*, *58*(1), 27–38. doi:10.12783/issn.2328-2967/58/1/3

Murray, S. (2012). *Library: An Illustrated History*. New York: W W. Norton.

Pappas, C. (2017, October 27). *Tips to create Flexible Online Training Courses*. Retrieved from eLearning Industry: https://elearningindustry.com

Peter, B. (2013). Adaptive and Intelligent Web-based Educational Systems. *International Journal of Artificial Intelligence in Education*, 159–172.

Peter, R. (2012, September 4). *Scanning: The Benefits of Digitization*. Retrieved from Smart Document Capture and Management blog: http:/www.athento.com

Radebaugh, R. G. (2014). *Understannding Metadata*. NISO Press.

Ranganathan, S. (1931). *The Five Laws of Library Scince*. London: Edward Goldston.

Reed, K. L. (2016). LIS Training for Support Staff. *Journal of Library Administration*, *56*(3), 317–325. doi:10.1080/01930826.2016.1146535

Reid, N. (2015, October 4). *NCBI-NIH*. Retrieved from Enhancing Library Impact Through Technology: https://www.ncbi.nlm.nih.gov

Selenay Aytac, M. K. (2013, December 2). *Emerging trends in Knowledge Organization and information Organization Course Curriculum*. Retrieved from Wiley Online Library: Onlinelibrary.wiley.com

Terry, F. (2008). *New Media: An Introduction*. Oxford University Press.

USCMarshall. (2017, March 13). *How Mobile Technologies Changes the Library Experience*. Retrieved from University of Southern Carolina: https:/ librarysciencedegree.usc.edu

Zeng, M. (2016). *Metadata Types and Functions*. NISO.

Chapter 7
Media Information Literacy:
The Answer to 21st Century Inclusive Information and Knowledge-Based Society Challenges

Darlington Musemburi
University of Zimbabwe, Zimbabwe

Collen Nhendo
University of Zimbabwe, Zimbabwe

ABSTRACT

Media and information literacy skills are critical contemporary skills to enable the 21st century citizen to effectively and efficaciously function in the information glut economy. This chapter explores what MIL is, outlining the relationship between media literacy and information literacy. The chapter builds a case for adoption of MIL by organizations, educators, and information practitioners. Significance of MIL against the backdrop of media convergence is interrogated. Various ways in which MIL can be integrated into the curriculum and necessary competencies required to deliver MIL by teachers and librarians are explored and a section on MIL into curriculum was developed from the UNESCO MIL curriculum for teachers. MIL evaluation was also tackled focusing on the capacity of teachers and students to evaluate sources and access information. The chapter concludes with MIL learning environment and resources.

DOI: 10.4018/978-1-5225-5840-8.ch007

INTRODUCTION: RE IMAGINING THE LITERACY LANDSCAPE

The 21st century now calls for new conceptualisation of literacy as it is characterised by evolving technologies, digital natives and heavy reliance on internet information communication technologies for information production, storage and dissemination. Cordes, S. (2009:2) states that, "the skills required to navigate and perform in today's information invite focus on a range of literacy." Tracing the etymology of literacy found in dictionaries refers to textual competency, the degree to which an individual is competent in the skills of reading and writing of a particular language (Leaning, 2009:1). However Gamble and Easingwood (2000) have argued that to be literate is more than being able to read and write. It is about access to ideas that challenge our thinking and create new ways of looking at the world. Kress 2003 cited by Leaning (2009:1) argued that literacy as a term has moved away significantly from referring only to textual understanding and now many facets of literacy can be identified and measured; these include information literacy, media literacy, ICT literacy, visual literacy multimedia literacy and many others. To add to these plethora of literacies, Koltay (2011:218), mentioned emerging technology literacy, a type of literacy worth considering in the reimagining the literacy landscape.

Emerging technology literacy, or the ability to ongoingly adapt to, understand, evaluate and make use of the continually emerging innovations in information technology so as not to be a prisoner of prior tools and resources, and to make intelligent decisions about the adoption of new ones. Clearly this includes understanding of the human, organizational and social context of technologies as well as criteria for their evaluation (Shapiro and Hughes, 1996 cited by Koltay 2011).

A number of researchers including Kapitzke (2003), Codes (2009) and Bowden (2008) expanded the concept of literacy to include hyper-literacy, multimodal literacies and digital literacy respectively.

UNESCO, E. S. (2004:13) perceived literacy as the ability to identify, understand, interpret, create, communicate, compute and use printed and written materials associated with varying contexts. UNESCO further argued that literacy involves a continuum of learning in enabling individuals to achieve their goals, to develop their knowledge and potential, and to participate fully in their community and wider society. It is evident that in this 21st century era, the conception of literacy is not static; it requires continuous and constant updating to encompass concepts and competences in accordance with the changing circumstances of the information environment (Bawden, 2008). Expanding the horizon of the concept and aspect of literacy to blended literacies in response to the contemporary world demands becomes a necessity for imparting complex set of skills which include: access, analysis, synthesis, evaluation, and use of information in a variety of modes.

INFORMATION LITERACY

Since the coining of the phrase information literacy (IL) by Zurkowski's in (1974), IL has been continually valued as a transferable life skill that the society wants. Lloyd, (2017: 93) affirms that IL is becoming an increasingly important form of literacy, which, when executed, enables a person to understand the sources and sites of knowledge and ways of knowing that contribute to becoming emplaced. Johnston & Webber, (2003:366) defined IL as the adoption of appropriate information behaviour to obtain, through whatever channel or medium, information well fitted to information needs, together with critical awareness of the importance of wise and ethical use of information in society. American Libraries Association (ALA) also defined as Information literacy is a set of abilities requiring individuals to "recognize when information is needed and have the ability to locate, evaluate, and use effectively the needed information (ALA, 2000:2). To encompass the contemporary world demands UNESCO, (2017) posited that Information literacy empowers people in all walks of life to seek, evaluate, use and create information effectively to achieve their personal, social, occupational and educational goals. It is a basic human right in a digital world and promotes social inclusion in all nations."

Critical thinking, problem solving and ethical use of information in a contemporary society are a consistent thread clearly echoed in the above definitions of IL as well as other various IL meanings and debates articulated in the literature (Lloyd 2017, and Todd 2017). UNESCO endorses IL as a basic human right in the digital world thus pacing IL as essential component to national development, active citizenship, economic well-being and educational standard.

ACRL (2000:3) contributed the IL standards which have immensely shaped the teaching of IL by outlining the attributes of an information literate person; these are

- Determine the extent of information needed
- Access the needed information effectively and efficiently
- Evaluate information and its sources critically
- Incorporate selected information into one's knowledge base
- Use information effectively to accomplish a specific purpose
- Understand the economic, legal and social issues surrounding the use of information, and access and use information ethically and legally.

To holistically develop an information literate person, in 2011 the Society of College, National and University Libraries (SCONUL) developed the Seven Pillars of Information Literacy. The core model which acknowledges that developing information literacy is a continuing holistic process with simultaneous activities encompassed with the seven pillars (Bent, M., & Stubbings, R. 2011: 3). The pillars

The model defines the core skills and competences (ability), attitudes and behaviours (understandings) at the heart of information literacy development in higher education. The model acknowledges that developing an information literate person is a continuous holistic process comprising of simultaneous activities which can be encompassed within the Seven Pillars. Within each "pillar" an individual can develop from "novice" to "expert" as they progress through their learning life, although, as the information world itself is constantly changing and developing, it is possible to move down a pillar as well as progress up it (Bent, M., & Stubbings, R. 2011:3)

Accordingly being information literate is to be able to use information and knowledge, to be informed in solving problems, make decisions and have control of one's world and be an active participant in a social context that shares a common reality, common objectives and a common learning culture (Hepworth and Walton 2009:27)

Figure 1. SCUNUL Seven Pillar of Information Literacy

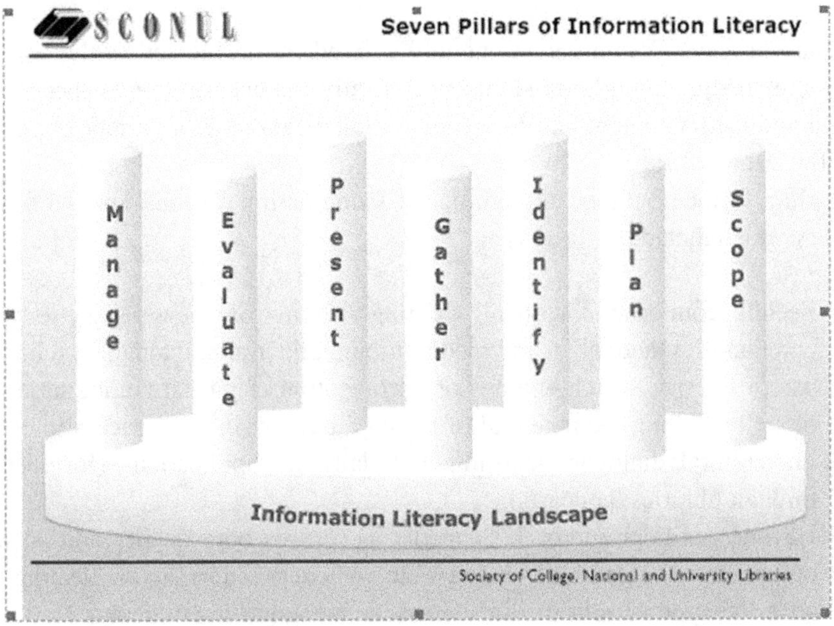

MEDIA LITERACY

As enunciated by the Article 19 of the Universal Declaration of Human Rights that "everyone has the right to freedom of opinion and expression; this right includes freedom to hold opinions without interference and to seek, receive and impart information and ideas through any media and regardless of frontiers", media literacy becomes a fundamental right in the a democratic society. Taking into cognisance the rise of social media and a general increase in media products corresponding to the major technological changes which the media landscape and media culture has experienced, it is critical to focus on media literacy's vital role of information in the development of democracy, cultural participation and active citizenship.

To put media literacy into perspective Rubin (1998:3-4) defined as;

The ability to access, analyze, evaluate, and communicate messages. ... as knowledge about how the media function in society ... understanding cultural, economic, political, and technological on the creation, production, and transmission of messages. Other definitions have included learning the formal features of media, critically processing media content, and comparing that content to reality ... all definitions emphasize specific knowledge, awareness, and rationality, that is, cognitive processing of information. Most focus on critical evaluation of messages, whereas some include the communication of messages. Media literacy, then, is about understanding the sources and technologies of communication, the codes that are used, the messages that are produced, and the selection, interpretation, and impact of those messages.'

The European Commission generally defined media literacy as the ability to access the media, to understand and to critically evaluate different aspects of the media and media content and to create communications in a variety of contexts (Koltay 20111:213).

Koltay further outlined the European Commission various levels of media literacy which include:

- Feeling comfortable with all existing media from newspapers to virtual communities; actively using media through, inter alia, interactive television, use of internet search engines or participation in virtual communities, and better exploiting the potential of media for entertainment, access to culture, intercultural dialogue, learning and daily-life applications (for instance, through libraries, podcasts);
- Having a critical approach to media as regards both quality and accuracy of content (for example, being able to assess information, dealing with advertising on various media, using search engines intelligently);

- Using media creatively, as the evolution of media technologies and the increasing presence of the internet as a distribution channel allow an ever growing number of Europeans to create and disseminate images, information and content;
- Understanding the media economy and the difference between pluralism and media ownership;
- Being aware of copyright issues which are essential for a 'culture of legality', especially for the younger generation in its double capacity of consumers and producers of content.

Tettey, (2013:5) emphasised that media literacy empowers citizens with skills to glean messages from a growing array of traditional print and electronic media, and multiple new media sources into credible, accurate, and informative resources on the basis of which to exercise their rights and responsibilities as citizens. Thus media literacy is not only critical for media practitioners but also to the 21st century citizens and other professionals to effectively and efficaciously sift through the quagmire of information that is churned out incessantly. Unfortunately, an overwhelming proportion of Africans do not have the capacity to undertake this distillation exercise in a manner that is efficacious, as far as their contributions to socio-economic and political development, as informed citizens, is concerned (Tettey 2013:5). United Nations Alliance of Civilisation (UNAOC) (2016:9) recognizes that;

The constant exposure of populations to media presents an educational challenge, which has increased in the electronic and digital age. Evaluating information sources requires skills and critical thinking and is an educational responsibility the importance of which is often underestimated. Separating fact from opinion, evaluating text and image for bias, as well as constructing and deconstructing a text based on principles of logic are teachable skills. Media literacy instruction is not widely recognized for its importance as an aspect of civic and peace education and therefore few instructional programs have been developed as part of basic modern education.

Media literacy proponents regard media knowledge as a critical factor to participation, active citizenship, competence development and lifelong learning. Therefore media literacy is a necessary component of a democratic society. To this effect, UNAOC recommended that media literacy programs should be implemented in schools, particularly at the secondary level, to help develop a discerning and critical approach to news coverage by media consumers and to promote media awareness and development of Internet literacy to combat misperceptions, prejudices and hate speech (UNAOC 2016:9).

DIGITAL LITERACY

Information Communication Technologies (ICTs) are impacting every sphere of today's society, hence digital literacy has become a prerequisite skill to effectively and efficiently operate in today's knowledge-based, technology-rich and culturally-diverse environment. Digital literacy has grown to be much more than skill to use computers but to comprise a set of basic skills which include the use and production of digital media, information processing and retrieval, participation in social networks for creation and sharing of knowledge, and a wide range of professional computing skills (UNESCO, 2011:2).

In a quest to simplify digital literacy, Spires, H. A., & Bartlett, M. E. (2012:9) expressed the cognitive and social processes for digital literacy into three categories: (a) locating and consuming digital content, (b) creating digital content, and (c) communicating digital content. This is clearly illustrated in Figure 2

From the literature, digital literacy is perceived as a concept that ties together literacies based on ICT competences and skills narrowed down to the softer skills of information evaluation and knowledge assembly. Central digital literacy competencies and skills aggregated by Bawden, (2008: 20) are;

- "Knowledge assembly," building a "reliable information hoard" from diverse source

Figure 2. Digital literacy practices involves the ability to locate and consume, create, and communicate digital content, while simultaneously employing a process of critical evaluation.

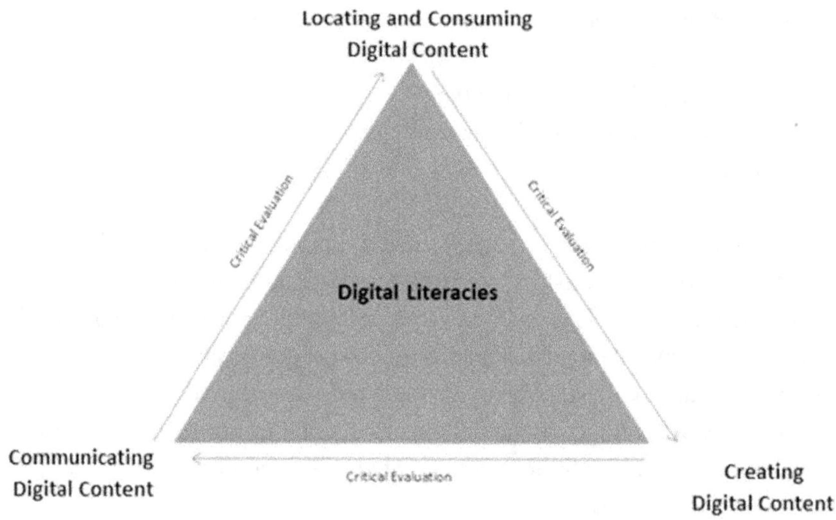

- Retrieval skills, plus "critical thinking" for making informed judgements about retrieved information, with wariness about the validity and completeness of internet sources
- Reading and understanding non-sequential and dynamic material
- awareness of the value of traditional tools in conjunction with networked media
- Awareness of "people networks" as sources of advice and help
- Using filters and agents to manage incoming information
- Being comfortable with publishing and communicating information, as well as accessing it

MEDIA LITERACY AND INFORMATION LITERACY NEXUS

The symbiotic relationship between information and democratic citizenship has cultivated the interest on the fusion media and information literacy as a concept from researchers, scholars and regional and international organisations across the globe. Media literacy's development is central to the ability to accessing the media, understand and critically evaluate different aspects of the media and media content as well as cultural expression which is marked by a critical dimension whereas

Information literacy has been developed in relation to various new digital systems for representing, accessing and distributing information. . This critical dimension is often missing in the current concept of "information literacy", which focuses more on "technical" skills, such as using ICT to find and gather and use. Media literacy, information literacy and digital literacy are no longer regarded as separate entities but interconnected and overlapping due to the requirement of all the competencies under each concept. The evolving of MIL is a lucid approach to the new types of literacy required to equip citizens with the necessary competencies to seek and enjoy the full benefits of universal human rights and fundamental freedoms, particularly freedom of expression and access to information. The proliferation of technologies has concealed the boundaries on media literacy, information literacy and digital literacy.

In contributing to promotion of universal human rights and fundamental freedoms through provision of information and freedom of expression, UNESCO (2013:17) defined;

MIL as set of competencies that empowers citizens to access, retrieve, understand, evaluate and use, create, as well as share information and media content in all formats, using various tools, in a critical, ethical and effective way, in order to participate and engage in personal, professional and societal activities.

MIL is concerned with the process of understanding and using media and other information providers, as well as information and communication technologies. Table 1 shows how the UNESCO MIL Curriculum and Competency Framework combines two distinct areas – media literacy and information literacy to bring out their key elements.

From the key elements of media and information literacy, Information literacy places emphasis on the critical aspects of access to information and the evaluation and ethical use of such information. Whilst media literacy places prominence on the ability to understand media functions, evaluate how those functions are performed and to rationally engage with media for self-expression. It is the object of interest that distinguishes the two, with Information literacy concerned on how data and information in any format and form are managed, using different technological tools while media literacy focuses on the media for good democracy and development.

Some researchers see the relationship between the two as subjective in nature depending on the school of thought one is coming from. The first school of thought is that information literacy is considered as the broader field of study, with media literacy subsumed into it, and the second school of thought is that, information literacy is merely a part of media literacy which is seen as the broader field.

Be that as it may, harmonising the two provides blended competencies required by a 21st century citizen to practice reflective engagement with information, thereby allowing users and producers to hone skills that promote critical inquiry in support of democratic citizenship (Tettey 2013:2). The Alexandria Declaration of 2005 places MIL at the core of lifelong learning. It recognizes how MIL "empowers people to seek, evaluate, use and create information effectively to achieve their personal, social, occupational and educational goals."

Table 1. Key Elements of media and information literacy

Information Literacy	Media Literacy
Define and articulate information needs	Understand the role and functions of media in democratic Societies
Locate and access information	Understand the conditions under which media can fulfil their functions
Assess information	Critically evaluate media content in the light of media Functions
Organize information	Engage with media for self-expression and democratic Participation
Make ethical use of information	Review skills (including ICTs) needed to produce user-generated content
Communicate information	
Use ICT skills for information processing	

UNESCO is one of the international organisations which have driven the MIL agenda, through commissioning various researches regarding to MIL, thus continual referral to UNESCO MIL Curriculum will be made as it has formed the bedrock of MIL curriculum implementation across the globe. According to the UNESCO MIL Curriculum for teachers, MIL provides knowledge on three aspects;

- The functions of mass media, internet, libraries, archives, museums, etc. in democratic societies
- The conditions under which media and information providers can effectively function
- How to evaluate the performances of these functions by assessing the content and processes of media and other information sources

The competencies acquired through MIL will in turn equip citizens with critical thinking skills allowing them to demand high-quality services from media and other information providers. The knowledge gained through MIL also equips citizens with competencies for self-expression (giving citizens a voice), a prerequisite of a knowledge society and a democratic society.

The UNESCO's MIL Curriculum for Teachers aggregated multiple and related literacies in the concept of MIL and these include; Computer Literacy, Digital Literacy, Freedom of Expression Freedom of Information Literacy, Information Literacy Internet Literacy Library Literacy Media Literacy News Literacy, Television literacy among others as illustrated in Figure 3.

MEDIA INFORMATION LITERACY COMPETENCIES IN THE 21ST CENTURY

The ultimate role of MIL is to develop citizens with multiple competencies to make their own decisions and be more engaged in civic and economic life: to be citizens who have moved beyond dependence on 'knowledge brokers,' to become knowledge builders (Moeller, 2011:12). MIL represents essential competencies and skills to equip citizens in the 21st century with the abilities to engage with media and information systems effectively and develop critical thinking and life-long learning skills to socialize and become active citizens (UNESCO, 2013:17)

In Lau, Jesus (2013:80) information literacy and media literacy conceptual relationship, MIL core skills are centred around three elements as shown in the Figure 4 related to media and information: 'access, evaluation/understanding and use'. The contextual focus is the main difference between them.

Figure 3. The Ecology of MIL: Notions of MIL

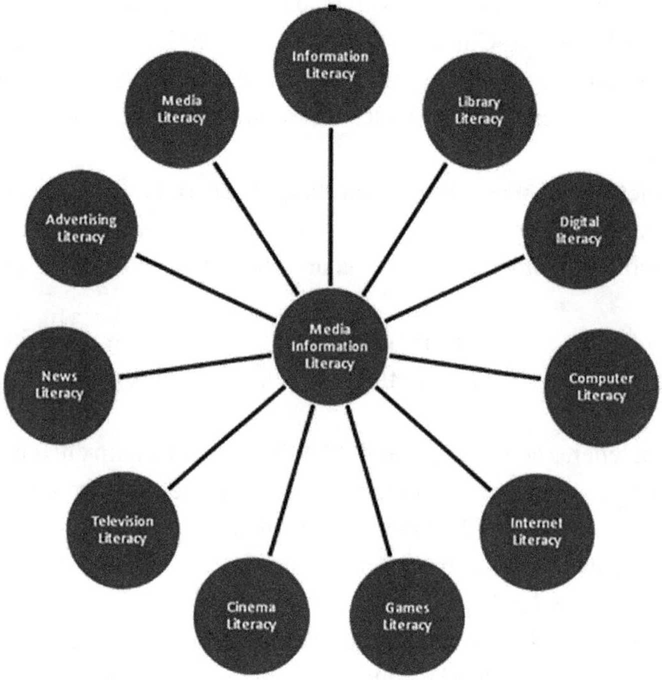

Figure 4. Lau, Jesus (2013) conceptual relationship of information literacy and media literacy

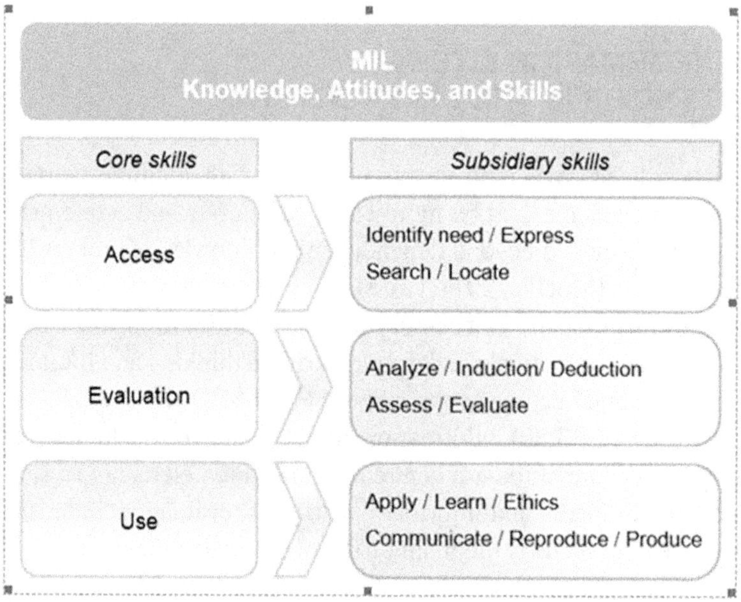

DW Akademie clearly outline the below composite of seven core MIL competencies capturing all the core skills and subsidiary skills illustrated in Figure 4:

- The ability to access and locate suitable media and information sources
- The ability to use and understand media and information in order to apply it to one's daily life
- The ability to evaluate the credibility, accuracy and objectivity of sources
- The ability to create and produce media and information
- The ability to participate by knowing how and where to interact with creators and editors of media and information
- The ability to understand the workings of media and information systems, their organization and how information is produced
- The ability to recognize, demand and defend quality media and information sources.

IMPORTANCE OF MEDIA INFORMATION LITERACY

The 21st century characteristics are learning, socialization, cultural exchange, political, and social activism (Grizzle 2016:21) being mediated by media, technology, the Internet and the flood of information they bring. Grizzle further affirms that media and information literacy empower all citizens to understand what new dimensions media and technology bring to their experiences.

MIL is a necessary subject of learning, a way of learning and self-awareness, self-guided socialization or self-regulation. It is a tool that can be applied to all forms of development issues and contexts. Finally, MIL is a set of 21stCentury competencies that can ultimately lead to citizens' empowerment, self-expression and intercultural and interreligious dialogue. (Grizzle 2016:21)

Tettey (2013:5) concurred with Grizzle by stating that

Media and information literacy is a critical necessity for Africa as it goes through significant political and socio-economic transformations. When citizens demonstrate competence as knowledgeable and discerning processors and producers of information, they can contribute effectively to democratic consolidation, political accountability, good governance, peaceful co-existence, national unity, and equitable socio-economic development.

From a bird's eye view, MIL thus becomes the conduit for formal learning and lifelong learning enabling both to enrich each other. MIL literally affects positively everyone's personal, professional and societal life as reflected in Figure 5.

UNESCO, (2013:36) compiled the below benefits of MIL which are synonymous to other scholars who researched on the importance of MIL.

- Fosters respect for and the protection of human rights and freedoms, and empowers all citizens to make informed decisions;
- Provides a comprehensive framework for cultivating a critical mass, among all citizens, of 21st century competencies that are required to respond to new challenges, risks, threats and opportunities, given the significant influence of information, media and ICTs on all spheres of personal, social and professional life;
- Helps to raise awareness, understanding and knowledge regarding the functions of media and information providers in democratic societies; provides understanding about the conditions required to perform those functions effectively and responsibly;
- Helps citizens to acquire the basic competencies required to access information and media content, to evaluate the performance of media and

Figure 5. Direct impact of MIL to society global media
UNESCO Global Media Country Readiness: 32.

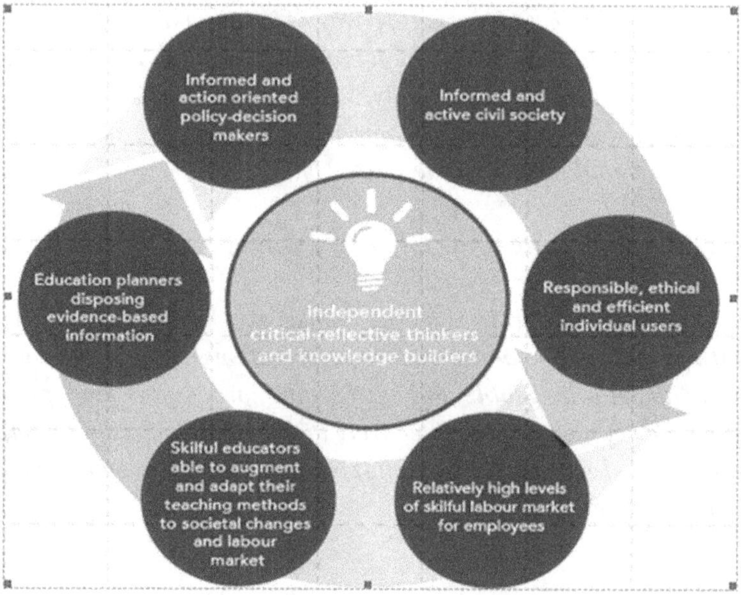

information providers in the light of the expected functions, and to create and share knowledge in an effective and ethical manner.

- Helps to enhance MIL competencies at institutional and individual levels, by creating an enabling environment at national levels. Conversely, the availability of MIL competencies increases demand for an enhanced environment and its associated outputs, such as new content, services and products, as well as employment, intercultural exchange and dialogue, leading to sustainable development and peace.
- MIL improves the teaching and learning process provided by teachers to young citizens by helping them to become independent, critical and reflective thinkers as well as effective, creative knowledge workers.

OPPORTUNITIES AND CHALLENGES OF THE POWER OF MEDIA AND INFORMATION LITERACY

The Internet World Statistics as at 30 June 2017 revealed that Africa accounts for 10% internet users across the globe and there is a 31.2% internet penetration rate from the year 2000 to 2017. Narrowing to Facebook Subscribers Statistics, Africa records the highest growth rate on the Internet World Stats with a scary 809.9% growth rate from the year 2010 to 2017. The increase in the use of internet and social media in Africa by these statistics reflect that the internet and social media has become an integral part of our lives. Abu-Fadil, M. (2016:13) affirmed that there has never been a more propitious time than the present to promote, teach, and engage with MIL in all its permutations across the Middle East/North Africa region notably the Arab states that are undergoing tectonic changes. It is high time African countries embrace MIL as a means for prerequisite for the 21st century citizen to deal with myriad of information and actively participate in a democratic society. Jolls (2012) cited by Tettey (2013:5) points out that today's global media promote values, behaviours and products through television programs, music, film, websites, games, apps and social media but the audiences are unprepared to filter this information with common tools for discernment that are widely taught and understood. MIL is best placed to seal this fissure.

Through its commitment to provision of access to information and freedom of expression as tenets for democratisation, UNESCO has over the years developed literature on MIL. UNESCO has developed a MIL curriculum concerned with helping teachers and students develop an informed and critical understanding of how various media and technologies operate, how they can be used, how they organize information and create meaning, and how to evaluate the information they present (Wilson, 2013:19). The curriculum also outlines a number of MIL goals and related teacher competencies in the areas of: policy development; curriculum and assessment; pedagogy; and teacher professional development. The explicitness of UNESCO MIL curriculum central concepts; tools of enquiry and structures of the discipline to create learning experiences and various literature on MIL presents an unprecedented opportunity to individual organisations, schools, universities and nations to engage in developing MIL competent citizens.

National policies or even institutional policies on MIL are crucial for it to be endorsed at all levels of education systems. For inclusion of MIL at a policy level, Wilson et al (2013:23) argued that an understanding of national education policies, enabling freedom of expression and freedom of information laws, and other related international instruments on freedoms and their intersection with media and information literacy policies should be the starting point. Where MIL policies do not exist, it is an opportunity for relevant stakeholders (teachers, librarians, professional associations) to play a role in advocating for MIL inclusion highlighting its close inclination to democracy and good governance.

INTEGRATING MEDIA INFORMATION LITERACY INTO CURRICULUM

Two groups within the library sector traditionally have been committed to MIL instruction—school librarians and academic librarians. This section presents several approaches to MIL instruction: from school libraries, the process approach exemplified by Guided Inquiry (Kuhlthau, Maniotes, & Casperi, 2007, 2012) and from academic libraries, the Framework for Information Literacy in Higher Education (ACRL, 2015). Several convergences between these approaches offer opportunities for "educators of educators"—school librarians, academic librarians, school teachers, college and university teachers, and educators of teachers and of librarians to draw upon and perhaps align their practices with the best in theories and practices of both sectors.

The concept of 'educators of educators' reflects the awareness that MIL instruction can be initiated in many different ways, by individuals, groups and institutions, carrying out many different roles in teaching and learning. "Educators of educators" oftenly denote to university faculty members prepare university students for professional practice as teachers and librarians, but in the context of MIL education, it is not always the case. For example, students in a college class experiencing difficulty with information searches necessary for completing an assignment might ask for help from their instructor who then accesses help for the class from the library staff. School librarians often provide informal professional development in MIL for their school leadership staff as part of initiating a whole-school approach to curriculum-integrated MIL instruction (Oberg, 2009). University faculty may reach out to academic librarians to discuss, making improvements to a course assignment (Shorten, Wallace, & Crookes, 2001). College accrediting bodies may require that colleges give evidence of student achievement of information literacy outcomes in the college curriculum, which brings academic librarians and faculty teaching staff together to revise, implement, and evaluate information literacy-based curricula (Thompson, 2002). From this explanation, MIL educators can range from school librarians, teacher librarians, faculty teaching staff, library staff among others.

MIL INSTRUCTION IN SCHOOL LIBRARIES

There are various strategies in which MIL instructions can be conducted in school libraries. These various strategies are explained below.

THE INFORMATION SEARCH PROCESS APPROACH

The Information Search Process approach to MIL emphasizes thinking about information and using information within a problem-solving perspective, it does not discard the knowledge from earlier approaches, such as the knowledge of tools, sources, and search strategies, but it does emphasize that this knowledge is to be developed within the teaching of thinking and problem-solving (Oberg, 1999, 2004).

Kuhlthau's Model of the Information Search Process showed the affective, cognitive, and physical changes that learners experience as they complete a research project from task initiation to presentation. The process approach to inquiry goes beyond the location of information to its usage, beyond the answering of a specific question to the seeking of evidence to shape a topic. It considers the process of an information search as well as the product of the search. This process also calls for an awareness of the complexity of learning from information which is not a routine or standardized task, but involves the affective as well as the cognitive domains. Throughout the process, learners benefit from support in dealing with the feelings, thoughts, and actions that are part of their information search processes.

The goal of instruction is "to instil in students a sense of the process of learning from a variety of sources of information" (Kuhlthau, 1995, p. 1). This is true for college and university students, high school students as well as professionals who engage in information use for solving problems e.g., research into the use of information by financial analysts and judges (Kuhlthau, 2003). Providing opportunities to information users, whatever their age and stage of life, to reflect on their feelings, thoughts, and actions in the process of learning, information users develop an awareness and understanding of their own personal learning experience as well as an awareness and understanding of their new content knowledge. This metacognitive aspect of the process approach to MIL is critical to developing abilities related to self-directed learning, lifelong and life-wide.

GUIDED INQUIRY INSTRUCTIONAL MODEL

Kuhlthau's Model of the Information Search Process is the basis of the Guided Inquiry Model (Kuhlthau et al., 2007). Guided Inquiry is a model to guide MIL instruction in schools; the model is based on six principles:

- Children learn by being actively engaged in and reflecting on experience.
- Children learn by building on what they already know.
- Children develop higher-order thinking skills through guidance at critical points in the learning process.
- Children have different ways and modes of learning.
- Children learn through social interaction with others.
- Children learn through instruction and experience in accord with their cognitive development (Kuhlthau et al., 2007, p. 25).

Guided Inquiry offers a process model for teaching content and information use in an integrated and meaningful way.

MIL INSTRUCTION IN ACADEMIC LIBRARIES

In academic libraries, MIL instruction is offered under many terms including bibliographic instruction, library instruction, information literacy, and informed learning. What is regarded as exemplary MIL instruction in academic libraries has changed over the years, however, the requirement of one-shot instructional models continues as a challenge in many academic library settings. Current approaches to MIL instruction in academic libraries are exemplified by the Framework for Information Literacy in Higher Education (ACRL, 2015) and Informed Learning (Bruce, 2008).

FRAMEWORK FOR INFORMATION LITERACY IN HIGHER EDUCATION

In North America, academic librarians and their partners in higher education have been looking for new approaches to enhance their longstanding guidelines for MIL instruction, the Information Literacy Competency Standards for Higher Education (ACRL, 2000). As noted by Johannessen in her chapter about source criticism, the 2000 Standards are based on a behaviouristic view of information literacy which emphasizes measurable skills that are not subject-specific, but generic and transferrable.

According to the ACRL 2000 Standards, the information-literate student:

- Determines the nature and extent of information needed;
- Accesses needed information effectively and efficiently;
- Evaluates information and its sources critically and incorporates
- selected information into his or her knowledge base and value system;
- Individually or as a member of a group, uses information effectively to accomplish a specific purpose;
- Understands many of the economic, legal, and social issues surrounding the use of information, and accesses and uses information ethically and legally (ACRL, 2000:8 &14).

Each of these five competencies has a number of performance indicators (22 in all) or measurable learning outcomes.

ACRL has recommended that the 2000 Standards be unseated from active use on July 1, 2016, in favour of the new Framework. The 2015 ACRL Framework for Information Literacy in Higher Education is built around six core concepts, or frames:

- Authority is constructed and contextual;
- Information creation as a process;
- Information has value;
- Research as inquiry;
- Scholarship as conversation; and
- Searching as strategic exploration.

Each core concept is illustrated through knowledge practices and dispositions. Knowledge practices are ways in which learners can demonstrate their understanding and use of the core concepts, or frames, while dispositions are related to the attitudes and values that underpin the core concepts. For example, one of the frames, Searching as Strategic Exploration, states that: "Searching for information is often nonlinear and iterative, requiring the evaluation of a range of information sources and the mental flexibility to pursue alternate avenues as new understanding develops." Learners who are developing their information literate abilities "utilize divergent (e.g., brainstorming) and convergent (e.g., selecting the best source) thinking when searching" (a knowledge practice) and "exhibit mental flexibility and creativity" (a disposition) (ACRL, 2015:9).

As Carncross (2015) notes, the implementation of the Framework requires a shift in the focus of instruction from skills to process. This is well illustrated by comparing the definitions of information literacy of the Standards and the Framework:

Information literacy is a set of abilities requiring individuals to recognize when information is needed and have the ability to locate, evaluate and use effectively the needed information. ACRL (2000: 2)

Information literacy is the set of integrated abilities encompassing the reflective discovery of information, the understanding of how information is produced and valued, and the use of information in creating new knowledge and participating ethically in communities of learning. ACRL (2015:3)

These core concepts and frames can be adopted for MIL, and be developed as an integrated approach to MIL instruction, as part of disciplinary or content learning, not taught in isolation from content.

INFORMED LEARNING

Informed Learning is "using information, creatively and effectively in order to learn" (Bruce, 2008: viii). The idea of Informed Learning builds upon Bruce's early research with university faculty in Australia from which emerged "seven faces of information literacy" (Bruce, 1997). Informed Learning is the kind of learning made possible through evolving and transferable capacity to use information to learn in education, in the workplace, and in community settings.

Three principles underpin Informed Learning:

1. Informed Learning takes into account learners' experiences.
2. Informed Learning promotes the simultaneous development of discipline learning and process learning.
3. Informed Learning is about changes in experience (Bruce, 2008:12-13).

Bruce's principles shape the work of librarians and teachers in developing programs of media and information education. Librarians and teachers must not only be aware of students' learning experience, but also help their students to be aware of their own learning experience. This means building relevant experiences into the curriculum, and ensuring that students have the opportunities to reflect on their experiences and apply what they have learned to "novel contexts." Librarians and teachers need to create learning activities that allow students to experience both information use and subject content in an integrated way. Librarians and teachers need to help students to critically see the world in new and complex way as they develop new and complex ways of working with information. This means that school librarians and academic librarians need to collaborate with teaching faculty in developing programs of MIL education that are integrated in the curriculum.

The seven faces of Informed Learning describe the different ways that information use can be experienced and suggest different focuses or goals for learning design:

1. The information awareness and communication experience;
2. The sourcing information experience;
3. The information process experience;
4. The information control experience;
5. The knowledge construction experience;
6. The knowledge extension experience;
7. The wisdom experience.

The six frames of Informed Learning provide a conceptual framework for analyzing theoretical influences that shape teaching and learning related to MIL instruction: Content; Competency; Learning to learn; Personal relevance; Social impact; and Relational.

Each frame or lens applies to a goal for learning about information and about subject content and includes a view of: information literacy; information; teaching and learning; curriculum focus; content; and assessment.

MIL CURRICULAR INTEGRATION MODEL

Wang (2010:1) investigated a "way to systematically integrate IL into an undergraduate academic programme". The key findings of her study centred around four categories: the key characteristics of IL integration, the key stakeholders in IL integration, IL curricular design strategies and the process of IL curricular integration. Based on her findings she developed an IL curricular integration model. The model sought to represent the different aspects of IL integration in the curriculum by defining the what, who and how. We recommend that the same model be adopted for MIL integration into the curriculum.

The element included what an institution expects its students to be taught and to learn through its educational system. The MIL guidelines could include student profiles, school or university teaching and learning policies, accrediting organisation requirements and MIL frameworks standards and strategies. This part of the model acts as a guideline to provide an MIL curricular working group with a solid understanding of why MIL education is important and a direction in planning and designing the curriculum (Wang, 2010: 21).

The ***Who*** element defines the key stakeholders in MIL integration and extends to all those who might have a role in providing MIL integration — people such as librarians, teaching staff, student learning advisors, learning designers and IT support staff.

The ***How*** element describes how MIL integration must be contextualised within courses or programmes; it must offer students ongoing opportunities to interact with information in single courses as well as across multiple courses and all of this must be applied through the curricular design process taking cognisance of learning theories, methods of delivery, Bloom's taxonomy, IL theories and frameworks and institutional IL curricula in a way that scaffolds students in their acquisition of MIL learning.

TEACHING MEDIA AND INFORMATION LITERACY

Pedagogical preparation is important for the simple and more fundamental reason that it is difficult to help students learn without a basic grounding in the theory and psychology of how students learn.MIL teachers without such preparation are, to borrow an example from Aristotle, like archers without a target to aim at: destined to be less successful than if they had a clear appreciation of their goal (Aristotle, N.E., I.3). Effective MIL teaching requires us to understand how our students learn and then to tailor our instruction accordingly. To truly become "student-cantered" educators, librarians need adequate training that is up-to-date on current best practices in educational theory and its application to the classroom context.

Is there a particular pedagogy that is useful in libraries and, if so, what characterizes this pedagogy? Henrichsen (2014:1) highlighted the joint task of teachers and librarians in library-based teaching by noting that:

It is about being able to read one's students and to make learning objectives concrete to them as well as working towards these aims through well-chosen contents and well-chosen working methods all on the background of the main aims and curriculum of the school.

Teachers and librarians need a common language for the pedagogical activity that takes place in the library. A challenge in this connection is that the school or university curriculum is divided into separate subjects and courses, whereas the use of the school or university library is not a particular subject, and it should not be. On the contrary, the use of literature and information sources should be integrated into the teaching of the different subjects to make certain that students learn better.

The school or university library can be understood as a learning centre. A learning centre is characterized by architecture and interiors that are designed for learning activities, and it is staffed with librarians, teachers, IT consultants, and others who all work together to promote the students' learning. Using the school library as a learning centre is an approach based on constructive and sociocultural theory. We learn by gradually building on what we already know and through our interaction with others.

Henrichsen (2014) suggests that we ask a series of questions much used in pedagogical planning when discussing the particular pedagogic challenges related to MIL and the use of the school library:

- Who is to learn? (Students);
- Why do the students need to learn? (Purpose);
- What objectives are to be obtained by the learning? (Objectives);
- What is to be learned? (Contents);
- From whom are the students to learn? (The teacher/the librarian);
- Where is the learning to take place? (Learning environment);
- By means of what are the students to learn? (Learning resources).

These questions all emphasize the need to focus on the students because the school and the school library exist for them.

PEDAGOGIES IN THE TEACHING AND LEARNING OF MIL

The writers recommend the UNESCO pedagogical approaches to teaching MIL:

Issue-Enquiry Approach

Issue-enquiry learning is a student-centred learning approach where the enquiry focus is on the issues related to media and information literacy in contemporary society. It incorporates many of the features associated with enquiry learning, problem-solving and decision-making, where the learners acquire new knowledge and skills through the following enquiry stages: identification of the issue; recognition of underlying attitudes and beliefs: clarification of the facts and principles behind the issue: locating, organizing and analyzing evidence: interpretation and resolution of the issue; and taking action and reconsidering the consequences and outcomes from each phase. It is an appropriate method to teach MIL as students can be given opportunities to explore issues in depth.

Examples of the issue-enquiry approach in MIL include: exploring gender and race portrayals through media analysis; exploring privacy and the media through primary and secondary document analysis; exploring cyber-bullying through ethnographic research.

Problem-Based Learning (PBL)

Problem-based learning is a curriculum development and instructional system that simultaneously develops students' interdisciplinary knowledge bases and skills, as well as critical thinking and problem-solving strategies. It originated in the Faculty of Medicine of McMaster University in Ontario, Canada. It is a highly structured, cooperative learning mode to enhance both individual and collective knowledge by engaging students in critical and deep enquiry of real-life problems. The learning objectives, enquiry questions and methods, and the outcomes are all managed by students.

An example of problem-based learning in MIL includes designing an effective social marketing campaign for a particular audience.

Scientific Enquiry

Scientific enquiry refers to a variety of techniques that scientists use to explore the natural world and propose explanations based on the evidence they find. The enquiry process is often expressed as a simplified set of steps called the enquiry cycle, which involves activities such as: making observations; posing questions; finding out what is already known; planning investigations; reviewing past knowledge in the light of experimental evidence; using tools to gather, analyze, and interpret data; proposing explanations; and communicating the results. This method could also be adapted for teaching media and information literacy.

Examples of scientific enquiry include: investigating the impact of media violence; investigating the roles of online communities.

Case Study

The case study method involves an in-depth examination of a single instance or event. It is practiced extensively at Harvard Business School where university students make use of real life incidents to see how theoretical knowledge might be applied to real cases. This approach is suitable in the teaching of MIL as students are exposed daily to various forms of messages from media and other information providers. It offers a systematic way of looking at the events, collecting data, analyzing information, and reporting the results, which in return supports enquiry learning among students. Students are able to gain a deeper and more thorough understanding of why the events or instances happened as they did. Case study also lends itself to the generation and testing of hypotheses.

For example, students could undertake a case study of the marketing campaign strategy and release of a very successful film, bestseller book, or other high profile media product.

Cooperative Learning

Cooperative learning refers to the instructional approach that puts students together to work towards accomplishing shared goals. Cooperative learning can range from simple paired work to more complex modes such as project learning, jigsaw learning, guided peer questioning and reciprocal teaching, all of which aim to produce learning gains such as the development of conceptual understandings and higher order thinking, better interpersonal skills, more positive attitudes toward schools and the self, and the exploration of how to manage academic heterogeneity in classrooms with a wide range of achievement in basic skills. This is an appropriate method in the learning and teaching of media education as it requires the sharing of ideas and learning from one another.

An example of cooperative learning: Working collaboratively in a wiki space.

Textual Analysis

Students learn to undertake textual analysis through identifying the codes and conventions of various media genres. This semiotic analysis should aim to reach further understanding of the key concepts. Therefore, students learn to identify how language codes and conventions are used to create particular types of representations that will appeal to certain audiences. Students are taught to identify the 'technical', 'symbolic' and 'narrative' codes of any media text. Where possible, this type of textual analysis occurs within meaningful contexts, rather than as an academic exercise for its own ends.

Example: students could be asked to select a piece of media text that is of interest to them. This could be a news article, a video from YouTube, or a video clip from an online news source. Put students in groups and guide them in analysing the audience, purpose, author, technique/textual features, and context.

Contextual Analysis

Students are shown how to undertake basic contextual analysis, particularly in relation to the key concepts of institutions and technologies, but also in relation to a range of theoretical approaches.

Examples of contextual analysis and pedagogy include: helping students learn about such topics as: the classification systems for film, television and video games that operate in Australia; how media ownership and concentration relates to questions of democracy and free speech.

Translations

This pedagogical approach can take many different forms and be used in a variety of media settings. Students can take a newspaper article they have written about an incident at the university and convert it into a podcast radio news story. Or they view a brief section of a children's film and then work in small groups to draw a storyboard that corresponds to the scene, identifying the shots, angles and transitions that have been used.

Further examples: Students can also take a fairytale and convert it into a storyboard to be filmed. Or they can collect a range of existing visual material related to a person's life and use this as the starting point to plan and make a short documentary about the person.

Simulations

Simulation is frequently used as a strategy in film and media curriculum units. The tutors use simulation to demonstrate to the students what media learning 'looks like'. That is, the tutor takes on the role of classroom teacher, and the trainees act as school-aged students, at least in terms of completing the activities. This strategy is discussed with the students as a pedagogic process.

Examples include: students taking on the roles of a documentary film team producing a youth-oriented television programme, or of radio/Internet-based journalists interviewing a media teacher for a podcast, or of a marketing team from the university making a promotional video for prospective students about life at university.

Production

This approach entails learning by doing which is an important aspect of knowledge acquisition in the twenty first century. Students should be encouraged to explore learning at a deeper and more meaningful level. The production of media and information content offers the opportunity for students to immerse themselves in learning through exploring and doing. Through the production of media texts (for example audio, video and print), students are able to explore the creativity and to express themselves through their own voices, ideas and perspectives.

Examples include: students use software such as iMovie or Moviemaker (or any other similar free and open source software) to make a one minute digital story about an environmental issue or any other subject of interest.

PARTICIPATORY TECHNOLOGIES PEDAGOGY 2.0 AND MIL

Meredith (2012) argued that the growth in use of participatory technologies has had a tremendous impact on the information environment. Instructors seeking to take advantage of participatory technologies in the classroom should also consider altering the classroom learning environment to one that embraces social constructivist and connectivist pedagogies. Use of technological tools enhance reflective and dialogical learning, increase student autonomy and help create learning communities in the classroom. Traditional approaches to teaching were developed in an environment where knowledge was scarce and only held by experts (Huang and Behara (2007). A teacher instructed learning approach was birthed out by this environment and students were considered unknowable black box and irrelevant to the process of learning. In today's era, the internet has liberalised the information such that people can access information at the point of need, rendering the ability to find information more important than mastery of knowledge in any one area. The internet has opened up a world of learning beyond the formal classroom, offering people opportunities to develop their own personal learning environments (Meredith, 2012) Today, people regularly take part in online communities where they share opinions, critique ideas, swap insights and comment on each other's plans and aspirations (Davidson and Goldberg et al., 2009). The social media has tremendously altered the teaching and learning environment. Tools like blogs, wikis, rating and review sites, Twitter and YouTube made it possible for anyone to share their ideas with the world. How an instructor teach must reflect how the students learn, it must also reflect the world they will emerge into, thus the 21st century style and approach to teaching must focus on knowledge acquisition, fostering critical thinking, collaboration and knowledge creation.

Key features for participatory technology pedagogy:

- Building technological, information and media fluencies
- Developing thinking skills (Lower Order Thinking Skills to Higher Order Thinking Skills)
- Makes use of project based learning
- Uses problem solving as a teaching tool
- Uses 21st Century assessments with timely, appropriate and detailed feedback and reflection
- Is collaborative in nature and uses enabling and empowering technologies
- Contextual learning bridging the disciplines and curriculum areas

The world, students are graduating into is a collaborative one, such that communication skills and team player abilities are the most sought after traits by the industry. Transforming pedagogies which will focus on the nurturing of clear thinking, discerning, flexible and creative problem-solvers who will exercise their developed capacity to make the world a better place becomes a pre-requisite. Vast arrays of collaborative tools are available at no cost to instructors;

- **Wikis:** Wet paint and wiki spaces
- **Classroom Blogs:** Edublogs, classroomblogmeister
- **Collaborative Document Tools:** Google documents, zoho documents
- **Social Networks:** Facebook, Twitter, My Space
- **Learning Managements Systems:** Moodle etc
- **Mobile Apps for Librarians:**
    - **Consuming Apps:** Miriam Webster Dictionary
    - **Curating Apps:** Facebook, Pintrest and Flipboard
    - **Creating Apps:** Iphoto, Google docs, Google Sheets, Keynote and etc
    - **Collaboration Apps:** Skype, Hangout, Dropbox and etc

All these tools are enablers of 21st century teaching and learning which foster greater participation and collaborative learning which the core tenets of learner centred approach. Utilisation of these tools will not limit collaboration to the confines of the classroom but facilitate students and teachers to collaborating across the world, and beyond the time constraints of the teaching day. While digital technologies can transform learning, MIL instructors the 21st century need to see themselves as co-learners and collaborators within the learning environment. In their role as learners instructors learn a great deal about and often from their students

EVALUATION OF MEDIA INFORMATION LITERACY

In everyday teaching, the development of a pupil's MIL literacy can be assessed through by comparing new skills to the pupil's original level. People can be on varying literacy levels, depending on their possibilities for media use and the support they get from adults.

The starting levels of pupils' MIL can be classified in the following way:

1. **Elementary Level:**
    a. No reading and writing skills or very poor skills in language
    b. Basic skills in technical use of media
    c. Poor or virtually non-existent chance to use media at home
2. **Basic Level:**
    a. Moderate reading and writing skills
    b. Experience on technical media use (using email, web browsing, chatting online)
    c. Possibility to use various media at home
3. **Advanced Level:**
    a. Good reading and writing skills, experience on self-expression through media (video, TV, radio)
    b. A lot of practice with technical devices
    c. Possibility to use various media at home

If a pupil's original level is not known to the teacher, his or her competence can be compared against the general levels of MIL, which are given below;

MEDIA AND INFORMATION LITERACY EVALUATION FRAMEWORK

1. **Creative and Aesthetic Skills:**
    a. Pupil creates and tells his/her own stories. He/she is aware of the construction of the plot and compares the protagonist of the story to his/her own experiences and feelings.
    b. Pupil mediates his/her feelings through words, images and music. Media is a source of enjoyment.
    c. Pupil knows his/her media needs and wants to develop his/her own taste in media.
    d. Pupil knows how to analyse messages. He/she mirrors the values and attitudes represented in media against his/her own.

e. Pupil expresses his/her persona and style through making media content.
f. He/she is aware of the basics of copyright.

2. **Interactive Skills:**
 a. Pupil identifies, takes turns, and takes on roles. He/she empathises with the situations of others.
 b. Pupil understands the different viewpoints represented in media. He/she can discuss, justify one's viewpoints, and not give in.
 c. Pupil knows the principles of free speech. He/she knows the difference between public and private spaces in media and is aware of the different kinds of media involvement.
 d. Pupil collaborates, gives peer support, and learns along with the others.
 e. Pupil tries on different roles.
 f. Pupil feels he/she can make a difference. He/she communicates purposefully through media and takes part in civic activities.
3. **Security Skills:**
 a. Pupil is aware of the age limits of various media contents, and knows how to contact adults if difficulties with media use occur.
 b. Pupil knows how to use the internet safely, how to protect his/her information and privacy online.
 c. Pupil is aware of courteous ways of interacting and behaving online, and abides by these rules.
 d. Pupil knows his/her legal rights and obligations as a media user.
 e. Pupil uses media in a diverse way, following the rules and laws of internet use.
4. **Critical Analysis Skills:**
 a. Pupil understands the difference between fact and fiction, advertisements and other media contents.
 b. Pupil is familiar with different genres and narrative devices, is aware that media contents are the result of choices and different framings.
 c. Pupil can parse, evaluate and control information, and is familiar with the way media communicates. He/she knows about the structures of media, and sees through and beneath media contents.
 d. Pupil questions media messages and understands how stereotypes work.
 e. Pupil is aware of the commercial, political, and ideological goals of media.
 f. Pupil understands the purpose and the target audience of sources and thinks about the reliability, accuracy, meaning, neutrality, and immediacy of provided information.
5. **Information Handling Skills:**
 a. Pupil can define central terms and concepts which describe his/her need for knowledge.

b. Pupil goes through various sources in order to satisfy his/her need for information, but knows how to limit this need or to modify it in order to find an easily controllable focus.
c. Pupil understands that available information can be combined with, and it can be set against, existing information in order to create new information.
d. Pupil knows how to search for information from various channels and in different ways, by varying and modifying his/her search strategies.
e. Pupil uses different techniques to handle his/her chosen information.
f. Pupil understands the main points of his/her sources and knows how to choose the most salient information for his/her text.
g. Throughout the process of information search, pupil understands the ethical and judicial points of view of this process and knows how to act accordingly.

LEARNING ENVIRONMENTS AND RESOURCES

In planning MIL instruction the learning area must be taken into account because these competencies could be taught and exercised in a variety of environments. MIL must be integrated into the ordinary curricula. To teach MIL, the school or academic library is a useful tool and there is need to look at the below learning environment in particular.

What Constitutes the School or Academic Library?

First, it is important to stress that libraries today cannot be understood only as physical places. They hold both physical and digital resources, and the competencies and methods they include are equally as important as the rooms and collections.

The digital library consists of databases and web resources, organized through efficient registration systems and with appropriate search tools. The physical room is the space for the collections, with reading space and work space, as well as room for MIL and library instruction. The library is a special room in the school. It can be used for teaching, as a classroom, but it is also a room for individual work or group work, as well as for reading and contemplation. It gives opportunities for silence and for recreation.

To be useful pedagogical resources, the library's collections of books and other media must be updated and be relevant to both staff and students. The teaching staffs needs to contribute actively in building both physical and digital collections to make them valuable resources in their educational work. Discarding of materials which are not relevant is an important as acquisition and must routinely and consistently carried out.

An efficient cataloguing system must be in place in order to find books and electronic resources. Both the physical and the digital collections must be organized according to standard cataloguing and classification principles.

The library must be equipped properly, with necessary ICTs while staffed with skilled professionals who have sufficient requisite competencies to effectively and efficiently assist students during their library allocated time. And lastly, there must be a library plan in place, which articulates how the library functions.

CONCLUSION

The expansion and harmonisation of information literacy and media literacy in-today's 21st century society is the answer for development of independent informed citizens and a democratic society. MIL becomes the medium to empower people and foster equitable access to information and knowledge, and building inclusive knowledge societies. To fully equip the citizens with MIL competencies, librarians and information practitioners have to integrate MIL into their institution's curriculums. Utilisation of participatory technology in MIL instruction creates an environment which contextualises learning and experience for the learners. An ICT learning space is a pre-requisite for equipping learners in the 21st century with abilities to engage with media and information systems effectively and develop critical thinking and life-long learning skills. In conclusion adoption of MIL as a new mode of literacy in schools and universities will ultimately develop competencies which enable learners to be work ready and be more be more engaged in civic and economic life: to be citizens who have moved beyond dependence on 'knowledge brokers,' to become knowledge builders.

REFERENCES

Abu-Fadil, M. (2016). Opportunities for Media and Information Literacy in the Middle East and North Africa. In J. Torrent & A. Grizzle (Eds.), International Clearinghouse on Children, Youth and Media at Nordicom. University of Gothenburg.

Bruce, C. S. (2008). Informed learning: realising the potential of the information society in our 21st century world. *International Conference on Libraries, Information and Society*, Petaling Jaya, Malaysia.

Buckingham, D. (2005). *The Media Literacy of Children and Young People. A review of the research literature on behalf of Ofcom*. Centre for the Study of Children, Youth and Media Institute of Education, University of London. Retrieved from http://www.ofcom.org.uk/advice/media_literacy/medlitpub/medlitpubrss/ml_children.pdf

Davidson, C. N., & Goldberg, D. T. (2009). *The Future of Learning Institutions in a Digital Age. MacArthur Foundation Reports on Digital Media and Learning*. Cambridge, MA: MIT Press. Retrieved from http://mitpress.mit. edu/sites/default/files/titles/free_download/9780262513593_ Future_of_Learning.pdf

Farkas, M. (2012). Participatory technologies, pedagogy 2.0 and information literacy. *Library Hi Tech*, *30*(Issue: 1), 82–94. doi:10.1108/07378831211213229

Grizzle, A. (Ed.). (2011). *Media and information literacy curriculum for teachers*. United Nations Educational, Scientific and Cultural Organization. Available at http://unesdoc.unesco.org/images/0019/001929/192971e.pdf

Grizzle, E. (2016). Preliminary Comparative Analysis of Media and Information Literacy in the MENA Region. *Opportunities for media and information literacy in the Middle East and North Africa*. Retrieved from http://www.unaoc.org/who-we-are/high-level-group

Huang, C. D., & Behara, R. S. (2007). Outcome driven experiential learning with Web 2.0. *Journal of Information Systems Education*, *18*(3), 329–333.

Kapitzke, C. (2003). Information literacy: A positivist epistemology and a politics of outformation. *Educational Theory*, *53*(1), 37–53. doi:10.1111/j.1741-5446.2003.00037.x

Koltay, T. (2011). The media and the literacies: Media literacy, information literacy, digital literacy. *Media Culture & Society*, *33*(2), 211–221. doi:10.1177/0163443710393382

Kuhlthau, C. C. (1991). Inside the search process: Information seeking from the user's perspective. *Journal of the American Society for Information Science*, *42*(5), 361–371. doi:10.1002/(SICI)1097-4571(199106)42:5<361::AID-ASI6>3.0.CO;2-#

Kuhlthau, C. C. (2007). Reflections on the development of the model of the Information Search Process (ISP): Excerpts from the Lazerow Lecture, University of Kentucky. *Bulletin of the Association for Information Science and Technology*, *3*(5), 32–37.

Kuhlthau, C.C., Heinström, J., & Todd, R.J. (2008). The 'information search process' revisited: Is the model still useful. *Information Research, 13*(4).

Lau, J. (2013). Conceptual relationship of information literacy and media literacy. *Conceptual Relationship of Information Literacy and Media Literacy in Knowledge Societies, 76.*

Lloyd, A. (2017). Information literacy and literacies of information: A mid-range theory and model. *Journal Of Information Literacy, 11*(1), 91–105. doi:10.11645/11.1.2185

Moeller, S., Joseph, A., Lau, J., & Carbo, T. (2011). Towards media and information literacy indicators. Academic Press.

Oberg, D. (2016). *Convergences of and for Media and Information Literacy Instruction in Higher Education in Media and Information Literacy in Higher Education: Educating the Educators*. Cambridge: Chandos Publishing.

Rubin Alan, M. (1998). Media Literacy. *Journal of Communication, 48*(1), 3–4. doi:10.1111/j.1460-2466.1998.tb02732.x

Spires, H. A., & Bartlett, M. E. (2012). *Digital literacies and learning: Designing a path forward.* Friday Institute White Paper Series, 5.

Stats, I. W. (n.d.). *Usage and Population Statistics.* Retrieved from http://www.internetworldstats.com/stats.htm

Tauzon, R. (2013). *Media and Information Literacy: Towards New Teaching-Learning Competencies*. Available online http://www.unescobkk.org/fileadmin/user_upload/ict/Workshops/RDTC_15ch/S6D3-Ramon.pdf

Tettey, W. (2013). *Media and information literacy, informed citizenship and democratic development in Africa: a handbook for media information producers and users*. Academic Press.

UNESCO. (2013). *Global Media and Information Literacy Assessment Framework: Country Readiness and Competencies*. Retrieved from http://www.unesco.org/new/en/communication-and-information/resources/publications-and-communication-materials/publications/full-list/global-media-and-information-literacy-assessment-framework

UNESCO. (2017). *Media and Information Literacy*. Available online. http://www.unesco.org/new/en/communication-and-information/media-development/media-literacy/mil-as-composite-concept/ (Accessed 20 July 2017)

Wang, L. (2011). An information literacy integration model and its application in higher education. *RSR. Reference Services Review*, *39*(4), 703–720. doi:10.1108/00907321111186703

Wilson, C. (2012). Media and Information Literacy: Pedagogy and Possibilities/ Alfabetización mediática e informacional: proyecciones didácticas. *Comunicar*, *20*(39), 15–24. doi:10.3916/C39-2012-02-01

Wilson, C., Grizzle, A., Tuazon, R., Akyempong, K., & Cheung, C. K. (2013). *Media and information literacy curriculum for teachers: Curriculum and Competency Framework*. UNESCO Publishing.

Chapter 8
Snapshot of the Status Quo of Selected Zimbabwe School Libraries

Sindiso Bhebhe
University of South Africa, South Africa

ABSTRACT

The aim of this chapter is to discuss the challenges and opportunities faced by selected school libraries in Zimbabwe. It is based on the observation that the school's library system in Zimbabwe, including rural schools, is plagued by a plethora of challenges ranging from neglect in relation to funding and policy issues. It is from this perspective that this chapter seeks to deeply understand and address the challenges and opportunities faced by Zimbabwe's school libraries. The study adopted interpretivism approach and was qualitative in nature. It is a multiple case study with purposively eight schools being selected to be part of the research. Some of the findings noted were that expensive schools mainly frequented by the elites had modern libraries which are manned by qualified librarians with most of them being well remunerated. This was not the case with rural schools in which there were no libraries whilst those with libraries had few outdated and irrelevant books and there were no trained librarians in those schools.

DOI: 10.4018/978-1-5225-5840-8.ch008

INTRODUCTION

The aim of this article is to discuss the challenges and opportunities faced by the selected school libraries in Zimbabwe. It is based on thc observation that the school's library system in Zimbabwe including rural schools is plagued by a plethora of challenges ranging from neglect in relation to funding and policy issues. It is from this perspective that this article would seek to deeply understand and address the challenges and opportunities faced by Zimbabwe's school libraries. The study adopted interpretivism approach and was qualitative in nature. It is a multiple case study with purposively eight schools being selected to be part of the research. Data was collected through interviews, relevant document analysis and observations on the ground. Interviews were mainly conducted with individuals from library fraternity and the experiences of the writer as a teacher in rural school were incorporated. Some of the findings noted were that expensive schools mainly frequented by the elites had modern libraries which are manned by qualified librarians with most of them being well remunerated. This was not the case with rural schools in which there were no libraries whilst those with libraries had few outdated and irrelevant books and there were no trained librarians in those schools. Therefore this paper would offer critical analysis to the subject.

BACKGROUND TO THE STUDY

According to Mchombu and Cadbury (2006: 2) it is sad that "while the west manufactures and ingests a glut of information every day the vast majority of Africans subsist on very little… books must often be shared between six or more pupils. Few schools have a school library…"The library school's system in Zimbabwe including rural schools is plagued by a plethora of challenges ranging from neglect in relation to funding and policy issues. This is worsened by the shortfalls of the National Library Documentation Services (NLDS) Act and the lack of National Library Policy. Writing about the importance of the library legislation and policies Mojapelo and Dube (2005: 111) said:

Clearly the policy would be an overarching and strategic framework that would inform school library development and practice by providing relevant canons, guidelines and frames. Without such a framework, there is likely to be a stalemate in critical aspects such as school library governance, support, appreciation, prioritisation, positioning, and resource-provisioning. These aspects are interrelated and interdependent.

So this means the lack of proper library legislative framework does not augur well with the development and empowerment of libraries.

IFLA (1998: 2) described the library situation in Zimbabwe as:

Well below the expected standards, largely due to the absence of libraries for the people...Even in the schools, the formerly whites only schools had superb library facilities, some of which have been further improved with the advent of new technology. The hardest hit people in terms of library provision in Zimbabwe are the rural people, who according to the 1992 National population Census results, constitute over seventy percent of the country's population.

The challenges bedevilling library schools are not unique to Zimbabwe as Agyekum and Filson (2012: 1) argue that "school library service provision has not seen remarkable change since the inception of the new educational reforms in Ghana. Some of these challenges are poor funding, untrained library staff, poor facilities among others".

The importance of libraries in impacting literacy skills cannot be overemphasised. Literacy skills help individuals to be active citizens in a society in which they can participate in developmental projects. It is therefore of paramount significance that school libraries can be used to impact that culture of reading within the learners so that they are able to effectively participate positively in societal challenges they face such as dealing with poverty and addressing their health issues. All this is feasible when school libraries can play their cardinal role of "supporting learners to acquire, maintain and develop their literacy" (Mchombu and Cadbury, 2006: 3).

However this is not always the case in Zimbabwe as most libraries in rural schools are the worst affected. School libraries in high density areas have challenges also, the exception being that of elite schools in low density areas. The general picture of school libraries in Matabeleland can be summarized by Montagnes, (2001) words quoted by Mchombu and Cadbury (2006: 5) which elucidated that "the majority of schools possessed no library. Where some semblance of a social library exists, it was often no more than a few shelves of outdated and worn out material, inadequately staffed." This has far reaching consequences as poor quality education and shortages of reading materials condemn many children to finish basic education with very limited literacy skills" (Mchombu and Cadbury, 2006: 3). Despite all these challenges there is a glimmer of hope as opportunities are there on the ground that can help improve the condition of school libraries in Matabeleland. For example there are now a reasonable number of tertiary institutions that train librarians.

School libraries if well-equipped can be the cornerstones for the transformation of the Zimbabwean education system into churning out of well literate and productive students into the society at large. The Library and Information Services (LIS)

Transformation Charter (2009: 37) has this to say about the importance of school libraries:

The school library equips students with lifelong learning skills and develops the imagination; enabling them to live as responsible citizens...The school library is more than a physical facility. It is rather a vital teaching and learning tool...The LIS is a force for social cohesion. An LIS that is open all day, after school hours, benefits the whole community. It provides a safe space for serious leisure – for personal, social, and cultural development. It's a place for exploring oneself and the wider world.

Same sentiments are echoed by Mojapelo and Dube (2015: 111) citing Frantsi, Kolu and Salminen 2002; Hoskins 2006; National Guidelines for School Library and Information Services 2012) argues that "there is evidence from the literature that where school libraries are well-resourced and functional, teachers and learners are likely to develop information literacy and media skills indispensable for life-long and independent study".

However all is not gloom as the formulation and adoption of vibrant new policies can positively turn around the school's library system. It is now encouraging that in addition to library and information science (LIS) diploma and certificate graduates from polytechnics there are now LIS degree graduates from National University of Science and Technology (NUST). This means the librarians are there on the ground and just need to be employed.

Statement of the Problem

School libraries in Zimbabwe are general bedevilled with a number of challenges some of which are being unsuitable library infrastructure, massive shortage of books, irrelevant donated books, lack of trained librarians and the lack of creativity amongst the administrators to tackle those problems. This is worsened by the vacuum in legislative framework guiding general all libraries in Zimbabwe. For example there is no National Library Policy in the country, the NLDS is outdated and currently there is no constituted NLDS Board. This has resulted in the country lacking a vibrant National library to the extent that the basic functions of any National Library in the world such as the issuance of International Standard Book Numbers (ISBN) have been usurped by National Archives of Zimbabwe because of that glaring vacuum when it comes to the visibility of the National Library in Zimbabwe. This is the library environment in a country that school libraries find themselves in, a situation worsened by the aloofness of the Government of Zimbabwe when it comes to the caring of school libraries. This observation is echoed by Mojapelo (2016) who argues that most governments, particularly in poor and developing African countries, are hesitant to pledge themselves in developing school libraries.

Objectives

The aim of the study was to uncover the state of the selected school libraries, the causes and consequences of the status quo. In particular the objectives of the study were:

1. To ascertain the state in which these school libraries are in.
2. The causes of the status quo.
3. The likely consequences of the status quo.
4. To come up with innovative ways of mitigating the challenges faced by school libraries

Research Questions

1. How can the state of the school libraries selected be described?
2. What has caused the state in which these school libraries find themselves in?
3. Given the status quo of these school libraries what are the likely consequences?
4. What are the innovative strategies that can be employed to mitigate these challenges faced by school libraries?

Research Methodology

The study adopted interpretivism approach and was qualitative in nature. It is a multiple case study with purposively eight schools being selected to be part of the research. These schools would be anonymised as School A, B, C, D, E, F, G, H. The table below summarizes the population of study:

Table 1. Population of the Study

Type of School	Location of the School
Bulawayo's elite schools (School A and B)	Low density areas
Bulawayo's secondary schools (School C and D)	High density areas
Missionary boarding schools (School E and F)	Matabeleland North and South
Rural secondary day schools (School G and H)	Matabeleland North and South

The data was collected through interviewing teachers and librarians in the above mentioned schools. Observations were again made in some of the schools. Specialist in the field of library and information science who is part of ZIMLA Executive was also purposefully targeted. Content analysis was also done on the empirical and theoretical literature concerning African libraries.

Limitations of the Study

The author acknowledges that the study does not claim to tell the complete story of school libraries in Zimbabwe. It rather attempts to provide a rich description of eight secondary school libraries in Matabeleland Provinces. As the scope of the study is restricted to eight secondary schools it is important to acknowledge that the findings may not be generalised to all Zimbabwean school libraries. Nevertheless, the author would show a detailed picture on the difficulties faced by eight secondary school libraries in Matabeleland Province of Zimbabwe, which could have relevance to similar schools in developing countries.

Guiding Lens of the Study

The guiding lens of this study would be the recommendations of International Federation of Library Associations and Institutions (IFLA, 2015) which are derived from School Library Guidelines. The data analysis of this study would be subjected to these recommendations. The IFLA (2015:10-11 Recommendations which would be used to come up with themes for discussion are:

Recommendation 1: The mission and purposes of the school library should be stated clearly in terms that are consistent with the principles of the IFLA/ UNESCO School Library Manifesto and the values expressed in the United Nations Declaration of the Rights of the Child, the United Nations Declaration on the Rights of Indigenous People, and in the Core Values of IFLA.

Recommendation 2: The mission and purposes of the school library should be defined in terms that are consistent with the expectations of national, regional, and local educational authorities, also the outcomes of the school's curricula.

Recommendation 3: A plan should be in place for the development of the three features necessary for the success of a school library: a qualified school librarian; a collection that supports the curriculum of the school; and an explicit plan for ongoing growth and development of the school library.

Recommendation 4: Monitoring and evaluating school library services and programs, as well as the work of the school library staff, should be conducted on a regular basis to ensure that the school library is meeting the changing needs of the school community.

Recommendation 5: School library legislation should be in place, at an appropriate governmental level or levels, to ensure that legal responsibilities are clearly defined for the establishment, support, and continuous improvement of school libraries accessible to all students.

Recommendation 6: School library legislation should be in place, at an appropriate governmental level or levels, to ensure that ethical responsibilities of all members of the school community are clearly defined, including such rights as equity of access, freedom of information and privacy, copyright and intellectual property, and children's right to know.

Recommendation 7: School library services and programs should be under the direction of a professional school librarian with formal education in school librarianship and classroom teaching.

Recommendation 8: The roles of a professional school librarian should be clearly defined to include instruction (i.e., literacy and reading promotion, inquiry-centred and resource-based), library management, school-wide leadership and collaboration, community engagement, and promotion of library services.

Recommendation 9: All school library staff-—professional, paraprofessional, and volunteer— should clearly understand their roles and responsibilities to work in accordance with library policies, including those related to equity of access, right to privacy, and right to know for all library users.

Recommendation 10: All school library staff should endeavour to develop collections of physical and digital resources consistent with the school's curriculum and with the national, ethnic, and cultural identities of members of the school community; they also should endeavour to increase access to resources through practices such as cataloguing, curation, and resource sharing.

Recommendation 11: The facilities, equipment, collections, and services of the school library should support the teaching and learning needs of the students and the teachers; these facilities, equipment, collections, and services should evolve as teaching and learning needs change.

Recommendation 12: The connections among school libraries and with public libraries and academic libraries should be developed to strengthen access to resources and services and to foster their shared responsibilities for the lifelong learning of all community members.

Recommendation 13: The core instructional activities of a school librarian should be focused on: literacy and reading promotion; media and information literacy instruction; inquiry-based teaching; technology integration; and professional development of teachers.

Recommendation 14: The services and programs provided through the school library should be developed collaboratively by a professional school librarian working in concert with the principal, with curriculum leaders, with teaching colleagues, with members of other library groups, and with members of cultural, linguistic, indigenous, and other unique populations to contribute to the achievement of the academic, cultural, and social goals of the school.

Recommendation 15: Evidence-based practice should guide the services and programs of a school library and provide the data needed for improvement of professional practice and for ensuring that the services and programs of a school library make a positive contribution to teaching and learning in the school.

Recommendation 16: The use and support of the services and programs of a school library should be enhanced by planned and systematic communication with school library users—current and potential—and with the library's stakeholders and decision-makers.

SUMMARY OF RESEARCH FINDINGS

Bulawayo's Elite Schools (School A and B)

1. The schools have properly built library buildings and infrastructure
2. The library shelves are well shelved with relevant and current books
3. E-resources are available for pupils
4. Well trained and well paid librarians are manning the libraries
5. Librarians are paid by the School Development Authorities' not the Government
6. Pupils are trained in literacy skills
7. Use of computers is widespread
8. Difficulty in collaboration between teachers and librarian
9. Recognition of teachers more than librarians

Bulawayo's School Libraries in High Density Areas (School C and D)

1. The schools have library buildings even though not originally meant for libraries
2. The library shelves are not well stocked with all that relevant and current books
3. E- resources are not available
4. Mostly manned by English teachers not trained librarians
5. Only getting the salary for their teaching duties from the government and nothing for their library duties
6. Pupils not trained in literacy skills

7. Inadequate funding from both the Government and School Development Authorities'
8. Book collection mainly from donations and book aids
9. Inadequate preservation infrastructure for library material
10. Inadequate intellectual control of the library material
11. Students utilize the library during free periods in their timetable

Missionary Boarding Schools (School E and F)

1. The schools have decent library buildings even though not originally meant libraries
2. The library shelves are stocked with both relevant, current and outdated books
3. School E is manned by a teacher cum librarian whilst school F is manned by trained librarian
4. Trained librarian paid by the School Development Authorities'
5. School F trains pupils on literacy skills
6. Inadequate funding from both the Government and School Development Authorities'
7. Book collection is mainly from donations, books aids and the mother church
8. School F has library in their subject timetable.
9. E-resources are not available

Rural Secondary Day Schools (Schools G and H)

1. The schools lack proper library buildings as even the conversion of classrooms to libraries is not feasible
2. The library shelves are stocked with mostly irrelevant outdated books for school H whilst school G has current and relevant books
3. School libraries are manned part time by teachers
4. Only paid for their teaching duties not the library
5. Pupils are not trained on literacy skills
6. Inadequate funding from both the Government and School Development Authorities'
7. Book collection is mainly from donations, book aids and national government organisations
8. E-resources not available
9. Selective use of library material by students, for example penchant appetite for vernacular novels
10. Inadequate finding aids or intellectual control of library material

The Role of Zimbabwe Library Association (ZIMLA) in the Management of School Libraries (Response From ZIMLA Member who was Interviewed)

1. Promotion of school libraries through the International School Library Month
2. Pre-Conferences for school libraries
3. Consultancy on library management issues
4. Setting up school libraries (For example in Sobukazi Secondary School in which Library Development Trust is also playing a role and Mavhurazi Primary School in Mutoko in the area in which 30 000 books have been donated recently).
5. Playing the role of advocacy

DATA ANALYSIS AND DISCUSSIONS

Using the 16 IFLA School Libraries Guidelines the following themes to be discussed along with data collected were chosen: Library infrastructure, collection development policies for school libraries, the role played by the Government in the development of school libraries, use of electronic resources in school libraries, societal perceptions of librarians, opportunities available for school libraries and governance issues in school libraries. In other words the data was analysed in such a way that how do the school libraries fare when it comes to the IFLA Recommendations in regard to the management of school libraries.

Library Infrastructure

The findings revealed that most school libraries are facing a lot of challenges in fulfilling their cardinal mandate of eradicating illiteracy and building literate citizenry which is able to compete in this knowledge based society. It can be deduced from the findings that most of the school libraries in Matabeleland except for elite schools are operating in unsuitable buildings. This is worse in rural areas where the classes themselves are not even enough for pupils. Libraries are then pushed into store rooms. Most of book shelves are also made of wood meaning that little which is there is going to suffer from preservation challenges such as termites. IFLA (1998: 2) commenting on the library situation in rural areas in Zimbabwe argues that

Unless government comes up with a policy on rural library development to bolster the efforts that have been started by the various donor agencies and non-governmental organisations, it will take ages to make freedom of access to information a reality for the majority of Zimbabweans. Maybe all the parties involved, including the

Zimbabwe Library Association, need to re-invigorate pressure on Government to come up with such a policy.

Proper library buildings are the first defence against disasters, be it physical, chemical or even biological. Mangemba (2012) described the school library system in Zimbabwe stating that it "is facing a myriad of challenges from lack of funding to lack of space … A general assessment of the situation shows that a school library may be a classroom block with boxes and is always closed and if opened it is under stocked". Failure to have proper library buildings means that in future these libraries will find it difficult to provide access to their collections. In one of the schools studied it was revealed that the classroom which was used as a library was burnt down by the fire. This shows the paucity of disaster management plans for these school libraries.

Instead of continuing with the centralised library for each school which is proving to be expensive for public schools, Zimbabwe can borrow a leaf from The National Policy Framework for School Library Standards (Department of Education, 1997) of South Africa which describes different models of school libraries from which it could be possible to choose, not to be locked only to the model of a centralised library in each school (Maud, 2005: 9). This framework proposes cheaper models which can be of benefit to Zimbabwe' school libraries which are struggling with library infrastructure. It proposes other models like classroom collections and a cluster of schools sharing resources that could be tested and encourages that the school library should be seen as a teaching method to enhance the school's curriculum and not just as a physical facility (Maud, 2005: 9).

Library Use

The research found that most of the libraries are still used in a traditional manner. The findings made by Paton-Ash and Wilmot in South Africa (2015: 8) apply also to this study that: "the school library is peripheral to as opposed to central to teaching and learning. The role of a school library is outdated and needs to change if the library is to play a pivotal role in promoting literacy and learning, facilitating and enabling quality education for all South African children".

Reader development is another aspect which is lacking in rural areas as the study found out a situation which was also observed by Rosenberg (2003-iv), when the author argued that "although reader development has dramatically increased in recent years, it is not yet regarded as a core aspect of service provision in libraries in developing countries." Reader development is defined by Anderson and Matthews (2010) as focusing on fostering a reading habit by developing positive attitudes towards reading, which in turn creates positive attitudes towards the development of reading skills.

Literacy skills are very important in national development hence the worrisome observation that some schools are not training their pupils in these lifetime skills. At this juncture it would be best to co-opt Chisita (2011) recommendation that the "Government through the NLDS should prioritize the development of school libraries" so that literacy skills are impacted to school pupils through their school libraries.

Library use for the handicapped group of students is still a challenge. For example in the study the mission and elite schools seem to be the only ones that are catering for the needs of handicapped especially the blind. This is not surprising but disappointing as Alemna (n.d:258) observed that general "in Africa, social services of any sort to any handicapped group is a very recent development. As such, in most African countries, established and organised library services to the blind and visually handicapped is almost non-existent". Alemna (n.d:258) further argues that

There is also the problem of lack of properly trained library personnel. In most library schools in Africa, the curricula is geared toward conventional librarianship courses. Library staff are therefore often unable to handle the needs of the blind. The idea that the needs of the blind may easily be ignored militates easily against the provision of services to the blind. Staff attitudes are an essential ingredient in making the library available to the blind.

Collection Development Policies for School Libraries

Pearce-Moses quoted by Ngulube (2012: 102) defined collection development as:

The function within an archives or other repository that establishes policies and procedures used to select materials that the repository will acquire, typically identifying the scope of creators, subjects, formats, and other characteristics that influence the selection process.

Ngulube (2012: 102) continued to state that collection development facilitates the:

1. Systematic acquisition of needed materials;
2. Effective discarding of the unwanted ones;
3. Determination of the suitability of acquiring materials in an archive;
4. Evaluation and analysis of collections;
5. Fostering of accountability in collection development;
6. Identification of the strengths and weaknesses of the materials in a collection;

7. Development of a collection that meets user needs; and judicious allocation of limited resources (e.g. funds, staff, equipment and space)

Collection development helps to "create some order out of chaos" as stated by Zamon (2012) quoted by Ngulube (2012: 102). However this is not happening in most of the school libraries as they tend to accept everything that comes their way to the extent that some secondary schools were having university textbooks. Even though beggars cannot be choosers there is need to accept only relevant material. African libraries seem to have relied much on donated materials from abroad. Issak (2000: 12) and Cramer (2012: 5) bemoaned this situation by stating that it has led to the accumulation of irrelevant and uninteresting materials. Cramer (2012: 26) observed that "many potential negative effects of book aid centre around supplying the wrong books. Book donation programs need to avoid "dumping", the practice of sending inappropriate books to economically challenged countries". Most but not all of the donations are acts of dumping rather than developing school libraries.

Greaney (1996) quoted by Cramer (2012: 26) argued that irrelevant donations may be solved by best practices on book donations and International library development programmes and that as such "cultural consideration are of utmost importance. Donors must work with the country to understand the cultural, linguistic, and educational conditions". Cramer (2012: 26) continued to argue that:

Purchase of books in native languages and that reflect local cultures and a knowledge system is very important and should be encouraged. Book donation and ILD programs need to link materials to the learners' cultural heritage (attributes of a society as inherited from ancestors, encompassing folklore, language, art, and architecture) in order to strengthen self-confidence and self-development.

Although it has been noted that most school libraries in Matabeleland have irrelevant books there is however a glimmer of hope as this situation is now being addressed by international donors. For example Plan International in Tsholotsho has bought books for schools by first contacting them to compile the list of books they need. By so doing the schools in Tsholotsho are now equipped with relevant books. The whole of Tsholotsho has 27 secondary schools and 83 primary schools. Out of these numbers 14 secondary and 33 primary schools managed to benefit from this noble book donation approach. This approach also benefits the local publishing industry as these books are bought from them.

The Africa Book Development Trust (ABDT) also seems to be taking this local based book donation approach. In 2012 it donated close to 2000 books for six schools in Tsholotsho. The books included in this donation were local books and set books for Ndebele and English literature. They have also taken the mantra of libraries reducing illiteracy and combating poverty into high levels. ABDT is now involving the local community in their book donations. At eMhlabangubo area in Tsholotsho they are assisting a group of women known as Mhlabangubo women club. They are helping them with their poultry projects. The books which are some of them donated to Mhlabangubo Primary School deal with issues of managing poultry projects. What happens then is that these books are also used by the community for their projects and in so doing combating poverty and creating successful partnerships between school libraries, community and Non-Governmental organisations. The interesting issue again is that some of these books are in local language and there are also pamphlets which are easy to be used by the local community. Such approach is favoured by Mchombu and Cadbury (2006: 8) who stated that:

In order for libraries to function effectively they depend on a good information environment, with access to appropriate resources. An important aspect of this is a thriving local book trade and media industry, which can help to ensure that people can access locally relevant information, including books and other reading materials in local language . . . it is vital that potential library users are not alienated by libraries which only contain material that is too detailed, too advanced or simply irrelevant to their needs. . . library book collections should be supplemented with basic pamphlets and audio-visual materials for easy transfer of information to a semi-literate community.

The Role Played by the Government in the Development of School Libraries

The data collected from these few selected schools showed that Government school's libraries are the ones struggling. Maybe this can be explained by Mojapelo (2016) who argues that "most governments, particularly in poor and developing African countries, are hesitant to pledge themselves through a legislated school library policy to roll out an active and sustainable library and information service for their schools to improve the quality of education". On the same vein of the Government's laxity when it comes to financial empowerment of libraries, Issak (2000: 12) writing about public libraries in Africa lamented that:

Considering that the government should be the principal supporter of the public library sector in Africa, there is declining support or even its total absence, which makes development of the sector difficult or impossible. In the majority of the cases, the government guarantees only the payment of salaries and does not finance any activity within the sector. Lack of recognition of the role and importance of libraries by government authorities is also affecting the development of the services.

Cramer (2012: 4) echoed the same sentiments by adding that "due to severe economic limitations, African governments consider libraries to be a lower priority than other concerns such as education, health, and securing necessities such as food, water, and electricity". These sentiments apply also to school libraries in Zimbabwe. Sithole (2012: 1) observed that the Zimbabwean Government's "support for school libraries is still elementary". Mangemba complements this by validating that:

Further assessment reveal that the position of a school librarian in Zimbabwe is not supported by the Public Service Commission (PSC) and Salary Service Bureau (SSB), human resource department of the government. This leaves the position of librarian being sponsored by the school development association offering poor remuneration and working conditions that give the position a bad image.

This was echoed by one of the ZIMLA official respondent who said that when they were campaigning for one school one librarian, the Government told them that the position of a librarian, nurse and bursar in schools has been removed from Public Service. Only the school boards can now pay those employed in those positions. It is disheartening to note that libraries as the nerves of the education system there are being relegated to the fringes by the Government. The Government cannot even pay one librarian per school. Given such a scenario it then calls for School Development Authorities' to be very creative in addressing these challenges. Recently public roads are awash with new school trucks and buses being bought by schools for their use. It is no longer the elite and missionary schools which used to have school buses, even day schools from high density areas are now having school buses. What then is difficult for the same school authorities' to buy books and pay one trained individual to mann the library? This calls for attitudinal changes to the extent that school authorities' can operate their libraries efficiently and effectively without any assistance from government. In order for teachers to get monetary incentives these days, schools sometimes organise civic days more than five times per term. Taking note of controversies surrounding such projects it then boggles the mind why such creativity is not used to fill library shelves with books and paying a reasonable salary to librarians hired by the school. The school authorities can even decide that a student can buy two books per term for the library. All these suggestions are possible for the schools to implement but the problem is that libraries seem to be not within their radar of pressing issues. Therefore attitudes have to change to the extent that libraries are given first priority in school budgets.

Lack of funding has always been touted as the main cause for the dearth of libraries. It has become a national anthem for librarians when describing Zimbabwean libraries. Maybe it can be the dearth of librarianship in Zimbabwe not the unavailability of funding as Sturges (2001: 44) quizzed that:

Unfortunately, but understandably, some librarians have more or less given up the struggle. There is a sad tendency to argue that only money will solve the multi-farious problems of the libraries. There is however, more to what Mchombu described as the librarianship of poverty than mere shortage of funds to run services.

The arms of Government of which one of them is Parliament have been found wanting in coming up with suitable legal framework for school libraries to operate in. Same challenges are mentioned in Ghana by Agyekum and Filson (2012:1) that "the absence of school library legislation in Ghana has enabled individuals and organizations to register schools without making the necessary provision for school libraries". In Zimbabwe while the Ministry of Primary and Secondary Education is empowered by the National Library and Documentation Services Act of 1985 (NLDS) to develop school libraries there appear to be no direct legislation that compels schools to have libraries in Zimbabwe (Tsekea, 2015).

Use of Electronic Resources in School Libraries

There is very limited use of electronic resources in the selected Matabeleland schools. It may appear that the use is only limited mainly to elite schools. In most of the day schools in rural areas the situation is worse. This is despite the fact that the President of Zimbabwe has over the years donated computers worth millions of dollars to schools in both rural and urban areas countrywide under the Presidential Computerisation Programme (Moyo, 2013: 2). Moyo (2013: 3) also noted that "computers donated by President Mugabe to promote E-learning are still lying idle at some schools in Matabeleland South Province because the institutions do not have computer laboratories". Other challenges being that some rural schools are not electrified. Another observation being made is that even those schools which have managed to use their computers are not able to partner the computer lab properly with the library.

Ngwenya (2013: 10) emphasised that:

School libraries must incorporate IT and computer activities into the library system. This would provide pupils with more information and broader information resource base. The internet and CD-ROM provide cheaper, multiple and faster access to information resources that are not physically available in the library.

The importance of Information Technology (ICTs) cannot be emphasised as The Library and Information Services Transformation Charter (2009: 72) observed that:

Diffusion of ICTs, essential for socio-economic development, impacts on all spheres of individual and collective life. In this global digital age, those who are unable to access ICTs are increasingly disadvantaged as the world's dependence on them grows in all spheres of human activity.

Many of the school libraries in Matabeleland are negatively affected by slow to zero provision of ICTs and this is a hindrance in their ability to deliver quality services, and also to be active agents in eliminating the digital divide and its dire consequences for the developing world. Tsekea (2015: 10) argues that the reasons why Zimbabwean schools are lagging behind in adopting the ICTs is "that while a lot of schools appreciate the importance of having their libraries automated, they are still facing challenges in doing so. Schools are still battling to get funding on the construction of the school library such that thinking of automating is still a dream". Some of the solutions to this is partnering of school libraries with University libraries as Bindura University of Science and Technology is doing (Tsekea, 2015). Through this partnering, Tsekea (2015: 5) describes the BUSE automation programme in the following way:

BUSE Library ventured into assisting school libraries in the Mashonaland Central Province to automate with a focus on mainly schools in and around Bindura though other schools from other provinces were assisted. Various workshops were done which include one on ICT and automation of libraries. Schools were then assisted in setting up their Library management system using one open source software called Open-biblio identified by the BUSE Library.

Such partnerships would go a long way in assisting school libraries to adopt ICTs.

Societal Perceptions of Librarians

One of the school librarian interviewed mentioned that there is no collaboration between the teacher and librarian in her school. She noted that the teachers tend not to visit the library and this sometimes makes her task difficult because she does not know the needs of a student in relation to what the teacher wants. Such scenarios seem to be as common as it appear on the literature. Miller (n.d: 9) explained that:

Many, perhaps most [teachers and administrators] do not understand the value and educational potential of libraries and librarians. . . Additional, some elementary teachers tend to view the librarian as a baby-sitter, while secondary teachers tend to take ownership of what they do, to the exclusion of the librarian.

Same sentiments are echoed by Tsekea (2015) who argues that "besides funding, the attitude of teachers and school administrators towards the library has not helped matters as according to Made (2000) the effectiveness of a school library rests on the attitudes of the teachers".

It is not surprising because of negative societal perceptions to witness that always the awards of excellence for student's good results being time and again given to teachers not librarians.

Opportunities Available for School Libraries

Ngwenya (2013: 10) argued that:

It must however be noted that, regardless of all these challenges faced by school libraries in Zimbabwe, the infrastructure for the promotion of information literacy skills training is there. A motion to the Ministry representative, that the position of the school librarian should be absorbed into the PSC (Public Service Commission) and SSB (Salary Services Bureau) structures was passed by ZimLA, and the month of October was made a month to promote the role of school libraries in Zimbabwe.

The Zimbabwe library Association (ZimLA) is playing a major role despite its challenges by lobbying the Government to improve school libraries. This current strong lobbying regarding school libraries as Sithole (2012: 1) has noted has led to "the Zimbabwe Library Association to embark on the one school, one library, and one librarian advocacy campaign". The resurrection of ZimLA from its death and its re-admission again to the International Federation of Library Associations (IFLA) and Institutions means that there is now a recognised representative that can act as a bridge between different stakeholders who may have interest in libraries. However it should be noted that ZimLA can be even more effective if proliferation of other library associations duplicating the same roles as ZimLA are discouraged so that there is only one voice voicing about the issues regarding libraries. Its membership should also be very national stretching to the remote areas of Zimbabwe.

The labour market is now having a reasonable number of librarians that can be employed as school librarians. Gone are the days when if one wanted to be a librarian has to study outside Zimbabwe. All this is happening because of the availability of tertiary institutions offering certificates, diplomas and degrees in Library and Information Science. In Matabeleland there is Bulawayo Polytechnic, National University of Science and Technology (NUST) and Zimbabwe Open University (ZOU). NUST has also recently introduced the post graduate diploma in library and information science which targets school teachers. This approach is recommended although it can be argued as Lance and Loertsher (2005) cited in Hughes, et al (2013: 20) puts it that:

While larger total library staff is often related to student achievements, the research emphasises that there is generally greater impact when staff includes qualified teacher-librarians. As teachers and information specialists, they make an impact by developing library collections to suit the curriculum, and enabling effective use of the resources in that collection to support learning.

The realisation of the importance of improving library services in rural areas is a positive development even though it's not a new idea. This has culminated to the launch of Zimbabwe Rural Schools Library Trust (ZRSLT) which aims to develop school libraries. What is needed now is the action on the ground.

The existences of public libraries although facing some difficulties are able to provide services to school children. The students who are benefiting from that are those residing and learning in urban areas. However the same cannot be said of rural students. This crisis was illustrated by Chisveto (2000: 196) with the analysis that:

The history of Zimbabwe has been such that libraries were provided in urban areas as a service and as a right for the people. No similar provision was ever made for rural communities. Since the independence in 1980 a quantitative expansion of rural schools has been made and the underlying principle of community participation has been embarked upon. Unfortunately no qualitative expansion was made to match the massive expansion of schools in terms of providing libraries in all rural schools and providing adequate and relevant information to rural communities. Schools remained with serious shortages of textbooks and reading materials. Rural communities generally continued to lag behind their urban counterparts, despite the fact that 75 per cent of the country's population live there.

This situation slowly changed with the entry of Rural Libraries and Resources Development Programme (RLRDP) which was founded in 1990. The objectives of RLRDP being that of providing "relevant reading materials identified by the rural communities themselves. These libraries are based mainly in primary schools with a few being found in secondary schools. The libraries are used by school children, teachers, community members, school leader and all interested parties around the school" (Chisveto, 2000: 196). At least from these libraries students are likely to benefit.

Mobile libraries are playing a major part in rural areas in reaching the far remote places. Banda (2012) outlined that credit should be given to the donkey mobile libraries, which made their debut in 1990 because they have helped in improving rural literacy by reaching remote areas cut off by bad roads and the unwillingness of qualified teachers to serve where basic amenities such as electricity and running water are lacking.

Governance Issues in School Libraries

The challenges of school library management can also be narrowed to the governance issues. All the difficulties mentioned above and explained to be caused by different actors, the issue of governance also cannot be ignored. When all is said it should be stated that issues of proper governance are also important in the management of libraries. As noted above, this study revealed that there is lack of innovative ideas in the management of school libraries even those which seem to be doing well. This therefore calls for the introduction of school library committees that may assist in the management of school libraries. This argument is propagated by Mojapelo and Dube (2015:113) referencing (Govender 2007; Hughes-Hassel and Wheelock 2001) avers that:

School library committees are a means by which power is devolved to schools. The essence of decentralising power is matched with the notion of a collaborative and inclusive model. The model is based on the conviction that the process of initiating, nurturing and sustaining a school library cannot depend on one person. It requires collaboration wherein a variety of participants act responsibly in their own roles, assuming shared leadership for promoting an agenda that aims to realise the common vision of a school library (Govender 2007; Hughes-Hassel and Wheelock 2001)

Mojapelo and Dube (2015:114) further explains that

school based library committees [are needed] as these will address the unique and differing needs of schools in the country, although this model can have its limitations. Regardless of the level where school library committees are situated they can spearhead and catapult effective and efficient functioning and running of school libraries. Although there is no legislated school library policy in South Africa to direct and guide schools to effectively constitute school library committees, institutionalisation of such library committees should be undertaken to resuscitate school libraries in all schools.

Way Forward

The Government despite the challenges it may be facing with the distribution of the national cake it should strive by all means possible to be involved in the development of school libraries and even coming up with a legislature which is pro-improvement of school libraries.

School librarians need to be included in the government payroll.

School leaders need to be creative enough to solve some of the problems affecting school libraries than to be always carrying a begging bowl.

Library associations should work flat out in trying to change the negative societal perceptions about librarians. They should take advantage of such programmes as October the international school library day to demystify the library profession. These celebrations should also take place in rural areas not only in urban areas. These opportunities should also be used to market library and information science courses offered by tertiary institutions in order to increase enrolment.

Whereas book donations can play a positive role in library development time has come for school libraries to have written collection development policies so that they are able to destroy unnecessary and irrelevant collections whilst acquiring and accepting the relevant books.

Disaster management plans should be put in place in order to protect the library material. Nothing complicated is needed but only basic response skills when the disaster strikes. Being able to use fire extinguishers and knowing who to phone in case of emergency. The phone numbers to be used in case of emergency should be clearly displayed for anyone to see them.

Whilst all the stakeholders are trying to improve school library services they should not forget the disabled or physical challenged pupils. Special facilities to cater for their needs should be there. For the blind, braille books should be provided. Entry points should cater for the students using wheel chairs.

The oral nature of African society should not be forgotten when designing programmes in school libraries. Indigenous or traditional literature encompassing proverbs, folktales, riddles and praise poetry should be provided to students in book form and sometimes in its oral form. It is joyous to note that the importance of such approach is now being realised in education sector. For example Memory Kumbota is quoted by Ndlovu (2013: 6) arguing for the revival of folk story telling during the 2013 Intwasa Arts festival as it present an opportunity to teach children vernacular languages and impart moral and cultural values while being entertained.

The uses of ICTs need to be promoted in school libraries because the proliferation of these ICTs gadgets has led to increase in the use of facebook, twitter, WhatsApp and computer games. This has resulted in the decline of reading culture in schools. This can be addressed by availing the e-book to the students.

CONCLUSION

Selected school libraries in Matabeleland that is the western part of Zimbabwe are facing a number of challenges such as the shortage of reading material and the libraries are mostly manned by untrained librarians. The support from the government is very minimal. Only the libraries in elite schools seem to be doing well. However all is not lost as there are opportunities that are available for these libraries to improve. For example there are now a number of tertiary institutions offering courses in library and information science.

REFERENCES

Agyekum, B. O., & Filson, C. K. (2012). The Challenges of School Libraries after the Implementation of the New Educational Reforms in Ghana. *Library Philosophy and Practice (e-journal),* 932. Retrieved from http://digitalcommons.unl.edu/libphilprac/932

Alemna, A. (n.d.). *Library provision for the blind.* Available at: https://forge.fh-potsdam.de/~IFLA/INSPEL/93-4alan.pdf

Anderson, J., & Matthews, P. (2010). A Malawian school library: Culture, literacy and reader development. *Aslib Proceedings*, *62*(6), 570–584. doi:10.1108/00012531011089685

Banda, I. (2011). *Government has a duty to enrich school libraries.* Available at: http://ipsnet.net

Chisita, C. T. (2011). *Role of public libraries in promoting literacy in Zimbabwe: Challenges of sustaining a reading culture.* Available at: http://conference.ifla.org/ifla77

Chisveto, E. (2000). Zimbabwe: The present position of public library services in Zimbabwe. In *Public libraries in Africa.* Available at: http://www.inasp.org.uk

Cramer, E. (2012). *International library development in Africa: Benefits, challenges, and sustainability.* Available at: libre.uncg.edu/ir/asu/f/Cramer,%20Elizabeth_2012_Dissertation.pdf

Hughes, H. (2013). *School libraries, teacher-librarians and their contribution to student literacy development in Gold Coast schools.* Available at: http://www.slag.org/research

IFLA. (2015). *IFLA School Library Guidelines*. Available at: https://www.ifla.org/files/assets/school-libraries.../ifla-school-library-guidelines.pdf

International Federation of library Associations (IFLA). (1998). *IFLA/FAIFE World Report: Libraries and Intellectual Freedom*. Available at: https://www.ifla.org/files/assets/faife/publications/ifla-world-report/zimbabwe.pdf

Issak, A. (2000). *Public libraries in Africa*. Available at: http://www.inasp.org.uk

Mangemba, K. (2012). *October is International school library month*. Available at: mangemba.blogspot.com/2012/10/0ctober-is international-school-library.html

Maud, H. (2005). *School Libraries in a Democratic South Africa – Curriculum Support, Information Literacy, Policy Development*. Available at: https://muep.mau.se/bitstream/handle/2043/4100/Maud_final_project.pdf?sequence=1

Mchombu, K., & Cadbury, N. (2006). *Libraries, literacy and poverty reduction: a key to African development*. Available at: www.bookaid.org/wp-content/uploads/2011/06/libraries-literacy-and-Poverty-Reduction-BAI.pdf

Miller. (n.d.). *Novice teacher's perceptions of the role of the teacher librarian*. Available at: tldl.pbworks.com/f/Miller.pdf

Mojapelo, M. S., & Dube, L. (2015). Repositioning school library committees to advance school library development in South Africa. *Innovation*, *50*, 110–122.

Mojapelo, S. M. (2016). *Challenges in establishing and maintaining functional school libraries: Lessons from Limpopo Province in South Africa*. Available at: http://journals.sagepub.com/doi/abs/10.1177/0961000616667801

Moyo, M. (2013). Computers donated by President lie idle. *The Chronicle*, *25*(September), 3.

Ndlovu, B. (2012, September 27). Revive story telling – Memory Kumbata. The Chronicle, p. 6.

Ngulube, P. (2012). Collection Development at the National Archives of Zimbabwe: Achilles Heel. In P. Ngulube (Ed.), *National Archives 75@30 75 years of archiving excellence at the National Archives of Zimbabwe* (pp. 101–111). Harare: *Printflow (Private) Limited.*

Ngwenya, S. (2013). *Promoting information literacy through government school libraries in Zimbabwe*. Paper presented in Zimbabwe Library Association 47th Conference, Mutare, Zimbabwe.

Paton-Ash and Di Wilmot. (2015, February). Issues and challenges facing school libraries in selected primary schools in Gauteng Province, South Africa. *South African Journal of Education, 35*(1). Available at http://www.sajournalofeducation.co.za

Rosenberg, D. (Ed.). (2003). *Reader Development and Reading Promotion: Recent Experiences from Seven Countries in Africa*. Oxford, UK: INASP.

Sithole, N. (2012). *Government has a duty to enrich school libraries*. Available at: http://ipsnews.net/

Sturges, P. (2001). *The poverty of librarianship: An historical critique of public librarianship in Anglophone Africa*. Available at: www.librijournal.org/pdf/2001-1pp38-48pdf

The Library and Information Services (LIS) Transformation Charter. (2009). Available at: http://www.dac.gov.za/.../Transformation%20charter-6th%20draft-2210

Tsekea, S. (2015). *Automation of school libraries in Zimbabwe: An evaluation of BUSE Library's community initiatives*. Available at: https://www.researchgate.net/publication/317433850

Zamon, C. (2012). *The Lone arranger: succeeding in a small repository*. Chicago: Society of American Archivists.

Chapter 9
A Comparison Study of Oral History Programs at National Archives of Botswana and Zimbabwe:
Postmodernism Approach to Oral History

Sindiso Bhebhe
University of South Africa, South Africa

Tshepho Mosweu
University of Botswana, Botswana

ABSTRACT

The influence of the postmodernist school of thought has touched archival science. This chapter looks into how one of the notions of postmodernism in archival science which advocates for the challenging of the dominant narrative discourse by equally including into the archives the voices of the minority, the marginalized, the ordinary, and the underrepresented people is faring both at National Archives of Zimbabwe and Botswana National Archives and Records Service.

DOI: 10.4018/978-1-5225-5840-8.ch009

INTRODUCTION

Zimbabwe and Botswana are nations born from colonial emancipation. During the colonial era, the history of the black population was neglected in favour of the colonial masters' history. Even though Botswana became a colonial protectorate, it was not spared cultural genocide. Westernisation was the norm during the colonial and protectorate periods. African philosophies in terms of knowledge production were being looked down at. Heritage institutions such as archives, galleries and museums became centres where the stories of European settlers were celebrated. This changed when Zimbabwe and Botswana became fully 'free' from the yokes of colonisation as there was a paradigm shift from Westernisation to Pan Africanism. This shift was also witnessed in national archival institutions of Botswana and Zimbabwe when oral history programmes were introduced which aimed to 'correct' the historical gap for the Black populations which was left by colonisation. It is therefore the thrust of this paper to perpend, discuss and inquire about the impact of oral history programmes to the documentation of once marginalised society and the minority groups being conducted by National Archives of Zimbabwe and Botswana. This will be a comparative study where notes will be shared and evaluated between the two countries.

BACKGROUND

Botswana, which was known as the British protectorate of Bechuanaland during the colonial era gained independence in 1966 and according to the 2016 population census has a population of around 2 million. Though Batibo & Smieja (2000) posits that it is difficult to determine the exact number of minority languages spoken in Botswana as a result of language clusters, the number of languages spoken in the country is estimated to be at least 25 whereby Setswana is the most dominant language in the country, spoken by at least 80% of a population. Setswana has been declared by the government as the national language while English is the official language in the country.

Minority rights group international [MRGI] (2015) has outlined that:

Botswana is home to eight Tswana tribes and around 37 non-Tswana tribes. Since independence in 1966, the government of Botswana has sought to emphasise the homogeneity of Botswana and pursued what it calls a policy of racial neutrality, downplaying the importance of ethnicity as reflected, for example, in the fact that information on ethnicity is not collected in the national census.

MRGI (2015) further quotes a High Court judgement which highlights the cultural genocide of these minority groups mainly but not limited to the blatant denial of having their own traditional chiefs:

A 2001 decision of the High Court of Botswana recognised that certain provisions of the Constitution were discriminatory towards non-Tswana tribes, as was legislation which only recognised the chiefs and the tribal lands of the eight Tswana tribes. Nevertheless, despite amendments to the Constitution and the adoption of legislation which allows in theory for the recognition of any tribal group and its chief, the Constitutional provisions remain discriminatory on the basis of tribe and no non-Tswana tribe or its chief has to date been officially recognised.

Unfortunately, such racial neutrality, viewed by successive governments as a necessary means to ensuring Botswana's peaceful development, has not been rooted in fundamental principles of non-discrimination and equality. Instead it has largely favoured the status quo that existed prior to independence and, as such, continued the dominance of the eight Tswana tribes.

It is therefore one of the objectives of this paper to scrutinise whether this perceived discrimination of minority groups [whose languages are not even recognised as official languages like Setswana] in Botswana can also be seen in the preservation of their cultural heritage at the National Archives in Botswana.

According to Kgabi (1986) before colonialism, Batswana could not read and write. She argues that as the accounts of their social activities were in the memory of people, the collection of oral history became crucial so that what was not documented could be captured after Independence. The first president of Botswana also underscored the need to collect oral histories as he believed that the advent of colonial rule weakened Batswana's social systems and cultural activities through the introduction of civilization influences;

It should be our intension to try to retrieve what we can of our past. We should write our own history books to prove that we did have a past, and that it was just as worth writing and learning about as any other. We must do this for the simple reason that a nation without a past is a lost nation, and a people without a past is a people without a soul (Sir Seretse Khama,1970).

In Zimbabwe the oral history programme at National Archives of Zimbabwe can be traced back to 1968 when it was mainly targeting the Whites who were part of the Pioneer Column and those who were in the public service or who were prominent. During this period in time the colonial regime did not view Africans as having had a history worthy of being recorded (Manungo, 2012). However later in the 1970s some few prominent Black Africans were interviewed such as the traditional chiefs, politicians and acclaimed philanthropist such as Jairos Jiri. It is from this background that Bhebhe (2015:44) argues that

the oral history programme by then was elitist as it excluded Africans from all ethnic groups who were deemed to be 'not prominent' or of poor 'uneducated' background. Such an approach to oral history meant that National Archives of Zimbabwe was a voice for the prominent: the conquerors, the vanquishers, the elites, the educated, whereas the voices of the grassroots' people: the defeated, the minorities, and the women were side-lined and forgotten.

Bhebhe (2015:44) continues to argue that

It has only been recently that this elitist approach to oral history is being abandoned for the more inclusive approach. The minority groups are now being targeted such as the Kalanga, the San, the Shangane, the Tonga, the Venda, the Xhosa, the Nambya, the Sotho, and the Nyanja. However it has not been an easy journey. The challenges such as the language of collecting these oral testimonies has come into play. The National Archives of Zimbabwe as a whole having none speakers of these minority languages means that 'dominant languages' such as Shona and Ndebele are used to interview these minority group of people.

It goes without saying that the collection and preservation of oral history has become an important undertaking in the postmodern era especially in African societies. Preserving such oral history stand to preserve the traditions of Batswana and Zimbabweans, thereby ensuring that the society of Botswana and Zimbabwe does not lose its roots and its history. By postmodern era or the influence of postmodernism at archives the authors are implying that archives should be of the people for the people even by the people (Ketelaar, 1999). Archives used to be the domain of State Governments whereby the national narrative churned out was that of the elites or those in power. This is what Cook says has changed with the coming influence of postmodernism in its influence over positivist traditional archival theory. Cook, (2001:18-19) avers that

the principal justification for archives to most users, and to the tax-paying public at large as also reflected in most national and state archival legislation rests on archives being able to offer citizens a sense of identity, locality, history, culture, and personal and collective memory . Simply stated, it is no longer acceptable to limit the definition of society's memory solely to the documentary residue left over (or chosen) by powerful record creators. Public and historical accountability demands more of archives and of archivists

In other words this means that the recent trends in Southern Africa's archiving is seeing national archives trying to fill the gaps in their collections by using oral history. Mainly these programmes are targeting those minority groups whose memories are lacking at mainstream archival institutions. Other countries such as South Africa have also invested much on promoting community archives which are owned by communities themselves. Zimbabwe and Botswana are yet to register any meaningful developments in community archiving.

Methodology

This is a qualitative study of two cases that is National Archives of Zimbabwe and Botswana National Archives and Records Services (BNARS). The study would be influenced by postmodernism reasoning in archival science.

Problem Statement

Traditional archives have been used by the powerful to tell their stories at the expense of the marginalised, underrepresented, minorities and the vanquished group of people. This has been observed by the authors that it has been the case both at NAZ and BNARS. In attempting to address those historical gaps oral history has been used. However these oral history programmes both at NAZ and BNARS have faced challenges ranging from respondents who are coming from minority groups of society who are not willing to be part of the programmes. Some of the challenges include but not limited to inadequate funding, un-innovative oral history methodologies and language barriers.

Research Objectives

1. To undertake comparative description of the oral history programmes at NAZ and BNARS
2. To analyse how postmodernism reasoning has affected oral history programmes at NAZ and BNARS
3. To interrogate with intention of coming up with mitigation measures on the challenges faced by NAZ and BNARS in their oral history programmes

Research Questions

1. What kind of oral history programmes are conducted by NAZ and BNARS?
2. How has postmodernism reasoning affected oral history programmes at NAZ and BNARS?
3. How can the challenges faced by NAZ and BNARS in their oral history programmes be mitigated?

Data Collection

The authors of this article have worked for more than 10 years in their respective national archives and they are heavily involved in the oral history section. Their observations throughout these years at the National Archives of Zimbabwe (NAZ) and Botswana National Archives and Records Services (BNARS) respectively would be the anchor of this article. The author from Botswana collected oral history around the country between the years of 2008 to 2018 while an employee of BNARS and coincidental this also applies to the author from Zimbabwe who has been conducting oral history programmes at NAZ since 2008 to present. These observations would be supplemented by specific literature review and document analysis.

Postmodernism in Oral History

McDonald (2008:10) observes that the coming in together of postmodernism and social history has made it possible to document the histories of the undocumented minority groups. Rodrigues (2013:75) avers that postmodernism and social history are of

the notion that there is a need to preserve a comprehensive documentary heritage of society by not only favouring the dominant narrative discourse, but by equally including the voices of ordinary people and the marginalised that may be underrepresented such as women, marginal religious groups, ethnic, linguistic and immigrant minorities, and so on

Oral history has come handy in documenting the stories of the marginalised because most of these groups use oral traditions as storage of their history including their culture. However some scholars believe that archival institutions should not concern themselves with conducting oral history interviews as they would be contributing to the record creation or that oral history cannot be validated as a true reflection of what actually transpired (Dryden 1982, Ritchie 2003). But Greene (2004) argues that Postmodernism is deeply relevant to archivists that is to everything from acquisition decisions to how they view and relate to their users. The word record in the era of postmodernism or post colonialism has been reconceptualised to include landscapes, oral traditions, and ritual performances (Yeo 2016).Yeo (2016) further argues that a record, as a kind of document merely reflect practices predominant in Western cultures at particular periods of history diminishing the notion that oral histories may not be classified as records. It then goes without saying that it is upon African scholars to devise ways of ensuring that oral histories are authentic, reliable and trustworthy just like other types of records. Klopfer (2001) argues that "If oral history is now being claimed as a source of heritage and as a more African form of historical documentation, then perhaps it requires its own institution with its own standards". Traditionally histories were passed from generation to generation through word of mouth among African societies as such archival Institutions play an important role in collecting these histories as they supplement written sources and fill the gaps that may exists in the people's history.

Fredriksson (2003:177) describes postmodernistic approach as fruitful in archival science as it "take full consideration of the societal context in which archives are produced and used". In this postmodern era Cook (2011:181) calls

for macroappraisal which focuses on governance rather than the structures and functions of government per se. Governance emphasises the dialogue and interaction of citizens and groups with the state as much as the state's own policies and procedures; focuses as well on documenting the impact of the state on society, and the functions and activities of society itself; encompasses all media rather than privileging written text; searches for multiple narratives and hot spots of contested discourse between citizen and state, rather than accepting the official policy line; and deliberately seeks to give voice to the marginalised, to losers as well as winners, to the disadvantaged and underprivileged as well as the powerful and articulate, which is accomplished through new ways of looking at case files and electronic data and then choosing the most succinct record in the best medium for documenting the diverse voices...

What can be taken from this quotation is the emphasis of diversity when it comes to archival holdings. Holdings that try by all means to represent all different groups of society without having amnesia when it comes to minorities. As Cook (2011:181) says

the result should be archives reflecting multiple voices, and not by default only the voices of powerful, an archival legacy shaped by an appraisal respecting diversity, ambiguity, tolerance, and multiple ways of archival remembering, celebrating difference rather than monoliths, multiple rather than mainstream narratives, the personal and local as much as the corporate and official.

Scwartz and Cook (2002:2) make it clear that archival institutions possess power in shaping, moulding and forming national, personal and collective identities and in the process validating the way we know ourselves as groups, nation, societies and individuals. Wales (2014:15) citing Cook argues that elsewhere archives can also inhibit this form of self-realisation, as they may be used as a tool for legitimising those with power and marginalising those without it resulting in many voices in society remaining absent from archival collections of the mainstream heritage sector, and are not given sufficient representation in the greater public record.

Documentation of Oral History of Minority Groups in Botswana

The collection of oral history in Botswana has been done on a national scale by the Department of BNARS, the Botswana National Museum and the Department of Broadcasting services (Mosweu 2011). This is unlike in South Africa where Klopfer (2001) reports that there was an upsurge of oral history collection initiated by community and academic groups, with a huge support by the state. Klopfer (2001:100-101) further points out that, in other post-war or post-trauma situations, it is usually victim groups or academics who initiate efforts to preserve or amplify oral narratives. This might explain the reason why in Botswana there has not been notable oral history collection projects by communities and pressure groups.

The Department of Botswana National Archives and Records Services (BNARS) was first established in 1967 with the Archives legislation passed by an Act of Parliament in 1978. In its endeavour to achieve its mandate of preserving the nation's documentary heritage, the BNARS has been collecting and managing oral histories over the years since 1982 (Mosweu 2011). Although BNARS mostly manage records in paper format (Mosweu 2011), there is the oral history collection which covers different areas that reflect some historical events and cultural activities of different ethnic groups in Botswana. Oral History collections have been undertaken in areas such as Kgalagadi South, North East, Chobe and Ngami Districts covering over 50 villages mostly from minority groups. This drew together not only the history of the villages but also the socio-cultural activities and events of historical value by the local people, investigating reasons which influenced them to come and settle in those particular areas. Other issues such as chieftainship structures, traditional food, attire, ceremonies and other events that are only unique to their tribes such as traditional hunting expeditions were also investigated (BNARS 2014).

Documentation of Oral History of Minority Groups in Zimbabwe

The motivation of oral history programmes in Africa is generally derived from addressing historical 'fictions' which were created by the imperialists during colonization of Africa. In case of Zimbabwe this is clearly captured by Chaterera and Mutsagondo (2015:1) who state that "the history of Zimbabwe, like the rest of post-colonial Africa is replete with bias, prejudice, inaccuracies and misconceptions, since some of it was a product of colonialists who had their own interests to serve. Oral history has come as a great relief". Nevertheless this statement should not be the cause of celebration because even after independence of African countries historical imbalances are still prevalent especially when it comes to the minority groups.

In Zimbabwe when NAZ was founded in 1935 oral history was not included, the focus and interest was the preservation of the early records and documents of the British South Africa Company (BSACo) and other personal records, manuscripts and photographs of the pioneers (Manungo, 2012:65). It took more than 30 years from the inception of NAZ for the Oral History Section to be established and that was in 1969. In its initial phases this new section of the archives activities was directed at recording oral information from Europeans, to supplement the documentary material held by the National Archives of Rhodesia. Interviews were held with prominent Europeans who had been in public service or prominent citizens in society (Manungo, 2012:65). Some of the prominent people interviewed who are mentioned by Manungo, 2012:65) are MacDonald Greenfield, Minister of Justice and Internal Affairs, Harry Reedman, a founder member of the Rhodesian Front and first speaker of the Rhodesian Parliament after the breakup of the Federation of Rhodesia and Nyasaland in 1963, Father Michael, a Jesuit, founding missionary of the Marymount Mission in Mt. Darwin and Sir Hugh Beadle, at first a politician in the 1940s and 60s, then later a judge and Chief Justice in Rhodesia. It is clear from this list that in its very first phases the oral history programme was elitist in its approach and excluded the Africans as "the colonial regime did not view [them] as having a history worthy of being recorded" (Manungo, 2012:65).

In the early 1970's that when the European Oral History Programme at the National Archives decided to target some few prominent Africans such as Chief Zvimba and Chief Chivero and African chiefs were mainly targeted by the colonial government for the purposes of acquiring history that would make it easier to understand and rule the Africans (Manungo, 2012:65). This was the case in the 1960s when the Native Affairs Department collected the oral history of the chiefs and their lineages. These became known as Delineation Reports which today are so valuable to researchers who are studying the history of the different ethnic groups in Zimbabwe (Manungo, 2012:65). It was with the coming of the African interviewer Dawson Munjeri that more prominent Africans were being interviewed such as Jairos Jiri, Ignatius Chigwewdere, Ndabaningi Sithole and Paul Nyathi. Even then the oral history programme was still elitist as it was targeting the only prominent black people not the povo. More prominent people such as Professor Stanlake Samkange, Mr Mike Hove, who were the Africans elected to the Federation Parliament, Mrs

Bona Mugabe, the mother of former President Robert Mugabe, Mrs Ruth Chinamano and the late Joshua Mqabuko Nkomo and it was in the mid-1980s that focus of oral history was shifted to the ordinary people (Manungo, 2012:66).

Despite the oral history programme in 1980's covering the testimonies of ordinary people it was still omitting what we may call the 'minority' groups both in terms of ethnicity and power relations. Bhebhe (2015) notes that in this period of 1980s and 1990s the focus was mainly on the Shona and Ndebele whilst nothing much was being done on ethnically minor groups such as the Venda, Xhosa, Nyanja/Chewa, Shangani, Tonga, Barwe, Sotho, Xhosa, Nambya and the Khoisan community. In regard to this matter Chabikwa (2016:66) also avers that societal archives are

selective memory and the voices of the socio-political and economic elites abound in the archive at the expense of the other voices. This is so because of the nexus between political power and archives. In the case of the National Archives of Zimbabwe (NAZ), public sector records and archives predominate. Minorities and the underrepresented are evident by their "silences" and "absences" from the archive.

Bhebhe (2015:50) further argues that "after noting that the oral archive of Zimbabwe has a gnawing gap when it comes to the minority groups, the institution started collecting their oral traditions. All this is being done in the spirit of national cohesion so that at least everyone will feel being part of Zimbabwe where pluralism or diversity of Zimbabweans is celebrated". This oral history programme of targeting minority groups became to be known as 'One Nation One Zimbabwe' which was launched in 2004 and it has managed to cover 4 districts of Gokwe, Bulilima, Chiredzi and Mangwe in which ethnically minority groups such as the Tonga, the Khalanga and the Tshangani are found (Chabikwa, 2016: 71).

Minority groups can also be understood not only from ethnical point of view but from power relations. In this regard when African countries got their independence some African political parties who were not part of the new African governments but who had fought in the liberation war found themselves being side-lined and omitted in the national memory/history. This was the case with Zimbabwe in which most of the recorded testimonies were those of the victors, the cadres of Zimbabwe African National Union (ZANU) and its military wing, Zimbabwe African National Liberation Army (ZANLA, while those who were vanquished (who did not win the first democratic elections leading to independence in 1980), for example the Zimbabwe African People's Union (ZAPU) and its military wing, Zimbabwe People's Revolutionary army (ZIPRA) were side-lined (Bhebhe, 2015: 47). SAHA (2012:5) further argues that "the Zimbabwean government has since 1980, been dominated by ZANU, a political party formed as a break-away from ZAPU in 1963. Within this context, the story of ZAPU's role in the liberation struggle has been eclipsed, deliberately underestimated by official Zimbabwean sources, and largely not understood by many sympathisers".

It is from this status quo that the NAZ, National Museums and Monuments (NMMZ) and the History department of University of Zimbabwe joined hands in trying to collect "true" and "endangered" oral record of the Zimbabwe war liberation struggle. The programme was known as the 'Capturing of the Fading National Memory'.

Challenges Faced by the Oral History Programmes in Both NAZ and BNARS

The challenges faced by NAZ and BNARS in collecting oral history testimonies are almost the same with few notable differences. There are challenges on the staffing of oral history sections; inadequate funding; lack of enough access to oral history collections; un-innovative oral history methodologies in collecting oral testimonies of the minority groups and the unwillingness of some minority groups in sharing their oral testimonies with mainstream national archives.

Skills and Staffing

Conducting oral history is a technical undertaking more especially in the postmodernism era and as such archivists need to have special skills and expertise to effectively undertake it (Mosweu 2011). Moatlhodi and Ramokate (2009) have also pointed out that BNARS was still faced with lack of skilled personnel whereby since 2000, the Department's trained professionals at any given time were not capable of dealing with all archives and records management functions of the Department. With the whole department struggling with inadequate skilled personnel, it means the oral history programme competes for manpower with other archives programmes where oral history becomes low priority. Ramokate and Moatlhodi (2010:77-78) noted that the activities of BNARS have been hampered by a lack of skilled personnel and an inability to retain staff due to pay issues. Same challenges of retaining staff at NAZ have also been experienced. Matangira (2012:118) notes that National Archives of Zimbabwe in the period of 2000 it experienced serious challenges because of the general meltdown of the Zimbabwean economy and this resulted in the "loss of professional staff; unfilled vacancies, especially of the professional and higher grades…". Matangira (2012:119) further explains that

for instance, by 2009, the Deputy Director post had been vacant for more than four years; three of the four Chief Archivist posts were; and many of the senior archivists had also left in a period of five years…The fact that more staff was leaving and more frequently, meant that there was not enough time for the skills transfer as was the tradition before. The young graduates who joined the National Archives received orientation from inexperienced colleagues, who themselves were still learning. There was more leakage of skills than was coming in. With no opportunities to transfer skills, professionalism slowly vanished. Those traditions, built over years and decades went down the drain!

The authors have observed that the situation is still the same at National Archives of Zimbabwe, worsened by the fact that the Government has frozen all new recruitments. These conditions have meant that there is not enough staff complement to efficiently and effectively carry out oral history programmes. The situation is more challenging in Provincial Centres which are manned by one Provincial Archivist per Provincial Centre as these provinces are too big for one officer to cover even the half of province doing oral history

The Unwillingness of Some of the Minority Groups to Tell Their Stories

The unwillingness by the minority groups to tell their stories have been a major challenge faced by the NAZ. As Bhebhe (2015) observed that there is gnawing gap when it comes to the minority groups in Zimbabwe and it has been difficult to collect their testimonies because they are sometimes not willing to cooperate because of archivists being outsiders and not even speaking their languages. This is not peculiar to Zimbabwe as it is the case with South Africa. Mhlanga (2014:82) argued:

that despite the efforts made by NARS [National Archives and Records of South Africa] to achieve equality, whereby the institution strives to include in their archives those social groups previously under-represented by the apartheid record-keeping regime, they encounter resistance from the groups they would have otherwise targeted as marginalised elements that merit inclusion in the documentary heritage of the country.

Both Zimbabwe and Botswana are home to the indigenous people of Khoisan origin. But despite that fact of the Khoisan being the 'first' people in these countries, the archives are 'silent' on that, not only that but also in the documentation of their way of life. This includes their rich indigenous knowledge systems which are not documented by both Zimbabwe and Botswana national archives. What may be found is nothing compared to what has been documented. Even in cases where they have been attempts to document the life testimonies of the San people, challenges of language have come in, unwillingness of the San people to get involved and the fact that this group of people lives on the margins of 'modern society' have worsened the situation of trying to document their oral testimonies.

Memorialisation of liberation struggle in Zimbabwe and some other Southern African countries has been bitter and contested in most cases. In regard to the selective memory of the liberation struggle in Zimbabwe, Hadebe (2016:1) mentions that since ZPRA did not win political power at the attainment of independence in 1980, its war effort has largely remained an untold story or where reference is made it is often anecdotal and their contribution is belittled by their competitors. However when NAZ attempts to close that gap, in some cases stern resistance has been mounted by former ZIPRA cadres who are not willing to tell their oral testimonies. Mainly this is caused by their mistrust of government and its departments such as NAZ because of their immediate post-wartime experiences in which soon after independence they were labelled dissidents and some of their compatriots and civilians were killed during what became known as the Gukurahundi atrocities hence their reluctance to participate in government sponsored oral history programmes (Bhebhe, 2015). Well for Botswana being a country that did not go through the confrontational war of liberation struggle with its colonisers it means there are spared from this specific politicisation of memory.

Access

The mandate of national archives is not only to collect and preserve but to also make accessible the nation's documentary heritage. How then do the archival institutions ensure that oral history collections are available to researchers? This paper has revealed that there is limited research on oral history collections at the two national archives that is Botswana and Zimbabwe. Those who visit these 2 archival institutions rarely consult oral sources. This may be due to the fact that some researchers still believe that oral sources cannot be trusted like their paper record counterparts. Filippelli (1976) has suggested that the most effective ways to inform scholarly community of the oral history holdings was through scholarly journals and publications of the catalogues. Wales (2014:36-37) citing National Archives of Australia argues that "there is little point in keeping records unless they can be accessed by interested researchers". Cannon (2009:17) echoes the same statements by stating that "an unused archive is a sad archive, indeed". Wales (2014:36) while noting the value of archives explains that access to community archives is compromised because of inadequate preservation and limited facilities that make archives accessible to the public. Both in Zimbabwe and Botswana there is still a need to vigorously adopt the Information and Communication Technologies (ICTs) and use of social media in order to improve access of oral history collections to the researchers.

In Zimbabwe public access to oral history collection has been a challenge because of the backlog of un-transcribed oral archive which might be attributed to shortage of manpower as alluded above. Writing about access at Bulawayo Archives (BA), Ngulube, Sibanda and Makoni (2013:134) bemoaned the status quo by stating that ICT's were not used effectively in the provision of access to archives and that the

Finding aids available at BA included indexes, accession registers for archival materials and descriptive inventories. Some finding aids were incomplete and were not compiled according to any international standard. Some finding aids available from NAZ website were not detailed enough. The inadequacy of finding aids means that the public is deprived of the right to access to archives of public bodies as enshrined in first Principle of ICA (2011).

Specifically writing about access of oral history interviews at NAZ, Moyo (2007:166) observes that cataloguing and indexing have received scant attention as most of the collection at Provinces is not accessioned and indexed. Moyo (2007:166) again mentions that most of the collection is yet to be transcribed thereby hindering access.

Funding

National archives are inadequately funded to undertake their programmes and as such, oral history programmes are also not given the amount of funding they require for the full implementation of the programmes. Fillippelli (1976) argues that one of the conditions under which archives can seriously undertake oral history programme is when it has money as anything less will result in a slipshod program. In Zimbabwe even though after the oral history programme became vibrant after independence in the 1980s and 1990s through a deliberate effort to "take the archives to the people" including the project "Capturing a Fading National Memory" – a project set-up in 2003 to document oral testimonies on experiences of the liberation struggle in Zimbabwe, nevertheless, in recent years, it has also suffered from the effects of the Zimbabwe crisis/economic meltdown. This status-quo led to Murambiwa (2009:33) arguing that 'the National Archives of Zimbabwe does not have the resources, goodwill or intention to be the sole custodian of the 'Zimbabwe Archive'.

Oral History Methodology Approaches Used in Both NAZ and BNARS

The oral history programmes run by these institutions that is NAZ and BNARS have a history of recording the testimonies of those who are 'important' in society such as the politicians whilst ignoring the subaltern. Even after independence this trend has continued even though on a milder scale. The minority groups in whatever format they come, have been neglected. Lopez (2013:2) citing Pareto argues that "history is nothing but a cemetery of the elites". In the archival world "archives have always reflected the influence of certain members of their community – often the social elites and their political and administrative allies" (Bloch 2013:153).

It has been in the year 2000s that NAZ has started to take the archives to the ordinary people as it has been seen by such oral history programmes like the 'Capturing the Fading Memory' and 'One Zimbabwe one Nation'. Even with these programmes that target the ordinary people and minority groups, challenges have been met especially on the issues of methodology. The authors have observed that the approach which is being used by NAZ and BNARS has tended to be an 'up to bottom', meaning tailored programmes are imposed to communities without much input from the locals. Meaning that even the languages used for interviewing are those of the archivists not the local communities. This has created tensions between the local communities and archivists as noted by Bhebhe (2015).

The approach used by NAZ and BNARS can be critiqued using Thompson's (1998:27) argument who argue that;

there have been telling criticisms of a relationship with informers in which a middle-class professional determines who is to be interviewed and what is to be discussed and then disappears with a tape of somebody's life which they never hear about again—and if they did, might be indignant at the unintended meanings imposed on their words.

This is one of the criticisms that have been levelled at conventional oral history methodologies, especially those used by national institutions such as NAZ and BNARS.

With community archiving taking centre stage in this postmodern world, archivists in both countries have an onus now of promoting these endeavours because of their advantage of empowering the community. Thompson (1998) avers that with community approach communities are empowered and then have confidence in writing their history. Thompson (1998: 21-28) seems to argue that a community approach method is recommended for oral history. This approach can be best for the NAZ and BNARS as it will also address the issue of the language. The minority groups as communities can tell their testimonies in a community set-up using their community language and thereby defusing the tensions that exist now whereby communities are forced to tell their oral testimonies in the language of the oral historian or the archivist.

RECOMMENDATIONS

There is a need for oral history programmes of NAZ and BNARS to be adequately resourced if ever the mandate of collecting oral histories is to be achieved. Filippelli (1976: 481) has recommended that the oral history project "should be administered separately with its own Director and its own support staff" a situation which is lacking in both NAZ and BNARS.

It is recommended that heritage institutions work together in the collection and preservation of oral histories. In other words partnerships can have favourable results as it was witnessed when NAZ, University of Zimbabwe and National Museums and Monuments (NMMZ) in the programme dubbed 'Capturing the Fading Memory' worked together in a positive way and producing positive results even though there were some challenges which were encountered in collecting the testimonies in the Provinces of Matabeleland. In Botswana, Institutions such as BNARS, the National Museum as well as the Department of Broadcasting Servies need to collaborate on documentation of oral histories in the country. Such partnerships are supported by Ngulube (2007:165) who argues that ESARBICA should foster partnerships between archives and records management professionals and those working in museums, art galleries, and other heritage institutions.

It is now high time that the NAZ and BNARS support community archives programmes that is the programmes that are community centred. The NAZ and BNARS can form synergies with these community archives in which they may come in but not in a full scale, in providing professional assistance here and there. Independence of these community archives is very important as it is one of its major characteristic and the one which makes some of them to be 'successful'. With these community archives which most of them are hybrid consisting of traditional archives, oral history and artefacts and seem to be minority based or though not always, it means the challenges faced now by NAZ and BNARS in documenting oral testimonies of the minority groups can be addressed. Steven (2008:30) argue that projects undertaken around the world to preserve indigenous knowledge such as a partnership between the University of Queensland in Australia and the Smithsonian National Museum of the American Indian in the United States, the GIS database developed to map knowledge of the Inuit people of Nunavut as well as the program delivered by the libraries of the Northern Territory in Australia illustrated how knowledge management tools can be implemented and adapted to accommodate indigenous knowledge systems and community needs. The projects also demonstrated how partnerships between communities, institutions, governments and other organizations can lead to creative solutions, sharing of resources, and projects that benefit multiple stakeholders. In the process strengthening knowledge systems in the country.

Both countries should do more in coming up with oral history programmes that target minority groups as the study revealed that much is not done in that section. Zimbabwe has tried to come up with few programmes targeting the minorities however inadequate funding has negatively affected the success of those initiatives. For Botswana there is a serious need to really come up with oral history programmes that are specifically meant for those locals who are not of the main Tswana tribe.

CONCLUSION

It may appear that both NAZ and BNARS are still having their archival holdings full of those archives that are mainly of major linguistic groups such as Shona, Ndebele, and Setswana-speaking.. When it comes to the minority groups such as Venda, the Xhosa, the Kalanga, the San, the Nambya, the Sotho among others in Zimbabwe, more still needs to be done. Same applies to Botswana which needs to vigorously document oral testimonies of such minority groups who are not of Setswana-speaking origins. Both NAZ and BNARS can make it a priority to try to construct inclusive/total archival holdings as this would lead to an improved social cohesion among different communities in both countries. While challenges which hinder that goal of coming up with inclusive archives are there especially the issue of funding, hope should not be lost. Some of the challenges can be mitigated by partnering with other institutions such as universities who have overlapping interest with archival institutions so that knowledge and resources can be shared.

REFERENCES

Batibo, H. M. S. B. (Ed.). (2000). *Botswana: The Future of the Minority Languages*. Frankfurt am Main: Peter Lang.

Bhebhe, S. (2015). Overview of the oral history programme at the National Archives of Zimbabwe: Implications for nation building and social cohesion. Oral History Journal of South Africa, 3(1), 43-56.

Bhebhe, S. (2015). Description of the oral history programme at the National Archives of Zimbabwe. *Oral History Australia Journal, 37*, 49-55.

Bloch, E. (2013). Interview: Med Tom Nesmith. *Nordisk Arkivnyt, 3*, 152–155.

Botswana National Archives and Records Services. (2014). *Preserving Our Past, Securing Our Future: An Insight In to the National Archives, 1967-2014 & Beyond*. Author.

Cannon, B. (2009). *Preserving communities: A guide to archiving for community organisations.* Retrieved from https://www.halifax.ca/archives/documents/GuideToArchivingForCommunityOrgs.pdf

Chabikwa, S. (2016). Minorities and Zimbabwean Archival Endeavour. *ESARBICA Journal, 35*, 65–78.

Chaterera, F., & Mutsagondo, S. (2015). Towards a complete documentary heritage of Zimbabwe. Whither oral history? *Information Development*, 1–8. doi:10.1177/0266666914568574

Cook, T. (2011). We are what we keep; We keep What We Are': Archival Appraisal Past, Present and Future. *Journal of the Society of Archivists, 32*(2), 173–189. doi: 10.1080/00379816.2011.619688

Dryden, J. (1981–1982). Oral History and Archives: The Case Against. *Canadian Oral History Association Journal, 5*(1), 34–37.

Filippelli, R. L. (1976). Oral History and the Archives. *The American Archivist, 39*(4). Online at http://americanarchivist.org/doi/pdf/10.17723/aarc.39.4.u3kw876j8127wl55?co de=same-site Accessed 10/02/17

Fredriksson, B. (2003). Postmordenistic Archival Science – Rethinking the Methodology of a Science. *Archival Science, 3*(2), 177–197. doi:10.1007/BF02435657

Greene, M. A. (2003-2004). The Messy Business of Remembering: History, Memory, And Archives. *Archival Issues, 28*(2).

Hadebe, S. (2016). Challenges in memorialising ZPRA legacy. Paper presented in The politics of armed struggle in Southern Africa, University of Witwatersrand.

Ketelaar, E. (1999). Understanding Archives of the People, by People, and for the People. In *Washington Conference on Holocaust-Era Assets Proceedings*. Washington, DC: Government Printing House.

Kgabi, D. (1986). Oral Traditions and the Archivist: The Case of Botswana. In Oral Traditions in Southern Africa. Overview of proceedings, Country Reports and Recommendations. Institute of African Studies. University of Zambia.

Klopfer, L. (2001, Fall). Oral History and Archives in New South Africa: Methodological Issues. *Archivaria, 52*, 100–125.

Lopez, M. (2013). *Elite theory*. doi: 10.1177/2056846013112

Manungo, K. (2012). Oral history as captured by the National Archives of Zimbabwe over the years. In P. Ngulube (Ed.), *National Archives 75@30: 75 years of archiving excellence at the National Archives of Zimbabwe* (pp. 64–67). Harare: National Archives of Zimbabwe.

Matangira, V. (2012). Seventy Five Years of Archiving and Excellence and a Decade of Loss. In P. Ngulube (Ed.), *National Archives 75@30: 75 years of archiving excellence at the National Archives of Zimbabwe* (pp. 112–124). Harare: National Archives of Zimbabwe.

McDonald, A. S. (2008). *Out of the Hollinger Box and into the streets: activists, archives and under-documented populations* (Unpublished thesis). University of North Carolina, Chapel Hill, NC.

Mhlanga, B. T. (2014). *The role of the National Archives and Records Service of South Africa in human rights promotion and protection*. Master of Management by Research and Dissertation at the University of the Witwatersrand, Johannesburg. Retrieved from wiredspace.wits.ac.za

Minority Rights Group International (MRGI). (2015). *Botswana: Recognising minority right*. Available at: http://minorityrights.org/what-we-do/botswana-recognising-minority-rights/

Molosiwa, A. (n.d.). *Language and Literacy Issues in Botswana*. Online at http://cpls.educ.ubc.ca/content/pdfs/4MolosiwaBotswana.pdf

Mosweu, T. (2011). Digitising the oral history collection at Botswana National Archives and Records Services: Problems and prospects. *Journal of the South African Society of Archivists*, *4*, 2011.

Moyo, C. (2007). *Capturing a fading national memory: an assessment of the impact of the oral history collections in augmenting archival sources at the national archives of Zimbabwe* (Unpublished dissertation). National University of Science and Technology, Bulawayo.

Murambiwa, I. (2009). Dismembering or remembering the 'Zimbabwe archive? *Journal of British Records Association, 34*(121), 25-33. Retrieved from www.britishrecordsassociation.org.uk/pages/list.htm

Ngulube, P. (2007). The Achilles Heel of the Preservation of Documentary Materials in Sub Saharan Africa: Knowledge and Skills or Funding? *Restaurator (Copenhagen)*, *28*(3), 159–168. doi:10.1515/REST.2007.159

Ngulube, P., Sibanda, P., & Makoni. (2013). Mapping access and use of archival materials held at the Bulawayo archives in Zimbabwe. *ESARBICA, 32*, 123-137.

Ramokate, K., & Moatlhodi, T. (2010). Battling the appraisal backlog: a challenging professional obligation for Botswana National Archives and Records Services. *ESARBICA Journal, 29*(1).

Ritchie, D. A. (2003). *Doing Oral History: A practical Guide*. New York: Oxford University Press.

Rodrigues, A. (2013). *An archival collecting framework for the records generated by South Africa's Portuguese community based organisations in Guateng*. Doctor of Literature and Philosophy in the subject information Science at the University of South Africa, Pretoria. Retrieved from uir.unisa.ac.za/handle/10500/13340

Schwartz, J., & Cook, T. (2002). Archives, Records and Power: The Making of Modern Memory. *Archival Science*, *2*(1-2), 1–19. doi:10.1007/BF02435628

Steven, A. (2008). A Different Way of Knowing: Tools and Strategies for Managing Indigenous Knowledge. *Libri*, *58*, 25–33.

Thompson, P. (1998). The voice of the past. In *The Oral History Reader*. Routledge.

Wales, J. (2014). *Community archives and the archival community*. A thesis submitted to Leiden University in partial fulfilment of the requirements for the degree of MA History in Archival Studies. Retrieved from https://openaccess.leidenuniv.nl/bitstream/handle/1887/28520/Josie%20Wale s%20 1405977%20MA%20Thesis.pdf?sequence=1

Yeo, G. (2016). Records. In Encyclopedia of Archival Science. Rowman & Littlefield Publishers.

Chapter 10
Documenting Nigeria's Social and Cultural History Through Cinema:
A Study of Biyi Bandele's *Half of a Yellow Sun* and Kunle Afolayan's *October 1*

Floribert Patrick C. Endong
University of Calabar, Nigeria

ABSTRACT

In recent times, cinema has emerged as an alternative technology to document reality. This could be seen in the fact that both fictional and non-fictional films are increasingly deployed to chronicle various aspects of history. In the Nigerian moving pictures industry (Nollywood), this paradigm could be illustrated by the recent release of historical epic movies such as Lancelot Imasuen's Invasion 1897, Jeta Amata's Black November, Biyi Bandele's Half of a Yellow Sun, and Kunle Afolayan's October 1, among others. Drawing on this relatively old trend, this chapter examines the extent to which some of Nollywood epic films are "trustworthy" records of Nigerian history. The chapter begins by examining the controversy over the nature of film as a historical document in its own right. It goes further to exploring the issue of historical film making in Nollywood and ends with a reading of Biyi Bandele's Half of a Yellow Sun and Kunle Afolayan's October 1 as forms of historical films.

DOI: 10.4018/978-1-5225-5840-8.ch010

INTRODUCTION

The act of documenting reality (people, places and events) has always been a central aspect of all human cultures. This is connected to the fact that the documentation of human experiences (particularly history and cultural heritage) does not only represent an excellent tool for cultural heritage preservation, but "a way of valuing people around the world who rightly want to see their unique expressions and identities recognized and valued as part of the human record" (SIL 2016). Thus, from time immemorial, man has designed various approaches to recording his activities in a realistic form; this has been in view of making them (these activities) rememorized from generations to generations. These approaches to documenting reality have been plural and formidable, ranging from the cave drawings done by early men to the ultra-modern audiovisual recording techniques.

In recent times, cinematography has emerged as a premium way of documenting events and people. Critical observations actually reveal that, all around the world, cinematically documented history has become a key instrument to safeguard traditions as well as a source of creativity among various ethnographic filmmakers (Camp 2006). Many visual anthropologists, ethnographers and culture conservation experts likewise construe the cinematic medium as being particularly valuable and important when it comes specifically to documenting both tangible and intangible culture (Engebrecht 2015; Hamar & Volanska 2015; Tari 2015). This may be attributed to the fact that the medium is a powerful visual source. In effect, through the use of the camera, a realistic rendition of history and cultural heritage may be done.

The cinematic genres which have mostly been used for this documentation purpose have been the non-story films (otherwise called documentary films) and alternatively, docudrama. This has principally been due to their non-fictional nature. However, in recent times, a number of schools of thought have underlined the potential of even story films (feature and epic films) to document history and socio-cultural heritage. In tandem with this, specific genres such as the historical epic films have been explored by some producers to record the socio-cultural heritage and political history of specific people and societies; or to simply preserve selected historical literature. Nigerian film producer Lancelot Imasuen underlines feature films' potential to record history when he notes that good or true epic films in particular do not only attempt to thrill viewers or audiences and to show them exotic landscapes. Rather, they most importantly deal with themes that are of historical, national, religious, or legendary importance. Such filmic productions use "an elevated style to celebrate heroic accomplishments" (cited in School of Media and Communication Studies, 2014). Some of these films are based on true historical events and serious ethnographic research. On these grounds, they often have strong elements of f/actuality. Others are purely fictional and though they sometimes muddle historical facts for the purpose of entertainment, they provide audiences with a certain image of the past which, to some schools of thought, is still a stride towards the good direction (Orubo, 2016; Ugwuede, 2015).

Despite the pertinence of the arguments given in support of the presence of f/ actuality in historical or epic films, it remains clear that the translation of historical literature into film is hardly perfect or authentic. Even when some producers claim to have kept costumes, props, and the overall *mise-en-scene* authentic, cinema remains a representation – and most often – a re-interpretation of reality. In the specific case of a historical epic filmmaking, movies constitute re-interpretations of history and so, factuality in them can only be to an extent. As argued by Ihidero (2016), in their attempt to narrate people's history from literature to film, new narratives are technically birthed. These new narratives are born out of two things: (i) the directors' voice in such films and (ii) the viewer's rapport with the original history. Inevitably, films are a complex mixture of historical records, fiction and the director's perspective (Marcus 2005).

This chapter seeks to examine the extent to which historical films produced in Nollywood (Nigerian film industry) could be considered as historical documents that record the socio-cultural heritage of specific peoples in the country. It does such examination through a critical reading of two Nollywood historical films namely Biyi Bamidele's *Half of a Yellow sun* and Kunle Afolayan's *October 1*. The chapter begins with a conceptual framework which gives attention to three key terms namely (i) history and cultural documentation, (ii) historical document and (iii) historical epic film. In its second part, the chapter explores the debate over cinema as a historical document. In its third part, it examines the phenomenon of historical/epic films in the Nigerian motion picture industry and in its fourth part, it finally offers a critical reading of *Half of a Yellow sun* and *October 1* vis-à-vis history and socio-cultural heritage documentation.

CONCEPTUAL FRAMEWORK

To ensure clarity of analysis in this paper, it will be expedient to provide a number of conceptual clarifications. This part of the study thus defines three key terms namely (i) history and cultural heritage documentation, (ii) historical document and (iii) historical film.

Culture and History Documentation

There have been various definitions of culture documentation. While some critics limit their definitions of the term to the act of capturing intangible cultural heritage with the help of audio and visual technologies (SIL 2015), others broaden their conception of the term to cover the recording of even tangible cultural heritage. Thus, according to LeBlanc and Eppich (2005), cultural heritage documentation include two main activities (i) the act of capturing information regarding intangible cultural practices, monuments, buildings, and sites, including their physical characteristics, history, and problems; and (ii) the interrelated processes of organizing, interpreting, and managing that information. Documentation is principally driven by the desire to preserve or conserve cultural heritage and make such heritage a focus of study. These two purposes can be broken down into the following:

- Assess the values and significance of the cultural heritage in question;
- Guide the process of conservation;
- Provide a tool for monitoring and managing heritage while creating an essential record; and
- Communicate the character and importance of cultural heritage.

Given its visual nature, the film medium has emerged as a valuable tool for the documentation of culture and history. While many ethnographical documentary projects have been rooted in the desire to preserve cultural heritage (Engebrecht 2015; Hamar & Volanska 2015; Tari 2015), it is extremely difficult to say whether all the historical films are strictly guided by cultural preservation motives. However, one thing remains observable: when they hinge on in-depth research and a *mis-en-scene* which is kept authentic, they (historical epic films) provide a view of the past and may intrinsically serve as historical documents. Based on this premise, it may be argued that, to some extent, historical films may document history (Aldgate 2015; Orubo 2015). This is in line with Marcus' (2005) contention that: "feature films are representations of history and can be primary and secondary resources. [...] Films are not stand-alone documents but contain interesting information about historical events" (p.64).

Historical Documents

Broadly defined, historical documents constitute one category of what is technically called historical evidences. They contain important and original information – most often in written form – which people can read, if only at face value. This information is about persons, places or events; and on the basis of their originality, they can be considered primary sources and valuable material for any historical methodology. Good examples of historical documents include treaties, deeds, old accounts of events such as battles (particularly given by victors or those sharing their opinion), contracts, newspapers and even the exploit of the powerful among others. One particular characteristic of historical document is that, they do not only detail the quotidian live of ordinary members of the society but they equally reveal the way(s) in which society functioned. Furthermore historical documents differ from artifacts in that, while they have writings (words), artifacts do not.

Historical Film Making

There have been various conceptions of historical films. Some of these conceptions are objectionable as they tend to associate historical films with any cinematic productions which are of large scale; have sweeping scope and spectacle and transport the viewers to settings of the old (Imasuen cited in School of Media and Communication 2014). In tandem with this, some Nigerian producers tend to think that historical filmmaking basically has to do with producing films which show mud houses, large crowd and people dressed in raffia palm skirts. However, historical films are filmic productions which engage with history or which in a way, construct a relationship to the past. This is regardless of the fact that such films purport to deal with 'real' people and events (Jack 2015; Raynaud 2015). Historical films explore themes that are of national, historic and legendary importance. Some of them basically utilize reality as historical context but does not claim that the primary plot line is representing events that have actually occurred.

Three major typologies of historical films include (i) history as drama, (ii) history as document and (iii) history as experiment (Rosenstone 2015). The first (history as drama) is dramatized history or dramas set in the past. This category includes films based on documentable peoples, events and movements and anchored on fictional plot lines and characters; but whose historical setting is intrinsic to the story and meaning of the work. The two films under study in this chapter (namely *Half of a Yellow Sun* and *October 1*) fall within this category.

The second typology regroups filmic productions which involve a narrator (as well as witnesses, history consultants and resource persons) talking while a number of footage of historical sites intercut with older ones (often from newsreel), along with photos of other historical documents such as newspaper and magazine clippings, paintings and graphics among others. The third typology (history as experience) includes films that are post-modern in nature as they do not follow the codes of representation of mainstream cinema. As defined by Rosenstone (2015), the term "history as experience" is an awkward concept used to refer to a variety of both dramatic and documentary films made by avant-garde or independent filmmakers. A peculiarity in these films is that they "struggle in one or more ways against the codes of representation of the standard film. All refuse to see the screen as a transparent «window» onto a «realistic» world".

CINEMA AS HISTORICAL DOCUMENT: THE CONTROVERSY

There has been a little controversy over whether or not (feature) films should be considered (reliable) historical documents. According to some schools of thought, despite the possibility that they constitute good reflections of the time during which they were made, films – particularly fictional ones – are liable to be extremely misleading when considered as historical documents. This position hinges on the fact that films are hardly truthful depictions of actual historical events. Most often, they simply represent the ideology or imaginations of their makers/directors. Furthermore, it has been observed that, though very popular as a tool for conveying knowledge, filmic texts are untrustworthy media. Sharing corollaries, Lavender (1997) posits that films should rather be read as artifacts of a time (that is a social and political reflection of the time in which they were made); rather than truthful depictions of the actual historical events (as historical documents). Lavender's contention exemplifies what Rosenstone (2015) refers to the "Explicit Approach" adopted by some historians when dealing with films.

This Explicit Approach may even be further rationalized by the fact that even genres such as historical films tend to partially – nay wholly – muddle or manipulate historical facts for entertainment or ideological motives. Films based on the adaptation of historical literature likewise tend to provide just a reinterpretation of the historical events they depict. As succinctly outlined by Ihidero (2016), "while translating historical literature into film, the history of the people that owns the historical material or shares the historical experience is being re/interpreted, rewritten, packaged and narrated as the f/actual version of the original history" (p.103). In other words, what is often presented in historical films may happen to be just a "subtle distortion" of the historical truth. This theory has been verified in the light of numerous great historical films in Hollywood. Two egregious examples are D.W. Griffith's *Birth of a Nation* (1915) and Lee Daniels's *The Butler* (2013). These two films have been taxed with departing in some sense and at various degrees, from historical facts. The former has mainly been read as a selective portrayal of historical events and a racist account of Black American communities in the early history of the U.S.A. (Bell 2011; Gunning 2016; Kuiper 1968; Lavender 1997); while the latter has been critiqued and profiled by some observers as a project which, glaringly, is devoted more to an exaggerative Black American rights advocacy than to the exposition of historical facts. In tandem with this, Turan Kenneth of the *Los Angeles Times* described the movie as "an ambitious and overdue attempt to create a Hollywood-style epic around the experience of black Americans in general and the civil rights movement in particular, it undercuts itself by hitting its points squarely on the nose with a 9-pound hammer" (p.49).

Similarly, films like *Millions Like Us* and *Our Aircraft is Missing* are egregious examples of filmic productions which are more propagandist in nature than oriented towards an authentic representation of historical events (British role in maintaining peace in the Second World War period). The two films have actually been taxed with being intended to engender pro-British feelings among the general population during the World War II period (Aldgate 2015; Marcus 2005). The often mitigated reception of historical films such as *The Birth of a Nation* is an indication that any filmic representation of the past is *ipso facto*, liable to be subject to debate or controversy. This observation is in line with Gunning's (2016) contentions that (i) "no picture of past events could be indisputable" and (ii) "all historical evidence should be subject to criticism" (p.4).

In the same line of thought, it has been argued that even non-story films like documentaries and docudramas are hardly neutral. On the basis of such lack of neutrality, they are liable to present biased depictions of history or reality. As Anderson (2016) puts it, "every documentary reflects a point of view. Even if the filmmaker has tried to present a balanced perspective, there will always be some sort of bias at work" (p.3). Unavoidable issues such as gate-keeping and selective attention by the filmmakers often result in a subtly doctored or biased (re)presentation of reality. No doubt, documentaries are popularly viewed as mere constructions of "truths". They are assemblies of director's cinematic choices and thus, virtually form a typology of distortion. It is therefore fair to enthuse that even documentary films hardly present the whole historical truth. They merely present directors' version of the historical truth. The situation is even worse with docudramas which integrate some elements of dramatization. Actually, docudrama producers most often tend to do a clumsy mixture of actuality and fiction thereby endangering the authenticity and trustworthiness of their contents (Ogunleye 2015). Based on all these indexes, many historians argue that films are disturbing as they distort and falsify history. They (films) trivialize, fictionalize and romanticize important people, events and movements. Bell (2011) highlights the skepticism of many historians towards films when he opines that:

Historians [...] regard history as a profession. Their discipline has its own standards of proof and of methodological consistency and accompanying practices of training and professional socialization. From this perspective the historical documentary can look like an applied and, let's face it, 'second-rate' form of doing history. Dependent for its factual accuracy on the mother discipline, the historical documentary film is viewed as an act of dissemination of previously accredited historical knowledge via an untrustworthy mass medium. (p.11)

A quasi antithetical school of thought is however of the persuasion that, though films may – in some specific circumstances – not authentically chronicle major historical events (like battles, elections and treaties among others), they offer an image of the life of ordinary people within the period they depict. On this basis, they may be considered valuable historical documents. As enthused by Gunning (2016), while classical historical documents (such as newspapers, a contracts or a treaties) tend to privilege great events and political leaders, feature films (the same as novels, memoirs and accounts of harvest), record the life of ordinary people within a specific period of time. "The best evidence of what it was like to walk down the streets of Paris in the 1890s, what a Japanese tea ceremony was like in the 1940s, what the World Series in 1950 looked like, or how people in factories did their work or spent a Sunday afternoon in the park" (Gunning 2016). Though all these subjects could be staged and distorted, causing reality to be misrepresented in various ways, films remain good records of time and motion. They "preserve gestures, gaits, rhythms, attitudes, and human interactions in a variety of situations" and teach their viewers one or two things about the past. No doubt, with close reference to the Nigerian context, Orubo (2015) posits that films have become "powerful historians" as they provide historical material that are even absent in Nigerian history textbooks.

Films, thus, often present vital elements of the social, cultural and economic life of a people. They capture bits of the past which may not be presented in detail in history textbooks. Issues like period costumes, dialogues, decorative masks, architecture and over-all *vise-en-scene*, when kept authentic by the film makers, are valuable tools to gain access and insights into the past (Aldgate 2015; Jack 2015; Reynaud 2015). The debate over the role of feature films (particularly historical epic films) as a medium for documenting, conveying and teaching history has thus led to various re-evaluation of cinema, vis-à-vis the representation of reality and vis-à-vis the act of recording history. Certain schools of historians are beginning to advocate the theory stipulating that, historical film making should be seen as a way film directors and specific critics look at history. Such schools of thought think that rather than viewing history in films automatically as a distortion of the past, it will be helpful to develop more flexible frames that accommodate the history presented in textbooks and the one offered in films. As rightly put by Rosenstone (2015),

To talk about the failures and triumphs, the strengths and weaknesses and the very possibilities of history on film, it is necessary to pull back the camera from a two-shot in which we see history on film and history on the page standing like opponents in a boxing ring. It is time to create a new frame, one which includes the larger realm of past and present in which both sorts of history are located and to which both refer. Seen this way, the question cannot be, Does the historical film convey facts or make arguments as well as written history? Rather, the appropriate questions are:

What sort of historical world does each film construct and how does it construct that world? How can we make judgments about that construction? [And] How does the historical world on the screen relate to written history? (p.2)

Viewed from this prism, history on the screen should no longer be read as being strictly antithetical to history on the page; but as a re-interpretation of past events. In other words, historical films are to be construed as a way of looking at the past. As put by Reynaud (2014), historical films should be envisaged as texts which, rather than revealing what really happened in history, show the importance of such historical events to later generations. "The most valuable use of historical movies is not so much as documents about the events, but as documents about the significance of the events for the culture that made the films' (p.52).

HISTORICAL FILM MAKING IN NOLLYWOOD

The idea of tapping into historical sources to produce filmic narratives is a tradition which has characterized the Nigerian cinema industry from its inception in the 1960s. One easily observes that the act of using theatre/drama to document history is as old as the Yoruba travelling theater tradition which has been at the genesis of the Nigerian film industry. One of the first three popular traveling theater practitioners (Duro Lapido) specialized in the writing and production of historical plays. Similarly, other prominent pioneers within the industry such as Akinwunmi Isola produced historical plays – notably *Efunseta Aniwura* – that was later adapted into films by a number of directors. *Efunsetan Aniwura* in particular is based on the life of a female Yoruba chief who died in 1874. The playwright, the same as the director of the film, immensely tapped into the history and popular traditions (cosmology) of the Yoruba people. He used reality as historical context. When adapted to film, the play turned out to be a major commercial success, inspiring many other productions of the same genre.

Two recent traditions in the Nollywood film industry have been to translate historical literature into films or to retell salient events of Nigeria history, using various cross-cultural and *cross-performative* narrative techniques. These types of filmic productions have most often been the fruit of international collaboration between Nollywood producers and their counterparts from Hollywood and from the British film industry. Two of such films which clearly illustrate this trend include Biyi Bandele' *Half of a Yellow Sun* (which retells the story of the 1967-1970 Nigerian civil war) and Jeta Amata's *Black November* (which is based on or chronicles the Niger Delta people's struggle, as championed by the martyred Ken Saro Wiwa). According to Ihidero (2016) the uniqueness of these two films is revealed by the fact that their narrative nucleus attempts to vividly represent the identities of particular peoples in Nigeria as well as the latter's distinct cultural heritage. The films equally record these peoples' struggle for self-determination and their conquest "as well as the merging of history with fiction". In fact, "the ways and manners [in which] these two Nollywood films fictionalize history and concoct a narrative for [these Nigerian peoples] throw up a substantial challenge for the Nigerian film critics and scholars to appraise" (p.105).

Other recent historical films produced in Nollywood dream world factory include Afolayan's October 1st (which is set against the backdrop of the Nigerian independence in 1960) and Lancelot Imasuen's *Invasion 1897* which chronicles the British invasion of the Benin Kingdom and the resultant looting of most of valuable works of art from the kingdom. Imasuen's film in particular is arguably considered the most ambitious of these historical epic films given the immense investments made by its director, in terms of in-depth research and resources. In effect, the film gulped up to 6 Million Naira only for research. Other heavy investments were made for the constructions of props to have an authentic reconstruction of life during the period of the British invasion (School of Media and Communication 2014).

One therefore remarks that the historical epic genre is an old cinematic paradigm in the Nollywood film industry. And today, many endogenous cinematography pundits and filmmakers advocate its use to document many historical events that happened in both pre and post-modern Nigeria. Nigerian film director, Tomi (2015) notes for instance that:

There have been many significant moments and periods in Nigerian history lost to the younger generation because they weren't taught in the classrooms and few books on them are available online or in print. Nigeria has had its fair share of tragedy in the last 70 years but very little of it has been captured in motion picture. Very few stories have been put on film and as a result many in the younger generation are unaware of the mistakes made in the past. (cited in Orubo 2015)

The pertinence of Tomi's exhortation is further revealed, by the fact that the Nigerian government has, in recent times, embarked on a number of curious and questionable educational policies which marginalize the teaching of history particularly in primary and secondary schools. From 2009 to 2016, history as a subject was removed from primary and secondary schools' curriculum for reasons which have never clearly been elucidated (Alalibo 2017; Ogunleye 2015). During this period, the subject was taught exclusively at the university level. Such a scenario has seriously been handicapping young Nigerians' learning of their history and has left the country's youths with the alternative of relying on historical literature or historical films which chronicle events in Nigeria. In view of such anti-history educational policies, critics have incessantly been making a case for the use of films to document or tell Nigeria history. A case in point is Ogunleye (2016) who posits that it is unthinkable that the depths of historical knowledge perpetually remain unplumbed by the cream of Nigerian youth. These youths deserve to know their past since they are compelled, as a cardinal social entity, to be part of the process of building the future of their country. This clearly introduces cases in favour of the use of docudrama and well research historical epic films as alternative sources of recording and disseminating historical facts.

The Role of Libraries, Museums and Archives in the Production of Historical Films in Nollywood

The production of historical films is a complex process involving a great deal of research. A film actually has greater probability to accurately/credibly reflect historical events only when it is based on sufficient or extensive research. Being authentic or truthful about the past requires cinematic paradigms which go beyond getting architectural and costume details right. A historical film therefore has to be based on serious research. This research can be facilitated only by resources or services which have a direct link with historical documentation, preservation and exhibition. Here, one will naturally think about such source centers as libraries, archives and museums among others, which offer a wide variety of documents that offer access to, or peepholes into the past.

There is no gainsaying that libraries, archives and museums have a great role to play when it comes to researching or making historical films. Libraries for instance most often provide a rich array of historical documents – ranging from oral history recordings and dairies to magazines, newspapers, letters, maps and footage. These documents may enable a filmmaker to crosscheck his or her facts, explore/find new versions of a story and produce a more detailed historical film. In the same manner, it is hard to think of researching a film without envisaging the use of archives and relevant museums. This is so as archival records are central to any serious film research. They represent the direct, uninterpreted and authentic voices of the past. As noted by the Archives Task Force (2016), archival materials could be viewed as "the primary evidence of what people did and what they thought; the look of places and events recorded through images – both still and moving; life's beginnings and life's endings; the growth and decline of industries and the ebbs and flows of communities and cultures. The archival record is the foundation on which are built all our histories, with their many and varied voices" (p.14).

In tandem with this, it could be argued that archives are the bedrock of film research. They could technically be viewed as the raw material that enables the historical film maker to analyse, compare and interpret facts, and to retain the best elements for the construction of his or her film. For instance, much of the materials used in the production of 2001's *Lost Battalion* were derived from the World War I's archives of the University of Kansas (Rizzo 2017). Similarly, Richard Rogers' 1997 movie (*A Midwife's Tale*) enormously relied on the historical accounts provided by specific historians as well as on various archival materials derived from Maine-based archives. As underscored by Kahn-Leavitt (the film's producer), exploring local museums and archives in the pre-production stage of the film enabled the director to put together a valuable database of thousands of images from the eighteenth century, as well as handwritten documents, paintings, maps, medical book illustrations, children's book illustrations, newspapers, broadsides, photos of buildings, and the artifacts of everyday life, which were all relevant for the film. She notes that "I found out what had been written about dialects and music and religious beliefs two hundred years ago. I learned as much as I could about the everyday work done by men and women in eighteenth century Hallowell, Maine: textile production, laundry, cooking, farming, surveying, etc" (Khan-Leavitt, 2016).

Nigeria is home to a multitude of museums, university libraries and archives which could facilitate historical film making in the country. The country actually harbors museums and archives such as the Benin City National Museum, the Jos museum, the Esie museum, the Nigerian National Museum, the Calabar Slave Museum, the National Archives and National Gallery of Modern Art among others, which may provide a wide database of archival material to Nigeria historical filmmakers. However, many of these source centers are not always well equipped or furnished. The unavailability of some important historical documents in Nigerian archives and museums have pushed many historical filmmakers to either depend on private collections (of antiquities or historical documents), foreign archives or historians and eye witnesses, to be able to recreate the historical period concerned by their films. Corroborating this observation, Nigerian cineaste Izu Ojukwu explains how herculean it was for him to obtain archival material for the production of his historical film *76* (a film chronicling the 1976 military coup d'état, which, like many other similar military punches, brutalized Nigeria and tarnished its image for decades. Ojukwu succinctly notes that:

We have poor communication practices in Africa. We have little respect for history. [...] The major part of our lives has been taken away. I couldn't access archival material. I had to get it from the Associated Press in the United States. We have a national television, we have a film corporation, but some of the events that occurred in our country are nowhere to be found" (cited in Tasha 2016).

Like Izu Ojukwu (cited above), many Nigerian filmmakers have been compelled to rather depend on foreign archives and museums to reconstruct history. Local

(Nigerian) museums and libraries have not always been relevant when it comes to researching films. It has therefore been common to find Nollywood epic filmmakers who largely depended on west-based archives or museums to research their films. A case in point is Lancelot Imasuen who immensely depended on such foreign heritage institutions as the British museum and the Metropolitan Museum of Art (New York, U.S.A.) to research his film *Invasion 1897*, a film which chronicles the historical events leading to the British invasion of the ancient Benin Kingdom, the fall of Oba Ovonramwen Nogbaisi and the looting of priceless ancient artifacts of the kingdom by British forces.

Biyi Bandele's *Half of a Yellow Sun* and Kunle Afolayan's *October 1* as Historical Documents

As earlier mentioned, historical films only use reality as a context and never claim that the primary plot is a representation of events that have actually happened in history. On this basis, exploring historicity or factuality in these films will mean considering the context in which the plots are set. Such a task will entail exploring the historical world which is created in the film and comparing such a world with the one created in history text books. This is going to be the main focus of this section of the paper. To set the stage for such a task, it will be helpful to provide brief summaries of the two films under study and thereafter, delve into the task of exploring their nature as historical documents.

Biyi Bandele's *Half of a Yellow Sun*

Half of a Yellow Sun is a 2013 filmic adaptation of Chimamanda Ngozi Adichie's 2006 award-winning epic novel of the same title, a bestseller arguably considered to be the most evocative literary account to date of the Biafran War which seriously ravaged Nigeria from 1967 to 1970. Written and directed by Biyi Bandele, the film movingly explores the effects of this large civil war on four characters. The film equally depicts the precariousness of social life in Nigeria during war. It presents the life of two twin sisters, Olanna (Thandie Newton) and Kainene (Anika Noni Rose) who, having completed their university education in England, return to Nigeria in the mid sixties and take a series of decisions that monumentally surprise their family. While Kainene decides to enter the family business and to pursue a career as a businesswoman falling in love with Richard (Joseph Mawie); Olanna moves to Nsuka to live with her lover, Odenigbo (Chiwetel Ejiofor) the radical academic who has been nicknamed the "revolutionary professor" and who later becomes her husband. Odenigbo and Olanna soon found a household and employ Ugwu (John Boyega), an uneducated teenaged homeboy whom Odemigbo takes as a kind of

Pygmalion project. As the Igbo people both clamour for and spiritedly labour to secede in view of establishing the Biafra as an independent and sovereign state, the two sisters are caught up in the untold violence of the bloody Nigerian Civil War and series of secretive betrayal which serious threaten to divide their family.

As a historical epic film, Bandele's *Half of a Yellow Sun* vividly chronicles a number of historical events which have marked the life of modern Nigeria. The film's director deploys various relevant tools to evoke life during the sixties and the seventies in the country. Some of these relevant tools include newsreel footage, authentic props and *mise-en-scene* and primordial costumes among other elements. The film captivatingly conveys the story of Nigerian independence through the Biafran civil war, deploying series of news clips which somehow enhance the documentary dimension of the production. Some of these news clips, include the footage of Queen Elizabeth II of England's visit to Nigeria, General Odemugwu Ojuku's strongly worded interviews, Ojuku's inspirational addresses on the question of the establishment of a sovereign Biafra Republic, Ojuku's search for asylum to Cote d'Ivoire, Phillip Effiong's surrender of the Biafra Republic and the massive displacement of people who were running away from federal troops among others. Through the instrumentality of these newsreel clips, the film presents some salient sequences of the Biafra Civil War. The clips equally presents some of the vivid glimpses of the horrors of the civil war, and unveil a number of facts which may not be found in current history textbooks; and which may not have been witnessed by the young generations of Nigerians.

The props, costumes and hairstyles deployed in the film are equally highly depictive of the 1960's Easter Nigeria. Throughout the film, the female actors are for instance, dressed in long and oversized dresses and hats. Some have well sprayed afros. All these features are notable aspects of feminine fashion and hairstyle in the sixties in Nigeria. Similarly, the cars used by characters in the film are appropriate models for the time setting of the film (the 60's in Eastern Nigeria) and one will naturally wonder where the director got these vehicles. Also noteworthy is the fact that the film opens with a folksong in the 1960's high-life music.

Kunle Afolayan's *October 1*

Written by Babalola Tunde and directed by Kunle Afolayan, *October 1* is a dark psychological thriller film which recounts the story of a police officer from Northern Nigeria, (Danladi Wazizi stared by Sadik Daba) who is sent on mission by the British colonial administration to investigate incidences of mysterious female murders in a remote town (Akote) situated in the south-western part of the country. The Officer's ultimate mission is to solve the mystery before the Nigerian flag is raised on October 1st, Nigeria's Independence Day. This film which is set in colonial Nigeria explores a variety of themes, some of which include the ills of colonialism, the shortcomings of western education and missionary activities in Nigeria, pedophilia as well as the persistent ethno-religious distrust/intolerance which has since independence characterized the Nigerian nation. In one of its sub-plots, the film captures the conflicting attitudes and reactions of two Nigerians named Prince Aderopo and Koya (respectively played by Demola Adedoyin Kunle Afoloyan) to (the ills of) western education as administered by missionary bodies. While enrolled in a missionary college, the two young men are sexually molested by a white ecclesiastic figure (Reverend Father Dowlin Colin played by David Reese). Vexed and traumatized by such a dehumanizing educational system, Koya abandons education and returns to his cocoa farm while Prince Aderopo develops erratic sexual desires which, in the long run, motivate him to mutate to a serial rapist and a dreaded killer of innocent maidens in his native land.

October 1 was shot in Lagos and Ondo State of Nigeria for a period of over 40 days following a four month pre-production stage. Apart from Sadiq Daba, the film stars Kayode Olaiya, Kehinde Bankole, Fabian Adeoye Lojede, Kayode Aderupoko, David Bailie, Nick Rhys, Bombo Manuel, Kanayo O. Kanayo, Kunle Afolayan, Femi Adebayo, Ibrahim Chatta and Demola Adedoyin. The film is the product of an extensive research. It received the support of a panoply of organizations major among which include Toyota Nigeria, Elisade Motors, the Sovereign Trust Insurance, Guiness and the Lagos State Government.

Afolayan's *October 1* is based on a fictive story. In spite of the fact that its title evokes Nigeria's Independence Day and much of its content is a stylish dramatization of a number of historical events, its plot and sub-plot cannot, at face value, be used to establish its nature as a historical document. However, from the director's intent or philosophy to the *mise-en-scene* and the context in which the film was premiered, there are sufficient evidences pointing to the film's historical nature. In a post-production interview, Kunle Afolayan succinctly revealed that, apart from entertaining viewers, his *October 1* has been aimed at telling Nigerian history through the instrumentality of cinema, particularly to the younger generations. He confides that:

For the older generation, especially those who were part of independence, they will be able to see themselves in this film. For the younger generation it's a platform for many of them who don't know the story of Nigeria [...] We want the younger generation to know where we are coming from and the older generation to see if we are moving in the right direction. (cited in Akande 2014)

Afolayan's view of his film is justified if one considers a number of factors ranging from props and styling to costumes and cinematography. In effect, *October 1* contains a number of documentary elements which enhance its nature as a historical document.

It for instance, features newsreel footages of the Queen's visit to Nigeria, Obafemi Awolowo and Tafawa Balewa's respective speeches on Nigeria's Independence Day, and various pictures of the Queen of England and the President of Nigeria at independence (Nnamdi Azikiwe). As in Bandele's *Half of a Yellow Sun*, the inclusion of such footage and images add to the documentary nature of the film. They provide glimpses of Nigeria history, particularly to the younger generations which may not have gotten the chance to witness the socio-political ambiance which reigned in the country during the 60s, particularly at the declaration of Nigeria's independence.

Besides the inclusion of footage of historical happenings in Nigeria, the director masterfully deploys relevant primordial costumes and antique props which help depict life in the 60s in Nigerian cities. Afolayan partnered with internationally acclaimed designer Deola Sagoe of Haute Couture to design the primordial costumes that were used in the films. These costumes are the fruit of systematic research into the kinds of style prevailing in Nigeria in the 1960s. The film costume designers actually had to watch series of documentaries on Nigeria in the sixties and exploit documentations on events that happened in Nigeria during the same period, to have an idea about the style that was prevalent in that era. Their efforts permit viewers of younger generations to have a non-exhaustive catalogue of fashion styles that prevailed in the country in the sixties.

Like the costumes and hair styles, the antique props deployed in the film are highly depictive of the independence period in Nigeria. From the old model cars, antique buses, bicycles and trains to the bush lamps and alarm clocks used in the film, all props reveal the mostly pre-modern state of life in Nigeria around the sixties. They are thus highly depictive of the 60s. Some of the props used in the film were imported from the United States of America and the United Kingdom. These include television sets and shotguns from the sixties. The importation of these props helped surmount the unavailability of such valuable historical items as costumes and antique weapons in the archives of the Nigerian Police Department. Other props such as old model vehicles were sourced in Nigeria. Most of the vehicles were refurbished from their original owners.

A striking feature in *October 1* is its strong reliance on thorough research, which is key to the production of good historical epic films intended to reconstruct historical reality/realism. In effect, research guided virtually all the stages the film's production, from scripting and costume to casting and scenery. With close reference to scripting and the *mis-en-scene*, Babalola (*October 1*'s script writer) clearly alludes to this fact when she notes that:

The rape of those boys [in the film] is a well-known fact. These things occurred. [...] it's a very open subject to deal with. I had to do research into the stories of people who were so abused when they were young. I wanted to make sure that when people see the film, they will be able to relate to it in a very sensitive manner. And I think Kunle did a pretty good job without putting it right there in your face. We don't have to be in the room to know what's going on, and he rightly portrayed the pain and anguish of these people. (Cited in Akande 2014).

Afolayan similarly relied on research during the casting of certain key actors, particularly those who played the role of some historical figures in the film. This can be illustrated by the fact that his choice of Sadiq Daba and Deola Sagoe (to respectively play the role of Danladi Wazizi [the lead character] and Funmilayo Ransome-kuti) has been informed by research. Danladi perfectly has the "look" commonly associated with people in the sixties while Deola Sagoe has a close resemblance with late Funmilayo Ransome-Kuti who is a leading historical figure of the sixties in Nigeria. Ransome-Kuti was a very powerful and influential political campaigner and woman right activist of the sixties in Nigeria. Her political prowess made her to earn such honorific titles and nicknames as "the Mother of Africa", "the doyen of female right activism in Nigeria" and the "Lioness of Lisabi".

The fact that *October 1* strongly hinges on systematic research is a strong index pointing to its maker's ardent desire to reconstruct the socio-historical context of Nigeria in the film. Afolayan's notable attention to details reveals his desire to adopt the posture of a historian. Such a posture is revealed the more by the fact that, the premiere and release of the film at Expo Centre (Eko Hotel and Suites) on September 28, 2014, integrated a series of activities aimed to showcase historical items in connection with the film. Firstly, celebrities that attended the ceremony were asked to dress in primordial native attires and hair styles. Secondly, the ceremony integrated an exhibition aimed among other things to display the antique props and costumes deployed in the film.

CONCLUSION

The use of epic films to document socio-cultural history is not a new tradition in the Nigerian motion picture industry (Nollywood). Though not pronounced, it has visibly marked the industry right from its genesis. Over the years, many Nigerian film pundits and ideologues have made a case for the increasing use of such approach to complement the efforts of conventional historians as well as to supplement the contents of history textbooks (and other historical sources) specifically devoted to the Nigerian context. In other words, many critics have advocated the increasing adoption of films to document various aspects of Nigerian history which are absent from history textbooks or which virtually overlooked by the conventional Nigerian historians. In line with this, there now exists a number of Nollywood films which are adaptation of historical literature or kinds of historical documents that reveal more or less overlooked historical events which have occurred in modern and antique Nigeria.

This chapter has attempted to illustrate this fact through a critical study of two Nollywood epic films namely Biyi Bandele's *Half of a Yellow Sun* and Kunle Afolayan's *October 1*. The chapter argued that though the two above mentioned films are based on fictive stories and re-interpretations of some historical events, they provide serious glimpses of life in the sixties in Nigeria. Various elements deployed in the films contribute an authentic or realistic rendition of Nigerian cultural history. History is documented in the films through the use of footage of socio-political events that happened in Nigeria around the sixties, particularly after the declaration of Nigerian Independence. Good example of such events are in connection with the Queen's visits to Nigeria, political speeches after the Declaration of Nigerian Independence and the Biafra War which took place from 1967 to 1970 among others. The use of these footage enhances the documentary nature of the films and informs particularly the younger generations (who may not have had the chance to witness the events in real time). In addition to this, the films display antique props and primordial costumes as well as hair styles which are highly depictive of life in Nigeria in the sixties. Even the dialogues in the films are constructed in a language that reveals a lot about life within this era. In view of all these indexes it may be argued that some Nollywood epic films – particularly the ones under study – have many characteristics of historical documents.

REFERENCES

Akande, V. (2014, August 16). As we await October 1. *The Nation*, pp. 34-35.

Alalibo, A. (2017, February 15). The reintroduction of history in Nigerian schools. *The Tide*, p. 6-7.

Aldgate, A. (2015). How can film be used as a historical source? *Groovy Historian.* Retrieved July 2017 from https://groovy-historian.com/2015/03/23/how-can-film-be-used-as-a-historical-source/

Anderson, A. (2016). *Looking at documentaries. Educational resource.* Toronto: Canadian Culture Online Strategy.

Archives Task Force. (2016). *Listening to the past, talking to the future. A report of the Archives Task Force.* London: The Archives Task Force.

Asantewa, Y. M. (2015, February 24). Crimes of empire: The invasion of Benin kingdom. *Pambazuka News*, pp. 23-38.

Bell, D. (2011). Documentary film and the poetic of history. *Journal of Media Practice*, *12*(1), 3–35. doi:10.1386/jmpr.12.1.3_1

Bordwell, D. (2008). Doing film history. *David Bordwell's Website on Cinema*. Retrieved March 20th, 2018 from http://www.davidbordwell.net/essays/doing.php

British Library. (2014). *How the British Library supports filmmakers*. Retrieved March 20th, 2018 from http://blogs.bl.uk/inspiredby/2014/11/how-the-british-library-supports-film-makers.html

Camp, M. A. (2006). *Die UNESCO-Konvention zur Bewahrung des immateriellen Kulturerbes. In Bulletin: Informationsblatt der Gesellschaft für die Volksmusik in der Schweiz GVS und der Schweizerischen Gesellschaft für Ethnomusikologie* (pp. 58–67). Paris: UNESO.

Cory, F. (2013, February 2). History according to Hollywood. *New York Times*. Retrieved March 20th, 2018 from http://www.nytimes.com/2013/02/23/opinion/History-According-to-Hollywood.html

Engelbrencht, B. (2015). Safeguarding intangible cultural heritage with film: Questions of documentation, protection and preservation. In N. V. Furlan (Ed.), *Documenting and preserving intangible cultural heritage on film* (pp. 25–38). Ljubljana: Sloveniski Etnograeski Muzej.

Gunning, T. (2016). Film as a social and cultural history. In T. Gunning (Ed.), *History matters: The US Survey on the web* (pp. 1–15). New York: MIT Press.

Hamar, J., & Valanska, L. (2015). The preservation and representation of the elements of the intangible cultural heritage in film. In N. V. Furlan (Ed.), *Documenting and preserving intangible cultural heritage on film* (pp. 63–74). Ljubljana: Sloveniski Etnograeski Muzej.

Ihidero, V.O. (2016). Meta-narratives and the challenges of narrating history in Half of a Yellow Sun and Black November. *A Journal of Theatre and Media Studies*, *1*(2), 103-117.

Jack, B. (2015). Feature film as history. *The Councilor. The Journal of Social Studies*, *76*(1), 1–23.

Khan-Leavitt, L. (2016). Process of making a historical film: Case Study: A Midwife Tale. *Do History*. Retrieved March 28th, 2018 from http://dohistory.org/film/process_preprod.html

Kuiper, J. B. (1968). The historical value of motion picture. *Library of Congress*, *31*(4), 385–390.

Maidabino, A. A. (2010). The availability, organization and use of archival records: A study of public archives agencies in the Northwestern states of Nigeria. *Library, Philosophy and Practice*. Retrieved March 20th, 2018 from http://www.webpages.uidaho.edu/~mbolin/maidabino2.htm

Marcus, A. (2005). "It is as it was": Feature film in the history class. *Social Studies, 96*, 61–67. doi:10.3200/TSSS.96.2.61-67

Ogunleye, F. (2015). *Television docudrama as alternative records of history*. Retrieved July 10, 2017 from http://documentaryisneverneutral.com/words/docalthis.html

Orubo, D. (2015). What role should Nollywood play in portraying our history? *Konbini Channels*. Retrieved July 13, 2017, from http://www.konbini.com/ng/entertainment/what-role-does-nollywood-have-in-portraying-our-history/

Raynaud, D. (2015). Dealing with historical movies in the history and English classroom. *TEACH: Research and Scholarship*, *2*(2), 48–52.

Rizzo, M. (2017). Arts department and the importance of research in pre-production. *The Film Business*. Retrieved March 24th, 2018 from http://masteringfilm.com/art-departments-and-the-importance-of-research-in-pre-production/

Rosenstone, A. R. (2015). The historical film as a real story. *Journalism History, 16*(2), 1–12.

School of Media and Communication. (2014). *The challenges of making a historical film in Nollywood*. Retrieved August 23, 2017, from http://smc.edu.ng/news/the-challenges-of-making-a-historical-film-in-nollywood/

Sefa-Boakye, J. (2016). Anika Noni Rose talks "Half of a Yellow Sun" and the need to revisit history. *Okay Africa Magazine*. Retrieved March 23rd, 2018, from http://www.okayafrica.com/7-things-we-learned-from-chimamanda-ngozi-adichie-and-reni-eddo-lodge-in-conversation/

SIL. (2014). *Language and culture documentation*. Paris: UNESCO.

Tari, J. (2015). Documentaring, preserving and digitizing Hungarian intangible cultural heritage. In N. V. Furlan (Ed.), *Documenting and preserving intangible cultural heritage on film* (pp. 53–62). Ljubljana: Sloveniski Etnograeski Muzej.

Tasha, R. (2016, September 28). How 'Nigerian Spielberg' Izu Ojukwu is taking advantage of the free speech in a changing industry. *The Verge*. Retrieved March 27th, 2018 from https://www.theverge.com/2016/9/28/13095648/izu-ojukwu-interview-nigerian-film-nollywood-76-movie

Turan, K. (2013, August 16). Review: Lee Daniels' The Butler: Significant but contrived. *The Los Angeles Times,* pp. 45-49.

Ugwuede, K. (2015). *13th, 76, October 1: Of numbers and the death of history in Nollywood.* Retrieved August 11, 2017, from http://amore.ng/13th-76-october-1-numbers-dearth-history-nollywood/

Compilation of References

Abu-Fadil, M. (2016). Opportunities for Media and Information Literacy in the Middle East and North Africa. In J. Torrent & A. Grizzle (Eds.), International Clearinghouse on Children, Youth and Media at Nordicom. University of Gothenburg.

Adams, R. (2017). Library Consortia: Models for Collaboration and Sustainability. *The Electronic Library*, *35*(5), 1067–1068. doi:10.1108/EL-07-2017-0147

AfLIA. (2017, October 21). *Public Libraries Network on Facebook*. Retrieved from AfLIA: aflia.net/

Agozzino, A. (2012). Building a Personal Relationship Throuigh Social Media. *Ohio Communication Journal*, 181-204.

Agyekum, B. O., & Filson, C. K. (2012). The Challenges of School Libraries after the Implementation of the New Educational Reforms in Ghana. *Library Philosophy and Practice (e-journal)*, 932. Retrieved from http://digitalcommons.unl.edu/libphilprac/932

Ahmed, A., Alreyaee, S., & Rahman, A. (2014). Theses and dissertations in institutional repositories: An Asian perspective. *New Library World*, *115*(9-10), 438–451. doi:10.1108/NLW-04-2014-0035

Akande, V. (2014, August 16). As we await October 1. *The Nation*, pp. 34-35.

Alalibo, A. (2017, February 15). The reintroduction of history in Nigerian schools. *The Tide*, p. 6-7.

Aldgate, A. (2015). How can film be used as a historical source? *Groovy Historian.* Retrieved July 2017 from https://groovy-historian.com/2015/03/23/how-can-film-be-used-as-a-historical-source/

Alemna, A. (n.d.). *Library provision for the blind.* Available at: https://forge.fh-potsdam.de/~IFLA/INSPEL/93-4alan.pdf

Alemneh, D., & Phillips, M. (2016). Indexing quality and effectiveness: An exploratory analysis of electronic theses and dissertations representation. *Proceedings of the Association for Information Science and Technology, 53*(1), 1–4. doi:10.1002/pra2.2016.14505301111

Alhaji, I. U. (2012). *Digitization of library resources and the formation of digital libraries: A practical approach.* Lagos: Usman.

Anderson, A. (2016). *Looking at documentaries. Educational resource.* Toronto: Canadian Culture Online Strategy.

Anderson, J., & Matthews, P. (2010). A Malawian school library: Culture, literacy and reader development. *Aslib Proceedings, 62*(6), 570–584. doi:10.1108/00012531011089685

Anna, K. (2016). Use of Social Networking Sites Tools and Services by LIS Professionals for. *DESIDOC Journal of Library and Information Technology,* 284–290.

Apurba, M. (2015). *Impact of Internet on LIS Education & Role of Future Librarians.* Assam: Gauhatti University.

Archives Task Force. (2016). *Listening to the past, talking to the future. A report of the Archives Task Force.* London: The Archives Task Force.

Ardalan, R., & Feyzbaksh, O. (2011). What are universities doing here? Migrating traditional dissertations into ETDs in Iran. *Library Hi Tech News, 28*(9), 7–11. doi:10.1108/07419051111195573

ARMA. (2014). *Generally Accepted Recordkeeping Principles, Information Governance Maturity Model.* Retrieved February 20, 2017, from: https://www.arma.org/docs/bookstore/theprinciplesmaturitymodel.pdf?sfvrsn=2

Armenui, M. (2014). Languages policy, national identity and politics. *European Scientific Journal*, *2*, 273–277.

Asantewa, Y. M. (2015, February 24). Crimes of empire: The invasion of Benin kingdom. *Pambazuka News*, pp. 23-38.

Banda, I. (2011). *Government has a duty to enrich school libraries*. Available at: http://ipsnet.net

Batane, T. (2013). Internet Access and Use among Young People in Botswana. *International Journal of Information and Education Technology (IJIET)*, *3*(1), 117–119. doi:10.7763/IJIET.2013.V3.246

Batibo, H. M. S. B. (Ed.). (2000). *Botswana: The Future of the Minority Languages*. Frankfurt am Main: Peter Lang.

Beall's List. (2015). Retrieved from http://scholarlyoa.com/publishers/

Begum, R. A. (2015). *Preserving Social Media (A case study at LTU archives)* (Master's Thesis). Luleå University of Technology, Department of Computer Science, Electrical and Space Engineering. Retrieved April 4, 2018, from: http://www.diva-portal.org/smash/get/diva2:1031685/FULLTEXT02

Bell, D. (2011). Documentary film and the poetic of history. *Journal of Media Practice*, *12*(1), 3–35. doi:10.1386/jmpr.12.1.3_1

Bhargava, G. D. (1986). Library resource sharing network, an evaluation. In Planning in library resource sharing. Lucknow: Print House.

Bhebhe, S. (2015). Description of the oral history programme at the National Archives of Zimbabwe. *Oral History Australia Journal, 37*, 49-55.

Bhebhe, S. (2015). Overview of the oral history programme at the National Archives of Zimbabwe: Implications for nation building and social cohesion. Oral History Journal of South Africa, 3(1), 43-56.

Blakes, E. F. (2006). *ICT Availability and Resource Sharing in some Academic Libraries in Nigeria*. Paper presented at the NLA Conference, Abuja.

Bloch, E. (2013). Interview: Med Tom Nesmith. *Nordisk Arkivnyt*, *3*, 152–155.

Bonn, M., Kendall, L., & McDonough, J. P. (2017). *Libraries, archives and the preservation of intangible cultural heritage: defining a research agenda*. Champaign, IL: University of Illinois.

Bordwell, D. (2008). Doing film history. *David Bordwell's Website on Cinema*. Retrieved March 20th, 2018 from http://www.davidbordwell.net/essays/doing.php

Botswana Government. (2012). *Botswana's National e-Government Strategy 2011-2016*. Retrieved March 31, 2018, from: http://workspace.unpan.org/sites/internet/documents/unpan048687.pdf

Botswana National Archives and Records Services. (2014). *Preserving Our Past, Securing Our Future: An Insight In to the National Archives, 1967-2014 & Beyond*. Author.

Boyd, D. M., & Ellison, N. B. (2007). Social network sites: Definition, history and scholarship. *Journal of Computer-Mediated Communication, 13*(1), 210–230. doi:10.1111/j.1083-6101.2007.00393.x

Brawley-Barker, T. (2015, March). *Integrating library, archives, and museum collections in an open source information management system: A case study at Glenstone*. Paper presented at the ARLIS/NA Conference.

British Library. (2014). *How the British Library supports filmmakers*. Retrieved March 20th, 2018 from http://blogs.bl.uk/inspiredby/2014/11/how-the-british-library-supports-film-makers.html

Bruce, C. S. (2008). Informed learning: realising the potential of the information society in our 21st century world. *International Conference on Libraries, Information and Society*, Petaling Jaya, Malaysia.

Buckingham, D. (2005). *The Media Literacy of Children and Young People. A review of the research literature on behalf of Ofcom*. Centre for the Study of Children, Youth and Media Institute of Education, University of London. Retrieved from http://www.ofcom.org.uk/advice/media_literacy/medlitpub/medlitpubrss/ml_children.pdf

Camp, M. A. (2006). *Die UNESCO-Konvention zur Bewahrung des immateriellen Kulturerbes. In Bulletin: Informationsblatt der Gesellschaft für die Volksmusik in der Schweiz GVS und der Schweizerischen Gesellschaft für Ethnomusikologie* (pp. 58–67). Paris: UNESO.

Cannon, B. (2009). *Preserving communities: A guide to archiving for community organisations.* Retrieved from https://www.halifax.ca/archives/documents/GuideToArchivingForCommunityOrgs.pdf

Chabikwa, S. (2016). Minorities and Zimbabwean Archival Endeavour. *ESARBICA Journal, 35*, 65–78.

Chapter 1 ETDs: From the Beginning. (2008). *Technical Services Quarterly, 25*(sup1), 1–10. 10.1080/07317130802127819

Chaterera, F., & Mutsagondo, S. (2015). Towards a complete documentary heritage of Zimbabwe. Whither oral history? *Information Development*, 1–8. doi:10.1177/0266666914568574

Chikaan, G. J., & Ahmad, I. J. (2011). *Mass communication for beginners.* Azaben Publishers.

Chirimuuta, C. (2017). *Empowering Zimbabweans through the use of indigenous languages in the media: A case of selected newspapers* (Unpublished doctoral dissertation). University of South Africa.

Chisita, C. T. (2011). *Role of public libraries in promoting literacy in Zimbabwe: Challenges of sustaining a reading culture*. Available at: http://conference.ifla.org/ifla77

Chisveto, E. (2000). Zimbabwe: The present position of public library services in Zimbabwe. In *Public libraries in Africa.* Available at: http://www.inasp.org.uk

Choi, K. S., Im, I., & Yoo, Y. (2013). *Liquid Communication: An Analysis of the Impact of Mobile Micro-blogging on Communication and Decision-Making.* Retrieved February 20, 2017, from: http://aisel.aisnet.org/cgi/viewcontent.cgi?article=1301&context=icis2013

Conway, P. (2010). Preservation in the age of google: Digitization in the age of google: digitization, digital preservation, and dilemmas. *The Library Quarterly*, *80*(1), 61–79. doi:10.1086/648463

Cook, T. (2011). We are what we keep; We keep What We Are': Archival Appraisal Past, Present and Future. *Journal of the Society of Archivists*, *32*(2), 173–189. doi:10.1080/00379816.2011.619688

Cory, F. (2013, February 2). History according to Hollywood. *New York Times*. Retrieved March 20th, 2018 from http://www.nytimes.com/2013/02/23/opinion/History-According-to-Hollywood.html

Cramer, E. (2012). *International library development in Africa: Benefits, challenges, and sustainability*. Available at: libre.uncg.edu/ir/asu/f/Cramer,%20Elizabeth_2012_Dissertation.pdf

Daramola, I., & Oyinade, B. (2015). Impact of cultural globalisation on Africa: The role of Western media. *International Journal of Education and Research*, *3*(3), 31–46.

Davidson, C. N., & Goldberg, D. T. (2009). *The Future of Learning Institutions in a Digital Age. MacArthur Foundation Reports on Digital Media and Learning*. Cambridge, MA: MIT Press. Retrieved from http://mitpress.mit. edu/sites/default/files/titles/free_download/9780262513593_ Future_of_Learning.pdf

Dean, J. (2002). *Planning Library Education Programmes* (E. Evans, Ed.). London, Worcester, Trinity Press.

Deirdre, B. (2015, August 27). *Public Relations Foundation*. Retrieved from Lynda.com: https://www.lynda.com

Di Bianca, M. (2014). *Discovery and Preservation of Social Media Evidence*. Retrieved February 20, 2018, from: https://www.americanbar.org/content/dam/aba/publications/blt/2014/01/social-media-evidence-201401.authcheckdam.pdf

Dryden, J. (1981–1982). Oral History and Archives: The Case Against. *Canadian Oral History Association Journal*, *5*(1), 34–37.

Duranti, L. (2014). *A clear sky forecast on a cloudy day: Making, Keeping and Preserving Records in a Public Cloud Environment.* Retrieved February 20, 2018, from: http://www.ffzg.unizg.hr/ada2014/wp-content/uploads/2014/07/08-Duranti-Making-Keeping-and-Preserving-Records-in-a-Public-Cloud-Environment.pdf

Duranti, L. (2015). Special Issue: Data, Records, and Archives in the Cloud. *Canadian Journal of Information and Library Science*, *39*(2), 91–96. doi:10.1353/ils.2015.0013

Eaton, N. L. (1995). Resource sharing: The public university library's imperative. *Journal of Library Administration*, *21*(1-2), 27–38. doi:10.1300/J111V21N01_03

EIFL. (2014). *Frequently Asked Questions - Consortium Management.* Available at http://www.eifl.net/faq/consortium-management

Ekwelem, V.O., Okafor, V.N., & Ukwoma, S.C. (2011). Preservation of cultural heritage: The strategic role of the library and information science professionals in south east Nigeria. *Library Philosophy and Practice, 562.*

Elsevier.com. (2015). Retrieved from http://www.elsevier.com

Engelbrencht, B. (2015). Safeguarding intangible cultural heritage with film: Questions of documentation, protection and preservation. In N. V. Furlan (Ed.), *Documenting and preserving intangible cultural heritage on film* (pp. 25–38). Ljubljana: Sloveniski Etnograeski Muzej.

Ezema, I. J., & Igbo, H. U. (2016). Electronic theses and dissertations and the promotion of scholarship in African universities: Prospects and challenges. *The International Information & Library Review*, *48*(1), 21–30. doi:10.1080/10572317.2016.1146038

Farkas, M. (2012). Participatory technologies, pedagogy 2.0 and information literacy. *Library Hi Tech*, *30*(Issue: 1), 82–94. doi:10.1108/07378831211213229

Filippelli, R. L. (1976). Oral History and the Archives. *The American Archivist, 39*(4). Online at http://americanarchivist.org/doi/pdf/10.17723/aarc.39.4.u3kw876j8127wl55?co de=same-site Accessed 10/02/17

Fithian, C., & Powell, A. (2009). *Cultural aspects of sustainable development.* Centre for Sustainable Development.

Franks, P., & Driskill, M. (2014). *Building Trust in Government through Social Media: An InterPARES Trust Research Project.* Retrieved May 16, 2018, from: https://interparestrust.org/assets/public/dissemination/FranksDriskill_ECSM2014_BuildingTrustInGovernmentThroughSocialMedia.pdf

Fredriksson, B. (2003). Postmordenistic Archival Science – Rethinking the Methodology of a Science. *Archival Science, 3*(2), 177–197. doi:10.1007/BF02435657

Freitas, A., & Curry, E. (2016). *Big data curation.* Galway: Insight Centre for Data Analytics. doi:10.1007/978-3-319-21569-3_6

Fuchs, C. (2014). *Social Media: A Critical Introduction.* London: Sage. doi:10.4135/9781446270066.n2

Fyffe, R., & Welburn, W. (2008). ETDs, scholarly communication, and campus collaboration: Opportunities for libraries. *College & Research Libraries News, 69*(3), 152–155. doi:10.5860/crln.69.3.7952

Gartner, Inc. (2016). *Information Governance.* Retrieved February 20, 2017, from: https://www.gartner.com/it-glossary/information-governance

Getz, M. (1991). Document delivery. *The Bottom Line (New York, N.Y.), 5*(4), 40–44. doi:10.1108/eb025354

Government of Botswana. (1978). *National Archives and Records Services Act Cap 59:04.* Gaborone: Government Printer.

Government of Botswana. (1996). *Vision 2016.* Gaborone: Government Printer.

Government of Botswana. (2007). *National Information and Communications Technology Policy (Maitlamo Policy).* Gaborone: Government Printer.

Government of Botswana. (2014). *Electronic Communications and Transactions Act.* Gaborone: Government Printer.

Greene, M. A. (2003-2004). The Messy Business of Remembering: History, Memory, And Archives. *Archival Issues*, *28*(2).

Grizzle, A. (Ed.). (2011). *Media and information literacy curriculum for teachers*. United Nations Educational, Scientific and Cultural Organization. Available at http://unesdoc.unesco.org/images/0019/001929/192971e.pdf

Grizzle, E. (2016). Preliminary Comparative Analysis of Media and Information Literacy in the MENA Region. *Opportunities for media and information literacy in the Middle East and North Africa*. Retrieved from http://www.unaoc.org/who-we-are/high-level-group

Gunning, T. (2016). Film as a social and cultural history. In T. Gunning (Ed.), *History matters: The US Survey on the web* (pp. 1–15). New York: MIT Press.

Hadebe, S. (2016). Challenges in memorialising ZPRA legacy. Paper presented in The politics of armed struggle in Southern Africa, University of Witwatersrand.

Hall, G. (2008). *Digitize This Book! Digitize This Book! The Politics of New Media, or Why We Need Open Access Now*. Minneapolis, MN: University of Minnesota Press. Retrieved from http://www.academia.edu/11922788/Digitize_This_Book_

Hamar, J., & Valanska, L. (2015). The preservation and representation of the elements of the intangible cultural heritage in film. In N. V. Furlan (Ed.), *Documenting and preserving intangible cultural heritage on film* (pp. 63–74). Ljubljana: Sloveniski Etnograeski Muzej.

Harnad, S., Brody, T., Vallieres, F., Carr, L., Hitchcock, S., Gingras, Y., ... Hilf, E. R. (2004). The Access/Impact Problem and the Green and Gold Roads to Open Access. *Serials Review*, *30*(4), 310–314. doi:10.1080/00987913.2004.10764930

Hartsock, R., & Alemneh, D. G. (2018). Electronic Theses and Dissertations (ETDs). In M. Khosrow-Pour (Ed.), Encyclopedia of Information Science and Technology, Fourth Edition (pp. 6748-6755). Hershey, PA: IGI Global. doi:10.4018/978-1-5225-2255-3.ch584

Hightower, C., & Soete, G. J. (1995). The consortium as learning organization: Twelve steps to success in collaborative collections projects. *Journal of Academic Librarianship, 21*(2), 87–91. doi:10.1016/0099-1333(95)90119-1

Hirshon, A. (1995). Library strategic alliances and the digital library in the 1990's. The OhioLINK Experiment. *Journal of Academic Librarianship, 21*(5), 383–386. doi:10.1016/0099-1333(95)90065-9

Hohman, C. (2011). *A records and information management guide to social media.* Retrieved May 13, 2018, from: http://www.incontextmag.com/articles/2011/a-records-and-information-management-guide-to-social-media.html

Huang, C. D., & Behara, R. S. (2007). Outcome driven experiential learning with Web 2.0. *Journal of Information Systems Education, 18*(3), 329–333.

Hughes, H. (2013). *School libraries, teacher-librarians and their contribution to student literacy development in Gold Coast schools.* Available at: http://www.slag.org/research

Huvila, I. (2014). Archives, libraries and museums in the contemporary society: Perspectives of the professionals. *Proceedings of the Perspectives of the Professionals*, 45-64.

Hyatt, M. (2014, June 26). *Paper or Screen? Exploring the Pros and Cons of the Ebook.* Retrieved from Rightly Designed: htttps://rightlydesigned.com/ebooks

Idang, G. E. (2015). African cultures and values. *Phronimon, 16*(2), 97–111.

IFLA. (2015). *IFLA School Library Guidelines.* Available at: https://www.ifla.org/files/assets/school-libraries.../ifla-school-library-guidelines.pdf

Ihidero, V.O. (2016). Meta-narratives and the challenges of narrating history in Half of a Yellow Sun and Black November. *A Journal of Theatre and Media Studies, 1*(2), 103-117.

INFLIBNET. (2017a). *ShodhGangotri: Repository of Indian Research in Progress: Home.* Retrieved from http://shodh.inflibnet.ac.in/

INFLIBNET. (2017b). *Shodhganga: a reservoir of Indian theses @ INFLIBNET.* Retrieved from http://shodhganga.inflibnet.ac.in/

International Federation of library Associations (IFLA). (1998). *IFLA/FAIFE World Report: Libraries and Intellectual Freedom.* Available at: https://www.ifla.org/files/assets/faife/publications/ifla-world-report/zimbabwe.pdf

Internet World Stats. (2017). *Internet Statistics users for Africa (Africa Internet Usage, 2017 Population Stats and Facebook Subscribers).* Retrieved February 08, 2018, from: http://www.internetworldstats.com/stats1.htm

InterPARES Trust. (2016). *The Social Media and Trust in Government.* Retrieved June 24, 2018, from: https://interparestrust.org/trust

ISO 15489. (2016). *Information and Documentation – Records Management. Part 1. General.* International Standards Organisation.

Issak, A. (2000). *Public libraries in Africa.* Available at: http://www.inasp.org.uk

Jack, B. (2015). Feature film as history. *The Councilor. The Journal of Social Studies*, *76*(1), 1–23.

Jansen, A., & Duranti, L. (2013). *The InterPARES Trust Project – Trust and Digital Records in an Increasingly Networked Society.* Retrieved April 10, 2018, from: https://interparestrust.org/assets/public/dissemination/203JansenDurantiTheInterPARESTrustProject.pdf

Kapitzke, C. (2003). Information literacy: A positivist epistemology and a politics of outformation. *Educational Theory*, *53*(1), 37–53. doi:10.1111/j.1741-5446.2003.00037.x

Kaplan, A. M., & Haenlein, M. (2012). Social media: Back to the roots and back to the future. *Journal of Systems and Information Technology*, *14*(1), 101–104. doi:10.1108/13287261211232126

Kaula, P. N. (1986). Towards resource sharing in libraries. In Planning in library resource sharing. Lucknow: Print House.

Kaul, V. (2012). Globalisation and crisis of cultural identity. *Journal of Research in International Business and Management, 2*(3), 341–349.

Kearney, M. H. (2015). Predatory Publishing: What Authors Need to Know. *Research in Nursing & Health, 38*(1), 1–3. doi:10.1002/nur.21640 PMID:25545343

Keetshabe, A. M. (2012). *Development of ICT legal and regulatory framework in Botswana.* Retrieved February 02, 2018, from: https://www.gov.bw/globalassets/.../ict.../e---legislation---ict-pitso-2012-legal-framework.ppt

Kent, A., & Galvin, T. (1979). *The Structure and Governance of Library Networks.* New York: Marcel Dekker.

Ketelaar, E. (1999). Understanding Archives of the People, by People, and for the People. In *Washington Conference on Holocaust-Era Assets Proceedings.* Washington, DC: Government Printing House.

Kgabi, D. (1986). Oral Traditions and the Archivist: The Case of Botswana. In Oral Traditions in Southern Africa. Overview of proceedings, Country Reports and Recommendations. Institute of African Studies. University of Zambia.

Khan, S., & Rahim, N. Z. A. (2016). *Factors Influencing Citizens Trust on Government Social media.* Retrieved October 25, 2018, from: http://ais.utm.my/paris2016/files/2016/11/3-Factors-Influencing-Citizens-Trust-on-Government-Social-Media.pdf

Khan-Leavitt, L. (2016). Process of making a historical film: Case Study: A Midwife Tale. *Do History*. Retrieved March 28th, 2018 from http://dohistory.org/film/process_preprod.html

Kieńć, W. (2015). *Green oa-vs-Gold-oa- Which one to choose*. Retrieved from http://openscience.com/green-oa-vs-gold-oa-which-one-to-choose

Kingma, B. R. (1996). *The economics of access versus ownership to scholarly information: The costs and benefits of access to scholarly articles via interlibrary loan and journal subscriptions*. Binghamton, NY: Haworth Press.

Kingma, B. R., & Eppard, P. (1992). Journal price escalation and the market for information: The librarian's solution. *College & Research Libraries, 53*(6), 523–535. doi:10.5860/crl_53_06_523

Klopfer, L. (2001, Fall). Oral History and Archives in New South Africa: Methodological Issues. *Archivaria, 52*, 100–125.

Koltay, T. (2011). The media and the literacies: Media literacy, information literacy, digital literacy. *Media Culture & Society*, *33*(2), 211–221. doi:10.1177/0163443710393382

Kuhlthau, C.C., Heinström, J., & Todd, R.J. (2008). The 'information search process' revisited: Is the model still useful. *Information Research, 13*(4).

Kuhlthau, C. C. (1991). Inside the search process: Information seeking from the user's perspective. *Journal of the American Society for Information Science*, *42*(5), 361–371. doi:10.1002/(SICI)1097-4571(199106)42:5<361::AID-ASI6>3.0.CO;2-#

Kuhlthau, C. C. (2007). Reflections on the development of the model of the Information Search Process (ISP): Excerpts from the Lazerow Lecture, University of Kentucky. *Bulletin of the Association for Information Science and Technology*, *3*(5), 32–37.

Kuiper, J. B. (1968). The historical value of motion picture. *Library of Congress*, *31*(4), 385–390.

Kwon, Y. J., & Kwon, K. N. (2013). Multifaceted appearance management as cultural practice. *Review of European Studies*, *5*(4), 19–29. doi:10.5539/res.v5n4p19

Lambers, H. (2014). *Why do authors publish in "predatory open access journals"?* Retrieved from http://www.researchgate.net/post/Why_do_authors_publish_in_predatory_open_access_journals

Lamprecht, E. (2017). *The Difference Between UX and UI Design - A Layman's Guide*. Retrieved from https://careerfoundry.com/en/blog/ux-design/the- difference-between-ux-and-ui-design-a-layman's-guide/

Langat, A. (2016). Adaptive Learning for Online Courses. *Digital Learning Conference* (pp. 193-227). Eldoret: Moi University Press.

Latham, R. (2014). *Information Management Advice 57 Managing Social Media. Records Part 1: Overview*. Retrieved November 26, 2017, from: https://www.informationstrategy.tas.gov.au/Records-ManagementPrinciples/Document%20Library%20%20Tools/Advice%2057%20Managing%20Social%20Media%20Records%20Part%201%20-%20Overview.pdf

Lau, J. (2013). Conceptual relationship of information literacy and media literacy. *Conceptual Relationship of Information Literacy and Media Literacy in Knowledge Societies, 76.*

Lenzerini, F. (2011). Intangible cultural heritage: The living cultures of peoples. *European Journal of International Law*, *22*(1), 101–120. doi:10.1093/ejil/chr006

Library and Archives Canada. (2013). *Governance and Records Keeping around the word.* Retrieved February 08, 2018, from: https://www.bac-lac.gc.ca/eng/services/government-information-resources/information-management/Documents/february-2013.pdf

Library and Archives Canada. (2017). *Governance and Records Keeping around the world.* Retrieved August 2, 2017, from: http://www.bac-lac.gc.ca/eng/services/government-information-resources/information-management/Documents/May2017vol5-no8.pdf

Liew, C. L. (2014). *Participatory cultural heritage: A tale of two institution's use of social media.* Wellington: University of Wellington.

Linke, A., & Zerfass, A. (2013). Social media governance: Regulatory frameworks for successful online communications. *Journal of Communication Management*, *17*(3), 270–286. doi:10.1108/JCOM-09-2011-0050

Litz, D. (2011). Globalisation and the changing face of educational leadership: Current trends and emerging dilemmas. *International Education Studies*, *4*(3), 47–61. doi:10.5539/ies.v4n3p47

Lloyd, A. (2017). Information literacy and literacies of information: A mid-range theory and model. *Journal Of Information Literacy*, *11*(1), 91–105. doi:10.11645/11.1.2185

Lopez, M. (2013). *Elite theory*. doi: 10.1177/2056846013112

Lowry, C. B. (1990). Resource sharing or cost shifting? The unequal burden of cooperative cataloging and ILL. *College & Research Libraries*, *51*(1), 11–19. doi:10.5860/crl_51_01_11

Magu, S. (2015). Reconceptualising cultural globalisation: Connecting the "cultural global" and the "cultural local". *Social Sciences*, *4*(3), 630–645. doi:10.3390ocsci4030630

Maidabino, A. A. (2010). The availability, organization and use of archival records: A study of public archives agencies in the Northwestern states of Nigeria. *Library, Philosophy and Practice*. Retrieved March 20th, 2018 from http://www.webpages.uidaho.edu/~mbolin/maidabino2.htm

Mangemba, K. (2012). *October is International school library month*. Available at: mangemba.blogspot.com/2012/10/0ctober-is international-school-library.html

Manungo, K. (2012). Oral history as captured by the National Archives of Zimbabwe over the years. In P. Ngulube (Ed.), *National Archives 75@30: 75 years of archiving excellence at the National Archives of Zimbabwe* (pp. 64–67). Harare: National Archives of Zimbabwe.

Marcus, A. (2005). "It is as it was": Feature film in the history class. *Social Studies*, *96*, 61–67. doi:10.3200/TSSS.96.2.61-67

Mas-Colell, A., Whinston, M. D., & Green, J. R. (1995). *Micro Economic Theory*. New York: Oxford University Press, Inc.

Matangira, V. (2012). Seventy Five Years of Archiving and Excellence and a Decade of Loss. In P. Ngulube (Ed.), *National Archives 75@30: 75 years of archiving excellence at the National Archives of Zimbabwe* (pp. 112–124). Harare: National Archives of Zimbabwe.

Maud, H. (2005). *School Libraries in a Democratic South Africa – Curriculum Support, Information Literacy, Policy Development*. Available at: https://muep.mau.se/bitstream/handle/2043/4100/Maud_final_project.pdf?sequence=1

McDonald, A. S. (2008). *Out of the Hollinger Box and into the streets: activists, archives and under-documented populations* (Unpublished thesis). University of North Carolina, Chapel Hill, NC.

Mchombu, K., & Cadbury, N. (2006). *Libraries, literacy and poverty reduction: a key to African development*. Available at: www.bookaid.org/wp-content/uploads/2011/06/libraries-literacy-and-Poverty-Reduction-BAI.pdf

Mhlanga, B. T. (2014). *The role of the National Archives and Records Service of South Africa in human rights promotion and protection*. Master of Management by Research and Dissertation at the University of the Witwatersrand, Johannesburg. Retrieved from wiredspace.wits.ac.za

Millar, L. (2004). Legal Status of E-Records. In *Problems of Authenticity in an Electronic Environment*. Academic Press. Retrieved April 23, 2017, from: http://www.wien2004.ica.org

Miller. (n.d.). *Novice teacher's perceptions of the role of the teacher librarian*. Available at: tldl.pbworks.com/f/Miller.pdf

Mills, E., Campana, K., & Goldsmith, A. (2017). Libraries as Learning Labs in a Digital Age. *Journal of Education for Library and Information Science*, *58*(1), 27–38. doi:10.12783/issn.2328-2967/58/1/3

Minority Rights Group International (MRGI). (2015). *Botswana: Recognising minority right*. Available at: http://minorityrights.org/what-we-do/botswana-recognising-minority-rights/

Moeller, S., Joseph, A., Lau, J., & Carbo, T. (2011). Towards media and information literacy indicators. Academic Press.

Mohammed, M. A. (2011). *Technology and Infrastructural Development: What the Future holds for the Book Industry in Nigeria?* Paper presented at the 9th and 10thNigeria International Book Fair, National Book Fairs and NPA General Meeting.

Mojapelo, S. M. (2016). *Challenges in establishing and maintaining functional school libraries: Lessons from Limpopo Province in South Africa*. Available at: http://journals.sagepub.com/doi/abs/10.1177/0961000616667801

Mojapelo, M. S., & Dube, L. (2015). Repositioning school library committees to advance school library development in South Africa. *Innovation*, *50*, 110–122.

Molosiwa, A. (n.d.). *Language and Literacy Issues in Botswana*. Online at http://cpls.educ.ubc.ca/content/pdfs/4MolosiwaBotswana.pdf

Mosweu, T. (2011). Digitising the oral history collection at Botswana National Archives and Records Services: Problems and prospects. *Journal of the South African Society of Archivists*, *4*, 2011.

Moyo, C. (2007). *Capturing a fading national memory: an assessment of the impact of the oral history collections in augmenting archival sources at the national archives of Zimbabwe* (Unpublished dissertation). National University of Science and Technology, Bulawayo.

Moyo, M. (2013). Computers donated by President lie idle. *The Chronicle*, *25*(September), 3.

Muhamed, R.A. (2012). The Roles of Library and Information Resource Sharing in the emerging Information Society. *Journal of Information and Knowledge Management, 2*(7), 79-85.

Murambiwa, I. (2009). Dismembering or remembering the 'Zimbabwe archive? *Journal of British Records Association, 34*(121), 25-33. Retrieved from www.britishrecordsassociation.org.uk/pages/list.htm

Murray, S. (2012). *Library: An Illustrated History*. New York: W W. Norton.

Muthu, M. (2013). *Resource Sharing in Libraries: A Vital Role of Consortia*. Academic Press.

National Archives and Records Administration. (2013). *Best Practices for the Capture of Social Media Records*. Retrieved April 20, 2017, from: https://www.archives.gov/files/records-mgmt/resources/socialmediacapture.pdf

Navy, U. S. (2012). *Navy Command Leadership Social Media Handbook*. Retrieved May 13, 2017, from: http://imagery.navy.mil/documents/Navy%20Social%20Media%20Handbook%20Fall%202012.pdf

Ndlovu, B. (2012, September 27). Revive story telling – Memory Kumbata. The Chronicle, p. 6.

Neal & McDevitt Intellectual Property and Marketing Attorneys. (2010). *Top 10 Legal Issues in Social Media*. Retrieved February 8, 2018, from: http://www.nealmcdevitt.com/assets/news/Top_10_Social_Media_Legal_Issues_FINAL.PDF

Ngoepe, M., & Keakopa, S. M. (2011). An assessment of the state of national archival and records systems in the ESARBICA region: A South Africa-Botswana comparison. *Records Management Journal*, *21*(2), 145–160. doi:10.1108/09565691111152071

Ngoepe, M., & Saurombe, A. (2016). Provisions for managing and preserving records created in networked environments in the archival legislative frameworks of selected member states of the Southern African Development Community. *Archives and Manuscript*, *44*(1), 24–41. doi:10.1080/01576895.2015.1136225

Ngulube, P., Sibanda, P., & Makoni. (2013). Mapping access and use of archival materials held at the Bulawayo archives in Zimbabwe. *ESARBICA*, *32*, 123-137.

Ngulube, P. (2007). The Achilles Heel of the Preservation of Documentary Materials in Sub Saharan Africa: Knowledge and Skills or Funding? *Restaurator (Copenhagen)*, *28*(3), 159–168. doi:10.1515/REST.2007.159

Ngulube, P. (2012). Collection Development at the National Archives of Zimbabwe: Achilles Heel. In P. Ngulube (Ed.), *National Archives 75@30 75 years of archiving excellence at the National Archives of Zimbabwe* (pp. 101–111). Harare: *Printflow (Private) Limited.*

Ngwenya, S. (2013). *Promoting information literacy through government school libraries in Zimbabwe*. Paper presented in Zimbabwe Library Association 47th Conference, Mutare, Zimbabwe.

Nocca, F. (2017). The role of cultural heritage in sustainable development: Multidimensional indicators as decision-making tool. *Sustainability*, *9*(1882), 1-29.

Norman, D., & Nielsen, J. (n.d.). *The Definition of User Experience (UX)*. Retrieved from https://www.nngroup.com/articles/definition-user-experience/

Nwagwu W.E. (2013). Open Access Initiatives in Africa- Structure, Incentives and Disincentives. *The Journal of Academic Librarianship*, *39*, 3-10. doi:10.1016/j.acalib.2012.11.024

Nwalo, K. I. N. (2006). Collaboration in the provision and utilization of IT facilities for library and information science education in Nigeria. Information Technology in Library and Information Science Education in Nigeria.

Nwalo, K. I. N. (2002). *Fundamentals of Library Practice: A Manual on Library Routines*. Ibadan: Stirling-Horden Publishers.

Nwegbu, M.U., Eze, C.C., & Asogwa, B.E. (2011). Globalisation of cultural heritage: Issues, impacts, and inevitable challenges for Nigeria. *Library Philosophy and Practice, 674.*

Oberg, D. (2016). *Convergences of and for Media and Information Literacy Instruction in Higher Education in Media and Information Literacy in Higher Education: Educating the Educators*. Cambridge: Chandos Publishing.

Odini, C. (1991). Problems and Prospects of Resource Sharing in Developing Countries. *African Journal of Library, Archives sand Information Science, 1*(2), 93-108.

Ogunleye, F. (2015). *Television docudrama as alternative records of history*. Retrieved July 10, 2017 from http://documentaryisneverneutral.com/words/docalthis.html

Ogunmodede, T. A., Apata, M. E., & Nwokeoma, N. M. (2017). Effect of Information Utilization on Decision-Making by Senior Managers: A Case Study. *International Journal of Library Science, 15*(2). Retrieved from http://www.ceser.in/ceserp/index.php/ijls/article/view/4813

Ohio Electronic Records Committee. (2014). *Social Media: The Records Management Challenge*. Retrieved June 12, 2017, from: http://ohioerc.org/wp-content/uploads/2014/09/OhioERC-Guideline-Social-Media1.pdf

Olurode L. (2017, March 30). Don seeks use of research findings. *The Nigeria Nation Newspaper.*

Omiunu O.G. (2014). Towards enhancing research qualities in African Universities and sustainable development: A phenomenological study. *International Research of Human and Social Sciences, 1*(4), 100-123.

Omiunu, O. G. (2014). Conceptualizing Information Need: A Phenomenological Study. *Journal of Library and Information Science*, *2*(2), 29–54.

Open Access Theses and Dissertations. (n.d.). *OATD – Open Access Theses and Dissertations*. Retrieved September 17, 2017, from https://oatd.org/

Orubo, D. (2015). What role should Nollywood play in portraying our history? *Konbini Channels*. Retrieved July 13, 2017, from http://www.konbini.com/ng/entertainment/what-role-does-nollywood-have-in-portraying-our-history/

Osho, S. A. (2011, July). *The uniqueness of African means of communication in contemporary world.* Paper presented at the seminar on cultural diplomacy in Africa and international conference on cultural diplomacy in Africa on strategies to confront the challenges of the 21st century: Does Africa have what is required, Berlin, Germany.

Panda, S. K. (2016). Shodhganga – a national level open access ETD repository of Indian electronic theses: Current status and discussions. *Library Hi Tech News*, *33*(1), 23–26. doi:10.1108/LHTN-09-2015-0062

Pappas, C. (2017, October 27). *Tips to create Flexible Online Training Courses*. Retrieved from eLearning Industry: https://elearningindustry.com

Paton-Ash and Di Wilmot. (2015, February). Issues and challenges facing school libraries in selected primary schools in Gauteng Province, South Africa. *South African Journal of Education*, *35*(1). Available at http://www.sajournalofeducation.co.za

Perrin, J. M., Winkler, H. M., & Yang, L. (2015). Digital preservation challenges with an ETD collection - A case study at texas tech university. *Journal of Academic Librarianship*, *41*(1), 98–104. doi:10.1016/j.acalib.2014.11.002

Peter, R. (2012, September 4). *Scanning: The Benefits of Digitization*. Retrieved from Smart Document Capture and Management blog: http:/www.athento.com

Peter, B. (2013). Adaptive and Intelligent Web-based Educational Systems. *International Journal of Artificial Intelligence in Education*, 159–172.

Peterson, A. T., Emmett, A., & Greenberg, M. I. (2013). Open Access and the Author-Pays Problem: Assuring Access for Readers and Authors in a Global Community of Scholars. *Journal of Librarianship and Scholarly Communication*, *1*(3), eP1064. doi:10.7710/2162-3309.1064

Potter, W. J. (2013). Synthesising a working definition of "mass" media. *Review of Communication Research*, *1*, 1–30.

Potvin, S., & Thompson, S. (2016). An analysis of evolving metadata influences, standards, and practices in electronic theses and dissertations. *Library Resources & Technical Services*, *60*(2), 99–114. doi:10.5860/lrts.60n2.99

Radebaugh, R. G. (2014). *Understannding Metadata*. NISO Press.

Ramokate, K., & Moatlhodi, T. (2010). Battling the appraisal backlog: a challenging professional obligation for Botswana National Archives and Records Services. *ESARBICA Journal, 29*(1).

Ramsay, J. (2009). *Government Communications in the Information Age*. Retrieved February 20, 2018, from: http://www.sundaystandard.info/government-communications-information-age

Ranganathan, S. (1931). *The Five Laws of Library Scince*. London: Edward Goldston.

Rao. (2017). C5 model for the consortium management: SWOT analysis. *Library Management, 38*(4-5). doi: 10.1108/LM-09-2016-0073

Raynaud, D. (2015). Dealing with historical movies in the history and English classroom. *TEACH: Research and Scholarship*, *2*(2), 48–52.

Reed, K. L. (2016). LIS Training for Support Staff. *Journal of Library Administration*, *56*(3), 317–325. doi:10.1080/01930826.2016.1146535

Reid, N. (2015, October 4). *NCBI-NIH*. Retrieved from Enhancing Library Impact Through Technology: https://www.ncbi.nlm.nih.gov

Ritchie, D. A. (2003). *Doing Oral History: A practical Guide*. New York: Oxford University Press.

Rizzo, M. (2017). Arts department and the importance of research in pre-production. *The Film Business*. Retrieved March 24th, 2018 from http://masteringfilm.com/art-departments-and-the-importance-of-research-in-pre-production/

Rodrigues, A. (2013). *An archival collecting framework for the records generated by South Africa's Portuguese community based organisations in Guateng*. Doctor of Literature and Philosophy in the subject information Science at the University of South Africa, Pretoria. Retrieved from uir.unisa.ac.za/handle/10500/13340

Rosenberg, D. (Ed.). (2003). *Reader Development and Reading Promotion: Recent Experiences from Seven Countries in Africa*. Oxford, UK: INASP.

Rosenstone, A. R. (2015). The historical film as a real story. *Journalism History*, *16*(2), 1–12.

Rubin Alan, M. (1998). Media Literacy. *Journal of Communication*, *48*(1), 3–4. doi:10.1111/j.1460-2466.1998.tb02732.x

Sarkar, P., & Mukhopadhyay, P. (2016). Full-text etd retrieval in library discovery system: Designing a framework. *Annals of Library and Information Studies*, *63*(4), 274–288. Retrieved from www.scopus.com

Sauti, L. (2013, March 11). Document Zim culture. *The Herald*. Retrieved from http://www.herald.co.zw/document-zim-culture/

Sawyer, R. (2011). The impact of new social media on intercultural adaptation. *Senior Honors Projects, 242*.

School of Media and Communication. (2014). *The challenges of making a historical film in Nollywood*. Retrieved August 23, 2017, from http://smc.edu.ng/news/the-challenges-of-making-a-historical-film-in-nollywood/

Schwartz, J., & Cook, T. (2002). Archives, Records and Power: The Making of Modern Memory. *Archival Science*, *2*(1-2), 1–19. doi:10.1007/BF02435628

Sefa-Boakye, J. (2016). Anika Noni Rose talks "Half of a Yellow Sun" and the need to revisit history. *Okay Africa Magazine*. Retrieved March 23rd, 2018, from http://www.okayafrica.com/7-things-we-learned-from-chimamanda-ngozi-adichie-and-reni-eddo-lodge-in-conversation/

Selenay Aytac, M. K. (2013, December 2). *Emerging trends in Knowledge Organization and information Organization Course Curriculum.* Retrieved from Wiley Online Library: Onlinelibrary.wiley.com

Shalini Ramdas Lihitkar, R. S. (2014). Electronic theses and dissertations (ETDs) in India: A comparative study. *Library Hi Tech News*, *31*(2), 9–14. doi:10.1108/LHTN-10-2013-0061

SIL. (2014). *Language and culture documentation*. Paris: UNESCO.

Sithole, N. (2012). *Government has a duty to enrich school libraries*. Available at: http://ipsnews.net/

Smit, F., Glaudemans, A., & Jonker, R. (Eds.). (2017). *Archives in Liquid Times.* Retrieved February 8, 2018, from: https://www.academia.edu/35423093/Archives_in_Liquid_Times

Spires, H. A., & Bartlett, M. E. (2012). *Digital literacies and learning: Designing a path forward.* Friday Institute White Paper Series, 5.

Stats, I. W. (n.d.). *Usage and Population Statistics.* Retrieved from http://www.internetworldstats.com/stats.htm

Steven, A. (2008). A Different Way of Knowing: Tools and Strategies for Managing Indigenous Knowledge. *Libri*, *58*, 25–33.

Sturges, P. (2001). *The poverty of librarianship: An historical critique of public librarianship in Anglophone Africa*. Available at: www.librijournal.org/pdf/2001-1pp38-48pdf

Suber, P. (2012). *Open Access*. Massachusetts Institute of Technology. Retrieved from https://mitpress.mit.edu/sites/default/files/9780262517638_Open_Access_PDF_Version.pdf

Sunday Standard Newspaper. (2016). *Botswana has highest rates of Facebook use in Africa*. Retrieved May 13, 2017 from http://www.sundaystandard.info/botswana-has-highest-rates-facebook-use-africa

Tari, J. (2015). Documentaring, preserving and digitizing Hungarian intangible cultural heritage. In N. V. Furlan (Ed.), *Documenting and preserving intangible cultural heritage on film* (pp. 53–62). Ljubljana: Sloveniski Etnograeski Muzej.

Tasha, R. (2016, September 28). How 'Nigerian Spielberg' Izu Ojukwu is taking advantage of the free speech in a changing industry. *The Verge*. Retrieved March 27th, 2018 from https://www.theverge.com/2016/9/28/13095648/izu-ojukwu-interview-nigerian-film-nollywood-76-movie

Tauzon, R. (2013). *Media and Information Literacy: Towards New Teaching-Learning Competencies*. Available online http://www.unescobkk.org/fileadmin/user_upload/ict/Workshops/RDTC_15ch/S6D3-Ramon.pdf

Terras, M. (2011). The digital Wunderkammer: Flickr as a platform for amateur cultural and heritage content. *Library Trends*, *59*(4), 686–706. doi:10.1353/lib.2011.0022

Terry, F. (2008). *New Media: An Introduction*. Oxford University Press.

Tettey, W. (2013). *Media and information literacy, informed citizenship and democratic development in Africa: a handbook for media information producers and users*. Academic Press.

The Library and Information Services (LIS) Transformation Charter. (2009). Available at: http://www.dac.gov.za/.../Transformation%20charter-6th%20draft-2210

The Networked Digital Library of Theses and Dissertations (NDLTD). (2017, August 2). *Mission, Goals, and History*. Retrieved August 28, 2017, from www.ndltd.org/about

Thompson, P. (1998). The voice of the past. In *The Oral History Reader*. Routledge.

Thurston, A. C. (2012). Trustworthy Records and Open Data. *The Journal of Community Informatics, 8*(2). Retrieved March 24, 2017, from: http://ci-journal.net/index.php/ciej/article/view/951/952

Topolsek, D., & Orthaber, S. (2011). Understanding the importance of internal integration and its implications for intercultural business communication. *Research in Logistics and Production*, *1*(3), 187–201.

Tsekea, S. (2015). *Automation of school libraries in Zimbabwe: An evaluation of BUSE Library's community initiatives*. Available at: https://www.researchgate.net/publication/317433850

Turan, K. (2013, August 16). Review: Lee Daniels' The Butler: Significant but contrived. *The Los Angeles Times,* pp. 45-49.

Ugwuede, K. (2015). *13th, 76, October 1: Of numbers and the death of history in Nollywood*. Retrieved August 11, 2017, from http://amore.ng/13th-76-october-1-numbers-dearth-history-nollywood/

UNESCO. (1985). *Information networking in population education*. Bangkok: Unesco.

UNESCO. (2013). *Global Media and Information Literacy Assessment Framework: Country Readiness and Competencies*. Retrieved from http://www.unesco.org/new/en/communication-and-information/resources/publications-and-communication-materials/publications/full-list/global-media-and-information-literacy-assessment-framework

UNESCO. (2017). *Media and Information Literacy*. Available online. http://www.unesco.org/new/en/communication-and-information/media-development/media-literacy/mil-as-composite-concept/ (Accessed 20 July 2017)

UNESCO. (n.d.). *Memory of the world.* Retrieved from https://en.unesco.org/programme/mow

US Department of Energy. (2010). *Managing Social Media Records*. Retrieved March 24, 2017, from: http://energy.gov/sites/prod/files/cioprod/documents/Social_Media_Records_and_You_Sept_2010.pdf

USCMarshall. (2017, March 13). *How Mobile Technologies Changes the Library Experience*. Retrieved from University of Southern Carolina: https:/librarysciencedegree.usc.edu

Valtolina, S. (2016). A storytelling-driven framework for cultural heritage dissemination. *Data Science and Engineering*, *1*(1), 114–123. doi:10.100741019-016-0007-z

Veisbergs, A. (2012). Semantic change in Latvian under the influence of English. *Baltic Journal of English. Language and Culture*, *2*, 103–121.

Wales, J. (2014). *Community archives and the archival community*. A thesis submitted to Leiden University in partial fulfilment of the requirements for the degree of MA History in Archival Studies. Retrieved from https://openaccess.leidenuniv.nl/bitstream/handle/1887/28520/Josie%20Wale s%20 1405977%20MA%20Thesis.pdf?sequence=1

Wamukoya, J., & Mutula, S. (2005). E-Records Management and Governance In East And Southern Africa. *Malaysian Journal of Library and Information Science*, *10*(2), 67–83.

Wang, L. (2011). An information literacy integration model and its application in higher education. *RSR. Reference Services Review*, *39*(4), 703–720. doi:10.1108/00907321111186703

Website report for shodhganga.inflibnet.ac.in. (2017). Retrieved from http://nibbler.silktide.com/en_US/reports/shodhganga.inflibnet.ac.in

Willinsky, J. (2006). *The Access Principle: The Case for Open Access to Research and Scholarship*. Cambridge, MA: MIT Press.

Wilson, C. (2012). Media and Information Literacy: Pedagogy and Possibilities/ Alfabetización mediática e informacional: proyecciones didácticas. *Comunicar*, *20*(39), 15–24. doi:10.3916/C39-2012-02-01

Wilson, C., Grizzle, A., Tuazon, R., Akyempong, K., & Cheung, C. K. (2013). *Media and information literacy curriculum for teachers: Curriculum and Competency Framework*. UNESCO Publishing.

World of Statistics. (2015). *Mobile Facebook, Twitter, Social Media Usage Statistics in Botswana.* Retrieved May 13, 2017, from: https://www.statsmonkey.com/table/21306-botswana-mobile-social-media-usage-statistics-2015.php

Xia, J., Harmon, J. L., Connolly, K. G., Donnelly, R. M., Anderson, M. R., & Howard, H. A. (2014). Who publishes in "predatory" journals?" *Journal of the Association for Information Science and Technology*. doi:10.1002/asi.23265

Yanqiu, Z. (2014, September). *Understanding China's media in Africa from the perspectives of constructive journalism*. Paper presented at the international conference on China and Africa media, communications and public diplomacy, Beijing, China.

Yeo, G. (2016). Records. In Encyclopedia of Archival Science. Rowman & Littlefield Publishers.

Zamon, C. (2012). *The Lone arranger: succeeding in a small repository*. Chicago: Society of American Archivists.

Zeng, M. (2016). *Metadata Types and Functions*. NISO.

Related References

To continue our tradition of advancing media and communications research, we have compiled a list of recommended IGI Global readings. These references will provide additional information and guidance to further enrich your knowledge and assist you with your own research and future publications.

Abashian, N., & Fisher, S. (2018). Intercultural Effectiveness in Libraries: Supporting Success Through Collaboration With Co-Curricular Programs. In B. Blummer, J. Kenton, & M. Wiatrowski (Eds.), *Promoting Ethnic Diversity and Multiculturalism in Higher Education* (pp. 219–236). Hershey, PA: IGI Global. doi:10.4018/978-1-5225-4097-7.ch012

Adebayo, O., Fagbohun, M. O., Esse, U. C., & Nwokeoma, N. M. (2018). Change Management in the Academic Library: Transition From Print to Digital Collections. In R. Bhardwaj (Ed.), *Digitizing the Modern Library and the Transition From Print to Electronic* (pp. 1–28). Hershey, PA: IGI Global. doi:10.4018/978-1-5225-2119-8.ch001

Adegbore, A. M., Quadri, M. O., & Oyewo, O. R. (2018). A Theoretical Approach to the Adoption of Electronic Resource Management Systems (ERMS) in Nigerian University Libraries. In A. Tella & T. Kwanya (Eds.), *Handbook of Research on Managing Intellectual Property in Digital Libraries* (pp. 292–311). Hershey, PA: IGI Global. doi:10.4018/978-1-5225-3093-0.ch015

Adesola, A. P., & Olla, G. O. (2018). Unlocking the Unlimited Potentials of Koha OSS/ILS for Library House-Keeping Functions: A Global View. In M. Khosrow-Pour (Ed.), *Optimizing Contemporary Application and Processes in Open Source Software* (pp. 124–163). Hershey, PA: IGI Global. doi:10.4018/978-1-5225-5314-4.ch006

Adigun, G. O., Sobalaje, A. J., & Salau, S. A. (2018). Social Media and Copyright in Digital Libraries. In A. Tella & T. Kwanya (Eds.), *Handbook of Research on Managing Intellectual Property in Digital Libraries* (pp. 19–36). Hershey, PA: IGI Global. doi:10.4018/978-1-5225-3093-0.ch002

Adomi, E. E., Eriki, J. A., Tiemo, P. A., & Akpojotor, L. O. (2016). Incidents of Cyberbullying Among Library and Information Science (LIS) Students at Delta State University, Abraka, Nigeria. *International Journal of Digital Literacy and Digital Competence*, *7*(4), 52–63. doi:10.4018/IJDLDC.2016100104

Afolabi, O. A. (2018). Myths and Challenges of Building an Effective Digital Library in Developing Nations: An African Perspective. In A. Tella & T. Kwanya (Eds.), *Handbook of Research on Managing Intellectual Property in Digital Libraries* (pp. 51–79). Hershey, PA: IGI Global. doi:10.4018/978-1-5225-3093-0.ch004

Agrawal, P. R. (2016). Google Search: Digging into the Culture of Information Retrieval. In E. de Smet & S. Dhamdhere (Eds.), *E-Discovery Tools and Applications in Modern Libraries* (pp. 210–239). Hershey, PA: IGI Global. doi:10.4018/978-1-5225-0474-0.ch012

Ahuja, Y., & Kumar, P. (2017). Web 2.0 Tools and Application: Knowledge Management and Sharing in Libraries. In B. Gunjal (Ed.), *Managing Knowledge and Scholarly Assets in Academic Libraries* (pp. 218–234). Hershey, PA: IGI Global. doi:10.4018/978-1-5225-1741-2.ch010

Ajmi, A. (2018). Developing In-House Digital Tools: Case Studies From the UMKC School of Law Library. In L. Costello & M. Powers (Eds.), *Developing In-House Digital Tools in Library Spaces* (pp. 117–139). Hershey, PA: IGI Global. doi:10.4018/978-1-5225-2676-6.ch006

Akakandelwa, A. (2016). A Glimpse of the Information Seeking Behaviour Literature on the Web: A Bibliometric Approach. In A. Tella (Ed.), *Information Seeking Behavior and Challenges in Digital Libraries* (pp. 127–155). Hershey, PA: IGI Global. doi:10.4018/978-1-5225-0296-8.ch007

Akande, F. T., & Adewojo, A. A. (2016). Information Need and Seeking Behavior of Farmers in Laduba Community of Kwara State, Nigeria. In A. Tella (Ed.), *Information Seeking Behavior and Challenges in Digital Libraries* (pp. 238–271). Hershey, PA: IGI Global. doi:10.4018/978-1-5225-0296-8.ch012

Al-Kharousi, R., Al-Harrasi, N. H., Jabur, N. H., & Bouazza, A. (2018). Soft Systems Methodology (SSM) as an Interdisciplinary Approach: Reflection on the Use of SSM in Adoption of Web 2.0 Applications in Omani Academic Libraries. In M. Al-Suqri, A. Al-Kindi, S. AlKindi, & N. Saleem (Eds.), *Promoting Interdisciplinarity in Knowledge Generation and Problem Solving* (pp. 243–257). Hershey, PA: IGI Global. doi:10.4018/978-1-5225-3878-3.ch016

Alenzuela, R. (2017). Research, Leadership, and Resource-Sharing Initiatives: The Role of Local Library Consortia in Access to Medical Information. In S. Ram (Ed.), *Library and Information Services for Bioinformatics Education and Research* (pp. 199–211). Hershey, PA: IGI Global. doi:10.4018/978-1-5225-1871-6.ch012

Allison, D. (2017). When Sales Talk Meets Reality: Implementing a Self-Checkout Kiosk. In E. Iglesias (Ed.), *Library Technology Funding, Planning, and Deployment* (pp. 36–54). Hershey, PA: IGI Global. doi:10.4018/978-1-5225-1735-1.ch003

Anglim, C. T., & Rusk, F. (2018). Empowering DC's Future Through Information Access. In A. Burtin, J. Fleming, & P. Hampton-Garland (Eds.), *Changing Urban Landscapes Through Public Higher Education* (pp. 57–77). Hershey, PA: IGI Global. doi:10.4018/978-1-5225-3454-9.ch003

Asmi, N. A. (2017). Social Media and Library Services. *International Journal of Library and Information Services*, *6*(2), 23–36. doi:10.4018/IJLIS.2017070103

Awoyemi, R. A. (2018). Adoption and Use of Innovative Mobile Technologies in Nigerian Academic Libraries. In J. Keengwe (Ed.), *Handbook of Research on Digital Content, Mobile Learning, and Technology Integration Models in Teacher Education* (pp. 354–389). Hershey, PA: IGI Global. doi:10.4018/978-1-5225-2953-8.ch019

Awoyemi, R. A. (2018). Adoption and Use of Innovative Mobile Technologies in Nigerian Academic Libraries. In J. Keengwe (Ed.), *Handbook of Research on Digital Content, Mobile Learning, and Technology Integration Models in Teacher Education* (pp. 354–389). Hershey, PA: IGI Global. doi:10.4018/978-1-5225-2953-8.ch019

Ayson, M. C. (2016). Maximizing Social Media Tools: Planning and Evaluating Social Media Strategies for Special Libraries. In J. Yap, M. Perez, M. Ayson, & G. Entico (Eds.), *Special Library Administration, Standardization and Technological Integration* (pp. 166–179). Hershey, PA: IGI Global. doi:10.4018/978-1-4666-9542-9.ch007

Babatope, I. S. (2018). Social Media Applications as Effective Service Delivery Tools for Librarians. In M. Khosrow-Pour, D.B.A. (Ed.), Encyclopedia of Information Science and Technology, Fourth Edition (pp. 5252-5261). Hershey, PA: IGI Global. doi:10.4018/978-1-5225-2255-3.ch456

Bakare, A. A. (2018). Digital Libraries and Copyright of Intellectual Property: An Ethical Practice Management. In A. Tella & T. Kwanya (Eds.), *Handbook of Research on Managing Intellectual Property in Digital Libraries* (pp. 377–395). Hershey, PA: IGI Global. doi:10.4018/978-1-5225-3093-0.ch019

Baker, W. (2016). Responding to High-Volume Water Disasters in the Research Library Context. In E. Decker & J. Townes (Eds.), *Handbook of Research on Disaster Management and Contingency Planning in Modern Libraries* (pp. 282–310). Hershey, PA: IGI Global. doi:10.4018/978-1-4666-8624-3.ch013

Baker-Gardner, R., & Smart, C. (2017). Ignorance or Intent?: A Case Study of Plagiarism in Higher Education among LIS Students in the Caribbean. In D. Velliaris (Ed.), *Handbook of Research on Academic Misconduct in Higher Education* (pp. 182–205). Hershey, PA: IGI Global. doi:10.4018/978-1-5225-1610-1.ch008

Baker-Gardner, R., & Stewart, P. (2018). Educating Caribbean Librarians to Provide Library Education in a Dynamic Information Environment. In S. Bhattacharyya & K. Patnaik (Eds.), *Changing the Scope of Library Instruction in the Digital Age* (pp. 187–226). Hershey, PA: IGI Global. doi:10.4018/978-1-5225-2802-9.ch008

Bassuener, L. (2016). Knowledge in the Shrinking Commons: Libraries and Open Access in a Market-Driven World. In E. Railean, G. Walker, A. Elçi, & L. Jackson (Eds.), *Handbook of Research on Applied Learning Theory and Design in Modern Education* (pp. 358–379). Hershey, PA: IGI Global. doi:10.4018/978-1-4666-9634-1.ch017

Baylen, D. M., & Cooper, O. P. (2016). Social Media and Special Collections: Exploring Presence, Prevalence, and Practices in Academic Libraries. In J. Yap, M. Perez, M. Ayson, & G. Entico (Eds.), *Special Library Administration, Standardization and Technological Integration* (pp. 180–201). Hershey, PA: IGI Global. doi:10.4018/978-1-4666-9542-9.ch008

Belden, D., Phillips, M. E., Carlisle, T., & Hartman, C. N. (2016). The Portal to Texas History: Building a Partnership Model for a Statewide Digital Library. In B. Doherty (Ed.), *Space and Organizational Considerations in Academic Library Partnerships and Collaborations* (pp. 182–204). Hershey, PA: IGI Global. doi:10.4018/978-1-5225-0326-2.ch009

Bengtson, J. (2017). Funding a Gamification Machine. In E. Iglesias (Ed.), *Library Technology Funding, Planning, and Deployment* (pp. 99–112). Hershey, PA: IGI Global. doi:10.4018/978-1-5225-1735-1.ch006

Bhebhe, S., & Ngwenya, S. (2016). Adoption and Use of Discovery Tools by Selected Academic Libraries in Zimbabwe. In E. de Smet & S. Dhamdhere (Eds.), *E-Discovery Tools and Applications in Modern Libraries* (pp. 168–180). Hershey, PA: IGI Global. doi:10.4018/978-1-5225-0474-0.ch009

Blummer, B., & Kenton, J. M. (2017). Access and Accessibility of Academic Libraries' Electronic Resources and Services: Identifying Themes in the Literature From 2000 to the Present. In H. Alphin Jr, J. Lavine, & R. Chan (Eds.), *Disability and Equity in Higher Education Accessibility* (pp. 242–267). Hershey, PA: IGI Global. doi:10.4018/978-1-5225-2665-0.ch011

Blummer, B., & Kenton, J. M. (2018). Academic and Research Libraries' Portals: A Literature Review From 2003 to the Present. In R. Bhardwaj (Ed.), *Digitizing the Modern Library and the Transition From Print to Electronic* (pp. 29–63). Hershey, PA: IGI Global. doi:10.4018/978-1-5225-2119-8.ch002

Blummer, B., & Kenton, J. M. (2018). International Students and Academic Libraries: Identifying Themes in the Literature From 2001 to the Present. In B. Blummer, J. Kenton, & M. Wiatrowski (Eds.), *Promoting Ethnic Diversity and Multiculturalism in Higher Education* (pp. 237–263). Hershey, PA: IGI Global. doi:10.4018/978-1-5225-4097-7.ch013

Bodolay, R., Frye, S., Kruse, C., & Luke, D. (2016). Moving from Co-Location to Cooperation to Collaboration: Redefining a Library's Role within the University. In B. Doherty (Ed.), *Space and Organizational Considerations in Academic Library Partnerships and Collaborations* (pp. 230–254). Hershey, PA: IGI Global. doi:10.4018/978-1-5225-0326-2.ch011

Boom, D. (2017). The Embedded Librarian: Do More With less. In B. Gunjal (Ed.), *Managing Knowledge and Scholarly Assets in Academic Libraries* (pp. 76–97). Hershey, PA: IGI Global. doi:10.4018/978-1-5225-1741-2.ch004

Bosire-Ogechi, E. (2018). Social Media, Social Networking, Copyright, and Digital Libraries. In A. Tella & T. Kwanya (Eds.), *Handbook of Research on Managing Intellectual Property in Digital Libraries* (pp. 37–50). Hershey, PA: IGI Global. doi:10.4018/978-1-5225-3093-0.ch003

Bradley-Sanders, C., & Rudshteyn, A. (2018). MyLibrary at Brooklyn College: Developing a Suite of Digital Tools. In L. Costello & M. Powers (Eds.), *Developing In-House Digital Tools in Library Spaces* (pp. 140–167). Hershey, PA: IGI Global. doi:10.4018/978-1-5225-2676-6.ch007

Brisk, A. T., Pittman, K., & Rosendahl, M. (2016). Collaborating Off Campus: Creating Communities of Practice with New Partners. In B. Doherty (Ed.), *Technology-Centered Academic Library Partnerships and Collaborations* (pp. 245–274). Hershey, PA: IGI Global. doi:10.4018/978-1-5225-0323-1.ch009

Brown, V. (2018). Technology Access Gap for Postsecondary Education: A Statewide Case Study. In M. Yildiz, S. Funk, & B. De Abreu (Eds.), *Promoting Global Competencies Through Media Literacy* (pp. 20–40). Hershey, PA: IGI Global. doi:10.4018/978-1-5225-3082-4.ch002

Carroll, V. (2016). Conservation Since 2000. In E. Decker & J. Townes (Eds.), *Handbook of Research on Disaster Management and Contingency Planning in Modern Libraries* (pp. 467–493). Hershey, PA: IGI Global. doi:10.4018/978-1-4666-8624-3.ch020

Chaiyasoonthorn, W., & Suksa-ngiam, W. (2018). Users' Acceptance of Online Literature Databases in a Thai University: A Test of UTAUT2. *International Journal of Information Systems in the Service Sector, 10*(1), 54–70. doi:10.4018/IJISSS.2018010104

Chandler, D. R. (2016). Prepared for Anything and Everything: Libraries, Archives, and Unexpected Small Scale Disasters. In E. Decker & J. Townes (Eds.), *Handbook of Research on Disaster Management and Contingency Planning in Modern Libraries* (pp. 240–256). Hershey, PA: IGI Global. doi:10.4018/978-1-4666-8624-3.ch011

Chaudron, G. (2016). After the Flood: Lessons Learned from Small-Scale Disasters. In E. Decker & J. Townes (Eds.), *Handbook of Research on Disaster Management and Contingency Planning in Modern Libraries* (pp. 389–411). Hershey, PA: IGI Global. doi:10.4018/978-1-4666-8624-3.ch017

Chaudron, G. (2016). Managing the Commonplace: Small Water Emergencies in Libraries. *International Journal of Risk and Contingency Management, 5*(1), 42–61. doi:10.4018/IJRCM.2016010104

Chaudron, G. (2018). Burst Pipes and Leaky Roofs: Small Emergencies Are a Challenge for Libraries. In K. Strang, M. Korstanje, & N. Vajjhala (Eds.), *Research, Practices, and Innovations in Global Risk and Contingency Management* (pp. 211–231). Hershey, PA: IGI Global. doi:10.4018/978-1-5225-4754-9.ch012

Chemulwo, M. J. (2018). Managing Intellectual Property in Digital Libraries and Copyright Challenges. In A. Tella & T. Kwanya (Eds.), *Handbook of Research on Managing Intellectual Property in Digital Libraries* (pp. 165–183). Hershey, PA: IGI Global. doi:10.4018/978-1-5225-3093-0.ch009

Chen, J., Lan, X., Huang, Q., Dong, J., & Chen, C. (2017). Scholarly Learning Commons. In L. Ruan, Q. Zhu, & Y. Ye (Eds.), *Academic Library Development and Administration in China* (pp. 90–109). Hershey, PA: IGI Global. doi:10.4018/978-1-5225-0550-1.ch006

Chigwada, J. P. (2018). Adoption of Open Source Software in Libraries in Developing Countries. *International Journal of Library and Information Services, 7*(1), 15–29. doi:10.4018/IJLIS.2018010102

Chisita, C. T., & Chinyemba, F. (2017). Utilising ICTs for Resource Sharing Initiatives in Academic Institutions in Zimbabwe: Towards a New Trajectory. In B. Gunjal (Ed.), *Managing Knowledge and Scholarly Assets in Academic Libraries* (pp. 174–187). Hershey, PA: IGI Global. doi:10.4018/978-1-5225-1741-2.ch008

Colmenero-Ruiz, M. (2016). Discussion on Digital Inclusion Good Practices at Europe's Libraries. In B. Passarelli, J. Straubhaar, & A. Cuevas-Cerveró (Eds.), *Handbook of Research on Comparative Approaches to the Digital Age Revolution in Europe and the Americas* (pp. 352–369). Hershey, PA: IGI Global. doi:10.4018/978-1-4666-8740-0.ch021

Costello, B. (2016). Academic Libraries in Partnership with the Government Publishing Office: A Changing Paradigm. In B. Doherty (Ed.), *Space and Organizational Considerations in Academic Library Partnerships and Collaborations* (pp. 87–110). Hershey, PA: IGI Global. doi:10.4018/978-1-5225-0326-2.ch005

Costello, L., & Fazal, S. (2018). Developing Unique Study Room Reservation Systems: Examples From Teachers College and Stony Brook University. In L. Costello & M. Powers (Eds.), *Developing In-House Digital Tools in Library Spaces* (pp. 168–176). Hershey, PA: IGI Global. doi:10.4018/978-1-5225-2676-6.ch008

Cowick, C., & Cowick, J. (2016). Planning for a Disaster: Effective Emergency Management in the 21st Century. In E. Decker & J. Townes (Eds.), *Handbook of Research on Disaster Management and Contingency Planning in Modern Libraries* (pp. 49–69). Hershey, PA: IGI Global. doi:10.4018/978-1-4666-8624-3.ch003

Cui, Y. (2017). Research Data Management: Models, Challenges, and Actions. In L. Ruan, Q. Zhu, & Y. Ye (Eds.), *Academic Library Development and Administration in China* (pp. 184–195). Hershey, PA: IGI Global. doi:10.4018/978-1-5225-0550-1.ch011

Das, T. (2016). Academic Library Collaborations to Strengthen Open Government Data and Expand Librarianship. In B. Doherty (Ed.), *Technology-Centered Academic Library Partnerships and Collaborations* (pp. 167–193). Hershey, PA: IGI Global. doi:10.4018/978-1-5225-0323-1.ch006 de Smet, E. (2016). E-Discovery with the ABCD Information Management System. In E. de Smet & S. Dhamdhere (Eds.), *E-Discovery Tools and Applications in Modern Libraries* (pp. 332–357). Hershey, PA: IGI Global. doi:10.4018/978-1-5225-0474-0.ch017

Decker, E. N., & Odom, R. Y. (2016). Publish or Perish: Librarians Collaborating to Support Junior Faculty to Publish within the Academic Environment. In B. Doherty (Ed.), *Space and Organizational Considerations in Academic Library Partnerships and Collaborations* (pp. 298–316). Hershey, PA: IGI Global. doi:10.4018/978-1-5225-0326-2.ch014

Desilets, M. R., DeJonghe, J., & Filkins, M. (2016). Better Together: The Successful Public/Academic Joint Use Library. In B. Doherty (Ed.), *Space and Organizational Considerations in Academic Library Partnerships and Collaborations* (pp. 1–21). Hershey, PA: IGI Global. doi:10.4018/978-1-5225-0326-2.ch001

Dhamdhere, S. N., De Smet, E., & Lihitkar, R. (2017). Web-Based Bibliographic Services Offered by Top World and Indian University Libraries: A Comparative Study. *International Journal of Library and Information Services*, *6*(1), 53–72. doi:10.4018/IJLIS.2017010104

Dhamdhere, S. N., & Lihitkar, R. (2016). Commercial and Open Access Integrated Information Search Tools in Indian Libraries. In E. de Smet & S. Dhamdhere (Eds.), *E-Discovery Tools and Applications in Modern Libraries* (pp. 41–55). Hershey, PA: IGI Global. doi:10.4018/978-1-5225-0474-0.ch002

Dixon, J., & Abashian, N. (2016). Beyond the Collection: Emergency Planning for Public and Staff Safety. In E. Decker & J. Townes (Eds.), *Handbook of Research on Disaster Management and Contingency Planning in Modern Libraries* (pp. 120–140). Hershey, PA: IGI Global. doi:10.4018/978-1-4666-8624-3.ch006

Doherty, B. (2016). Marriage after Divorce: The Challenges and Opportunities of a Shared Library after Institutions Separate. In B. Doherty (Ed.), *Space and Organizational Considerations in Academic Library Partnerships and Collaborations* (pp. 22–44). Hershey, PA: IGI Global. doi:10.4018/978-1-5225-0326-2.ch002

Dongardive, P. (2016). Digital Libraries as Information Superhighway. In A. Tella (Ed.), *Information Seeking Behavior and Challenges in Digital Libraries* (pp. 304–315). Hershey, PA: IGI Global. doi:10.4018/978-1-5225-0296-8.ch015

Dougan, K. (2016). Music Information Seeking Opportunities and Behavior Then and Now. In P. Kostagiolas, K. Martzoukou, & C. Lavranos (Eds.), *Trends in Music Information Seeking, Behavior, and Retrieval for Creativity* (pp. 42–57). Hershey, PA: IGI Global. doi:10.4018/978-1-5225-0270-8.ch003

Eiriemiokhale, K. A. (2018). Copyright Issues in a Digital Library Environment. In A. Tella & T. Kwanya (Eds.), *Handbook of Research on Managing Intellectual Property in Digital Libraries* (pp. 142–164). Hershey, PA: IGI Global. doi:10.4018/978-1-5225-3093-0.ch008

El Mimouni, H., Anderson, J., Tempelman-Kluit, N. F., & Dolan-Mescal, A. (2018). UX Work in Libraries: How (and Why) to Do It. In L. Costello & M. Powers (Eds.), *Developing In-House Digital Tools in Library Spaces* (pp. 1–36). Hershey, PA: IGI Global. doi:10.4018/978-1-5225-2676-6.ch001

Emiri, O. T. (2017). Digital Literacy Skills Among Librarians in University Libraries In the 21st Century in Edo And Delta States, Nigeria. *International Journal of Library and Information Services*, *6*(1), 37–52. doi:10.4018/IJLIS.2017010103

Entico, G. J. (2016). Knowledge Management and the Medical Health Librarians: A Perception Study. In J. Yap, M. Perez, M. Ayson, & G. Entico (Eds.), *Special Library Administration, Standardization and Technological Integration* (pp. 52–77). Hershey, PA: IGI Global. doi:10.4018/978-1-4666-9542-9.ch003

Esposito, T. (2018). Exploring Opportunities in Health Science Information Instructional Outreach: A Case Study Highlighting One Academic Library's Experience. In S. Bhattacharyya & K. Patnaik (Eds.), *Changing the Scope of Library Instruction in the Digital Age* (pp. 118–135). Hershey, PA: IGI Global. doi:10.4018/978-1-5225-2802-9.ch005

Esse, U. C., & Ohaegbulam, H. (2016). Library and Information Services for Open and Distance Learning: Assessing the Role of Mobile Technologies and Distance Learning in Higher Education. In G. Eby, T. Yuzer, & S. Atay (Eds.), *Developing Successful Strategies for Global Policies and Cyber Transparency in E-Learning* (pp. 29–45). Hershey, PA: IGI Global. doi:10.4018/978-1-4666-8844-5.ch003

Fagbohun, M. O., Nwokocha, N. M., Itsekor, V., & Adebayo, O. (2016). Responsive Library Website Design and Adoption of Federated Search Tools for Library Services in Developing Countries. In E. de Smet & S. Dhamdhere (Eds.), *E-Discovery Tools and Applications in Modern Libraries* (pp. 76–108). Hershey, PA: IGI Global. doi:10.4018/978-1-5225-0474-0.ch005

Fagbola, O. O. (2016). Indexing and Abstracting as Tools for Information Retrieval in Digital Libraries: A Review of Literature. In A. Tella (Ed.), *Information Seeking Behavior and Challenges in Digital Libraries* (pp. 156–178). Hershey, PA: IGI Global. doi:10.4018/978-1-5225-0296-8.ch008

Fan, Y., Zhang, X., & Li, G. (2017). Research Initiatives and Projects in Academic Libraries. In L. Ruan, Q. Zhu, & Y. Ye (Eds.), *Academic Library Development and Administration in China* (pp. 230–252). Hershey, PA: IGI Global. doi:10.4018/978-1-5225-0550-1.ch014

Farmer, L. S. (2017). ICT Literacy Integration: Issues and Sample Efforts. In J. Keengwe & P. Bull (Eds.), *Handbook of Research on Transformative Digital Content and Learning Technologies* (pp. 59–80). Hershey, PA: IGI Global. doi:10.4018/978-1-5225-2000-9.ch004

Farmer, L. S. (2017). Data Analytics for Strategic Management: Getting the Right Data. In V. Wang (Ed.), *Encyclopedia of Strategic Leadership and Management* (pp. 810–822). Hershey, PA: IGI Global. doi:10.4018/978-1-5225-1049-9.ch056

Farmer, L. S. (2017). Managing Portable Technologies for Special Education. In V. Wang (Ed.), *Encyclopedia of Strategic Leadership and Management* (pp. 977–987). Hershey, PA: IGI Global. doi:10.4018/978-1-5225-1049-9.ch068

Fujishima, D., & Kamada, T. (2017). Collective Relocation for Associative Distributed Collections of Objects. *International Journal of Software Innovation*, *5*(2), 55–69. doi:10.4018/IJSI.2017040104

Gaetz, I. (2016). Processes, Opportunities, and Challenges Creating and Managing a Scholarly Open Access Journal: An Investigation of "Collaborative Librarianship". In B. Doherty (Ed.), *Space and Organizational Considerations in Academic Library Partnerships and Collaborations* (pp. 205–229). Hershey, PA: IGI Global. doi:10.4018/978-1-5225-0326-2.ch010

Galloup, A. (2016). One Plan, Four Libraries: A Case Study in Disaster Planning for a Four-Campus Academic Institution. In E. Decker & J. Townes (Eds.), *Handbook of Research on Disaster Management and Contingency Planning in Modern Libraries* (pp. 166–183). Hershey, PA: IGI Global. doi:10.4018/978-1-4666-8624-3.ch008

Gamtso, C. W., Vogt, R. B., Donahue, A., Donovan, K., & Jefferson, J. (2016). Librarian and Peer Research Mentor Partnerships that Promote Student Success. In B. Doherty (Ed.), *Space and Organizational Considerations in Academic Library Partnerships and Collaborations* (pp. 255–279). Hershey, PA: IGI Global. doi:10.4018/978-1-5225-0326-2.ch012

Ghani, S. R. (2017). Ontology: Advancing Flawless Library Services. In T. Ashraf & N. Kumar (Eds.), *Interdisciplinary Digital Preservation Tools and Technologies* (pp. 79–102). Hershey, PA: IGI Global. doi:10.4018/978-1-5225-1653-8.ch005

Gibbons, P. (2016). Disaster Management and Exhibition Loans: Contingency Planning for Items on Display. In E. Decker & J. Townes (Eds.), *Handbook of Research on Disaster Management and Contingency Planning in Modern Libraries* (pp. 141–165). Hershey, PA: IGI Global. doi:10.4018/978-1-4666-8624-3.ch007

Gibbons, P. (2016). Assessing Risk and Safeguarding Rare Library Materials During Exhibition Loans. *International Journal of Risk and Contingency Management, 5*(1), 15–25. doi:10.4018/IJRCM.2016010102

Gibson, R. (2016). Wearable Technologies in Academic Information Search. In J. Holland (Ed.), *Wearable Technology and Mobile Innovations for Next-Generation Education* (pp. 122–146). Hershey, PA: IGI Global. doi:10.4018/978-1-5225-0069-8.ch007

Goldman, B. (2016). Two Fires and a Flood: Lasting Impact on a Public Library, Its Staff, and Community. In E. Decker & J. Townes (Eds.), *Handbook of Research on Disaster Management and Contingency Planning in Modern Libraries* (pp. 560–581). Hershey, PA: IGI Global. doi:10.4018/978-1-4666-8624-3.ch024

Goovaerts, M., Nieuwenhuysen, P., & Dhamdhere, S. N. (2016). VLIR-UOS Workshop 'E-Info Discovery and Management for Institutes in the South': Presentations and Conclusions, Antwerp, 8-19 December, 2014. In E. de Smet, & S. Dhamdhere (Eds.), E-Discovery Tools and Applications in Modern Libraries (pp. 1-40). Hershey, PA: IGI Global. doi:10.4018/978-1-5225-0474-0.ch001

Gu, J. (2017). Library Buildings on New Campuses. In L. Ruan, Q. Zhu, & Y. Ye (Eds.), *Academic Library Development and Administration in China* (pp. 110–124). Hershey, PA: IGI Global. doi:10.4018/978-1-5225-0550-1.ch007

Guan, Z., & Wang, J. (2017). The China Academic Social Sciences and Humanities Library (CASHL). In L. Ruan, Q. Zhu, & Y. Ye (Eds.), *Academic Library Development and Administration in China* (pp. 31–54). Hershey, PA: IGI Global. doi:10.4018/978-1-5225-0550-1.ch003

Gul, S., & Shueb, S. (2018). Confronting/Managing the Crisis of Indian Libraries: E-Consortia Initiatives in India - A Way Forward. In R. Bhardwaj (Ed.), *Digitizing the Modern Library and the Transition From Print to Electronic* (pp. 129–163). Hershey, PA: IGI Global. doi:10.4018/978-1-5225-2119-8.ch006

Gunjal, B. (2017). Managing Knowledge and Scholarly Assets in Academic Libraries: Issues and Challenges. In B. Gunjal (Ed.), *Managing Knowledge and Scholarly Assets in Academic Libraries* (pp. 270–279). Hershey, PA: IGI Global. doi:10.4018/978-1-5225-1741-2.ch013

Guo, J., Zhang, H., & Zong, Y. (2017). Leadership Development and Career Planning. In L. Ruan, Q. Zhu, & Y. Ye (Eds.), *Academic Library Development and Administration in China* (pp. 264–279). Hershey, PA: IGI Global. doi:10.4018/978-1-5225-0550-1.ch016

Hallis, R. (2018). Leveraging Library Instruction in a Digital Age. In S. Bhattacharyya & K. Patnaik (Eds.), *Changing the Scope of Library Instruction in the Digital Age* (pp. 1–23). Hershey, PA: IGI Global. doi:10.4018/978-1-5225-2802-9.ch001

Hamilton, R., & Brown, D. (2016). Disaster Management and Continuity Planning in Libraries: Changes since the Year 2000. In E. Decker & J. Townes (Eds.), *Handbook of Research on Disaster Management and Contingency Planning in Modern Libraries* (pp. 1–24). Hershey, PA: IGI Global. doi:10.4018/978-1-4666-8624-3.ch001

Hamilton, R., & Brown, D. (2016). Disaster Management and Continuity Planning in Libraries: Literature Review. *International Journal of Risk and Contingency Management, 5*(1), 26–41. doi:10.4018/IJRCM.2016010103

Hartsock, R., & Alemneh, D. G. (2018). Electronic Theses and Dissertations (ETDs). In M. Khosrow-Pour, D.B.A. (Ed.), Encyclopedia of Information Science and Technology, Fourth Edition (pp. 6748-6755). Hershey, PA: IGI Global. doi:10.4018/978-1-5225-2255-3.ch584

Haugh, D. (2018). Mobile Applications for Libraries. In L. Costello & M. Powers (Eds.), *Developing In-House Digital Tools in Library Spaces* (pp. 76–90). Hershey, PA: IGI Global. doi:10.4018/978-1-5225-2676-6.ch004

Hill, V. (2017). Digital Citizens as Writers: New Literacies and New Responsibilities. In E. Monske & K. Blair (Eds.), *Handbook of Research on Writing and Composing in the Age of MOOCs* (pp. 56–74). Hershey, PA: IGI Global. doi:10.4018/978-1-5225-1718-4.ch004

Horne-Popp, L. M., Tessone, E. B., & Welker, J. (2018). If You Build It, They Will Come: Creating a Library Statistics Dashboard for Decision-Making. In L. Costello & M. Powers (Eds.), *Developing In-House Digital Tools in Library Spaces* (pp. 177–203). Hershey, PA: IGI Global. doi:10.4018/978-1-5225-2676-6.ch009

Huang, C., & Xue, H. F. (2017). The China Academic Digital Associative Library (CADAL). In L. Ruan, Q. Zhu, & Y. Ye (Eds.), *Academic Library Development and Administration in China* (pp. 20–30). Hershey, PA: IGI Global. doi:10.4018/978-1-5225-0550-1.ch002

Hunsaker, A. J., Majewski, N., & Rocke, L. E. (2018). Pulling Content out the Back Door: Creating an Interactive Digital Collections Experience. In L. Costello & M. Powers (Eds.), *Developing In-House Digital Tools in Library Spaces* (pp. 205–226). Hershey, PA: IGI Global. doi:10.4018/978-1-5225-2676-6.ch010

Ibrahim, H., Mustapa, R., Edzan, N., & Yahya, W. A. (2016). Profiling Prominent Malaysians in Bernama Library and Infolink Service. In J. Yap, M. Perez, M. Ayson, & G. Entico (Eds.), *Special Library Administration, Standardization and Technological Integration* (pp. 315–336). Hershey, PA: IGI Global. doi:10.4018/978-1-4666-9542-9.ch014

Idiegbeyan-Ose, J., Ifijeh, G., Iwu-James, J., & Ilogho, J. (2016). Management of Institutional Repositories (IR) in Developing Countries. In E. de Smet & S. Dhamdhere (Eds.), *E-Discovery Tools and Applications in Modern Libraries* (pp. 306–331). Hershey, PA: IGI Global. doi:10.4018/978-1-5225-0474-0.ch016

Idiegbeyan-ose, J., Nkiko, C., Idahosa, M., & Nwokocha, N. (2016). Digital Divide: Issues and Strategies for Intervention in Nigerian Libraries. *Journal of Cases on Information Technology, 18*(3), 29–39. doi:10.4018/JCIT.2016070103

Ifijeh, G., Adebayo, O., Izuagbe, R., & Olawoyin, O. (2018). Institutional Repositories and Libraries in Nigeria: Interrogating the Nexus. *Journal of Cases on Information Technology, 20*(2), 16–29. doi:10.4018/JCIT.2018040102

Ifijeh, G., Idiegbeyan-ose, J., Segun-Adeniran, C., & Ilogho, J. (2016). Disaster Management in Digital Libraries: Issues and Strategies in Developing Countries. *International Journal of Risk and Contingency Management, 5*(1), 1–14. doi:10.4018/IJRCM.2016010101

Iglesias, E. (2017). Insourcing and Outsourcing of Library Technology. In E. Iglesias (Ed.), *Library Technology Funding, Planning, and Deployment* (pp. 113–123). Hershey, PA: IGI Global. doi:10.4018/978-1-5225-1735-1.ch007

Ikolo, V. E. (2018). Transformational Leadership for Academic Libraries in Nigeria. In M. Khosrow-Pour, D.B.A. (Ed.), Encyclopedia of Information Science and Technology, Fourth Edition (pp. 5726-5735). Hershey, PA: IGI Global. doi:10.4018/978-1-5225-2255-3.ch497

Jaafar, T. M. (2016). Law Library Consortium in Metro Manila: A Proposed Model and the Management of Law Libraries. In J. Yap, M. Perez, M. Ayson, & G. Entico (Eds.), *Special Library Administration, Standardization and Technological Integration* (pp. 134–164). Hershey, PA: IGI Global. doi:10.4018/978-1-4666-9542-9.ch006

Joe, J. A. (2018). Changing Expectations of Academic Libraries. In M. Khosrow-Pour, D.B.A. (Ed.), Encyclopedia of Information Science and Technology, Fourth Edition (pp. 5204-5212). Hershey, PA: IGI Global. doi:10.4018/978-1-5225-2255-3.ch452

Johnson, H., & Simms, S. (2016). Concept, Conversion, Cultivation, and Consequence: The Four Cs of Successful Collaboration. In B. Doherty (Ed.), *Space and Organizational Considerations in Academic Library Partnerships and Collaborations* (pp. 280–297). Hershey, PA: IGI Global. doi:10.4018/978-1-5225-0326-2.ch013

Jones, A. (2016). Shortcomings and Successes: A Small-Scale Disaster Case Study. In E. Decker & J. Townes (Eds.), *Handbook of Research on Disaster Management and Contingency Planning in Modern Libraries* (pp. 412–435). Hershey, PA: IGI Global. doi:10.4018/978-1-4666-8624-3.ch018

Juliana, I., Izuagbe, R., Itsekor, V., Fagbohun, M. O., Asaolu, A., & Nwokeoma, M. N. (2018). The Role of the School Library in Empowering Visually Impaired Children With Lifelong Information Literacy Skills. In P. Epler (Ed.), *Instructional Strategies in General Education and Putting the Individuals With Disabilities Act (IDEA) Into Practice* (pp. 245–271). Hershey, PA: IGI Global. doi:10.4018/978-1-5225-3111-1.ch009

Kalusopa, T. (2018). Preservation and Access to Digital Materials: Strategic Policy Options for Africa. In P. Ngulube (Ed.), *Handbook of Research on Heritage Management and Preservation* (pp. 150–174). Hershey, PA: IGI Global. doi:10.4018/978-1-5225-3137-1.ch008

Kamau, G. W. (2018). Copyright Challenges in Digital Libraries in Kenya From the Lens of a Librarian. In A. Tella & T. Kwanya (Eds.), *Handbook of Research on Managing Intellectual Property in Digital Libraries* (pp. 312–336). Hershey, PA: IGI Global. doi:10.4018/978-1-5225-3093-0.ch016

Karbach, L. (2016). Public Libraries: Analysis of Services for Immigrant Populations and Suggestions to Improve Outreach. In K. González & R. Frumkin (Eds.), *Handbook of Research on Effective Communication in Culturally Diverse Classrooms* (pp. 153–182). Hershey, PA: IGI Global. doi:10.4018/978-1-4666-9953-3.ch008

Karmakar, R. (2018). Development and Management of Digital Libraries in the Regime of IPR Paradigm. *International Journal of Library and Information Services, 7*(1), 44–57. doi:10.4018/IJLIS.2018010104

Kasemsap, K. (2016). Mastering Digital Libraries in the Digital Age. In E. de Smet & S. Dhamdhere (Eds.), *E-Discovery Tools and Applications in Modern Libraries* (pp. 275–305). Hershey, PA: IGI Global. doi:10.4018/978-1-5225-0474-0.ch015

Kasemsap, K. (2017). Mastering Knowledge Management in Academic Libraries. In B. Gunjal (Ed.), *Managing Knowledge and Scholarly Assets in Academic Libraries* (pp. 27–55). Hershey, PA: IGI Global. doi:10.4018/978-1-5225-1741-2.ch002

Kehinde, A. (2018). Digital Libraries and the Role of Digital Librarians. In A. Tella & T. Kwanya (Eds.), *Handbook of Research on Managing Intellectual Property in Digital Libraries* (pp. 98–119). Hershey, PA: IGI Global. doi:10.4018/978-1-5225-3093-0.ch006

Kenausis, V., & Herman, D. (2017). Don't Make Us Use the "Get Along Shirt": Communication and Consensus Building in an RFP Process. In E. Iglesias (Ed.), *Library Technology Funding, Planning, and Deployment* (pp. 1–22). Hershey, PA: IGI Global. doi:10.4018/978-1-5225-1735-1.ch001

Kohl, L. E., Lombardi, P., & Moroney, M. (2017). Moving from Local to Global via the Integrated Library System: Cost-Savings, ILS Management, Teams, and End-Users. In E. Iglesias (Ed.), *Library Technology Funding, Planning, and Deployment* (pp. 23–35). Hershey, PA: IGI Global. doi:10.4018/978-1-5225-1735-1.ch002

Kowalsky, M. (2016). Analysis of Initial Involvement of Librarians in the Online Virtual World of Second Life. In B. Baggio (Ed.), *Analyzing Digital Discourse and Human Behavior in Modern Virtual Environments* (pp. 126–148). Hershey, PA: IGI Global. doi:10.4018/978-1-4666-9899-4.ch007

Kumar, K. (2018). Library in Your Pocket Delivery of Instruction Service Through Library Mobile Apps: A World in Your Pocket. In S. Bhattacharyya & K. Patnaik (Eds.), *Changing the Scope of Library Instruction in the Digital Age* (pp. 228–249). Hershey, PA: IGI Global. doi:10.4018/978-1-5225-2802-9.ch009

Kwanya, T. (2016). Information Seeking Behaviour in Digital Library Contexts. In A. Tella (Ed.), *Information Seeking Behavior and Challenges in Digital Libraries* (pp. 1–25). Hershey, PA: IGI Global. doi:10.4018/978-1-5225-0296-8.ch001

Kwanya, T. (2018). Social Bookmarking in Digital Libraries: Intellectual Property Rights Implications. In A. Tella & T. Kwanya (Eds.), *Handbook of Research on Managing Intellectual Property in Digital Libraries* (pp. 1–18). Hershey, PA: IGI Global. doi:10.4018/978-1-5225-3093-0.ch001

LaMoreaux, N. E. (2016). Collaborating to Create a Fashionable Event: A Guide for Creating a Library-Sponsored Conference. In B. Doherty (Ed.), *Space and Organizational Considerations in Academic Library Partnerships and Collaborations* (pp. 317–334). Hershey, PA: IGI Global. doi:10.4018/978-1-5225-0326-2.ch015

Lewis, J. K. (2018). Change Leadership Styles and Behaviors in Academic Libraries. In M. Khosrow-Pour, D.B.A. (Ed.), Encyclopedia of Information Science and Technology, Fourth Edition (pp. 5194-5203). Hershey, PA: IGI Global. doi:10.4018/978-1-5225-2255-3.ch451

Lillard, L. L. (2018). Is Interdisciplinary Collaboration in Academia an Elusive Dream?: Can the Institutional Barriers Be Broken Down? A Review of the Literature and the Case of Library Science. In M. Al-Suqri, A. Al-Kindi, S. AlKindi, & N. Saleem (Eds.), *Promoting Interdisciplinarity in Knowledge Generation and Problem Solving* (pp. 139–147). Hershey, PA: IGI Global. doi:10.4018/978-1-5225-3878-3.ch010

Lock, M. B., Fansler, C., & Webb, M. (2016). (R)Evolutionary Emergency Planning: Adding Resilience through Continuous Review. *International Journal of Risk and Contingency Management*, *5*(2), 47–65. doi:10.4018/IJRCM.2016040103

Long, X., & Yao, B. (2017). The Construction and Development of the Academic Digital Library of Chinese Ancient Collections. In L. Ruan, Q. Zhu, & Y. Ye (Eds.), *Academic Library Development and Administration in China* (pp. 126–135). Hershey, PA: IGI Global. doi:10.4018/978-1-5225-0550-1.ch008

Lowe, M., & Reno, L. M. (2018). Academic Librarianship and Burnout. In *Examining the Emotional Dimensions of Academic Librarianship: Emerging Research and Opportunities* (pp. 72–89). Hershey, PA: IGI Global. doi:10.4018/978-1-5225-3761-8.ch005

Lowe, M., & Reno, L. M. (2018). Emotional Dimensions of Academic Librarianship. In *Examining the Emotional Dimensions of Academic Librarianship: Emerging Research and Opportunities* (pp. 54–71). Hershey, PA: IGI Global. doi:10.4018/978-1-5225-3761-8.ch004

Lowe, M., & Reno, L. M. (2018). Why Isn't This Being Studied? In *Examining the Emotional Dimensions of Academic Librarianship: Emerging Research and Opportunities* (pp. 90–108). Hershey, PA: IGI Global. doi:10.4018/978-1-5225-3761-8.ch006

Lowe, M., & Reno, L. M. (2018). Research Agenda: Research Ideas and Recommendations. In *Examining the Emotional Dimensions of Academic Librarianship: Emerging Research and Opportunities* (pp. 109–125). Hershey, PA: IGI Global. doi:10.4018/978-1-5225-3761-8.ch007

Luyombya, D., Kiyingi, G. W., & Naluwooza, M. (2018). The Nature and Utilisation of Archival Records Deposited in Makerere University Library, Uganda. In P. Ngulube (Ed.), *Handbook of Research on Heritage Management and Preservation* (pp. 96–113). Hershey, PA: IGI Global. doi:10.4018/978-1-5225-3137-1.ch005

Mabe, M., & Ashley, E. A. (2017). The Natural Role of the Public Library. In *The Developing Role of Public Libraries in Emergency Management: Emerging Research and Opportunities* (pp. 25–43). Hershey, PA: IGI Global. doi:10.4018/978-1-5225-2196-9.ch003

Mabe, M., & Ashley, E. A. (2017). I'm Trained, Now What? In *The Developing Role of Public Libraries in Emergency Management: Emerging Research and Opportunities* (pp. 87–95). Hershey, PA: IGI Global. doi:10.4018/978-1-5225-2196-9.ch007

Mabe, M., & Ashley, E. A. (2017). Emergency Preparation for the Library and Librarian. In *The Developing Role of Public Libraries in Emergency Management: Emerging Research and Opportunities* (pp. 61–78). Hershey, PA: IGI Global. doi:10.4018/978-1-5225-2196-9.ch005

Mabe, M., & Ashley, E. A. (2017). The CCPL Model. In *The Developing Role of Public Libraries in Emergency Management: Emerging Research and Opportunities* (pp. 15–24). Hershey, PA: IGI Global. doi:10.4018/978-1-5225-2196-9.ch002

Mabe, M., & Ashley, E. A. (2017). The Local Command Structure and How the Library Fits. In *In The Developing Role of Public Libraries in Emergency Management: Emerging Research and Opportunities* (pp. 44–60). Hershey, PA: IGI Global. doi:10.4018/978-1-5225-2196-9.ch004

Mabe, M. R. (2016). Libraries to the Rescue. *International Journal of Risk and Contingency Management*, *5*(1), 62–81. doi:10.4018/IJRCM.2016010105

Mabe, M. R. (2016). The Library as Lifeboat. In E. Decker & J. Townes (Eds.), *Handbook of Research on Disaster Management and Contingency Planning in Modern Libraries* (pp. 494–515). Hershey, PA: IGI Global. doi:10.4018/978-1-4666-8624-3.ch021

Manzoor, A. (2018). Social Media: A Librarian's Tool for Instant and Direct Interaction With Library Users. In R. Bhardwaj (Ed.), *Digitizing the Modern Library and the Transition From Print to Electronic* (pp. 112–128). Hershey, PA: IGI Global. doi:10.4018/978-1-5225-2119-8.ch005

Maringanti, H. (2018). A Decision Making Paradigm for Software Development in Libraries. In L. Costello & M. Powers (Eds.), *Developing In-House Digital Tools in Library Spaces* (pp. 59–75). Hershey, PA: IGI Global. doi:10.4018/978-1-5225-2676-6.ch003

Markman, K. M., Ferrarini, M., & Deschenes, A. H. (2018). User Testing and Iterative Design in the Academic Library: A Case Study. In R. Roscoe, S. Craig, & I. Douglas (Eds.), *End-User Considerations in Educational Technology Design* (pp. 160–183). Hershey, PA: IGI Global. doi:10.4018/978-1-5225-2639-1.ch008

Marks, A. B., & Owen, E. (2016). It Is Everywhere: Handling a Mold Outbreak in a Library's High-Density Storage Collection. In E. Decker & J. Townes (Eds.), *Handbook of Research on Disaster Management and Contingency Planning in Modern Libraries* (pp. 311–339). Hershey, PA: IGI Global. doi:10.4018/978-1-4666-8624-3.ch014

Mavodza, J. (2016). Relationship between Knowledge Management and Academic Integrity in a Middle Eastern University. In A. Goel & P. Singhal (Eds.), *Product Innovation through Knowledge Management and Social Media Strategies* (pp. 241–264). Hershey, PA: IGI Global. doi:10.4018/978-1-4666-9607-5.ch011

Maynor, A. (2016). Response to the Unthinkable: Collecting and Archiving Condolence and Temporary Memorial Materials following Public Tragedies. In E. Decker & J. Townes (Eds.), *Handbook of Research on Disaster Management and Contingency Planning in Modern Libraries* (pp. 582–624). Hershey, PA: IGI Global. doi:10.4018/978-1-4666-8624-3.ch025

McFall, L. M., Simons, J. T., Lord, G., MacDonald, P. J., Nieves, A. D., & Young, S. (2016). Collaborations in Liberal Arts Colleges in Support of Digital Humanities. In B. Doherty (Ed.), *Technology-Centered Academic Library Partnerships and Collaborations* (pp. 31–60). Hershey, PA: IGI Global. doi:10.4018/978-1-5225-0323-1.ch002

Na, L. (2017). Library and Information Science Education and Graduate Programs in Academic Libraries. In L. Ruan, Q. Zhu, & Y. Ye (Eds.), *Academic Library Development and Administration in China* (pp. 218–229). Hershey, PA: IGI Global. doi:10.4018/978-1-5225-0550-1.ch013

Nagarkar, S. P. (2017). Biomedical Librarianship in the Post-Genomic Era. In S. Ram (Ed.), *Library and Information Services for Bioinformatics Education and Research* (pp. 1–17). Hershey, PA: IGI Global. doi:10.4018/978-1-5225-1871-6.ch001

Natarajan, M. (2016). Exploring the E-Discovery Tools on the Use of Library Collections by Users. In E. de Smet & S. Dhamdhere (Eds.), *E-Discovery Tools and Applications in Modern Libraries* (pp. 122–137). Hershey, PA: IGI Global. doi:10.4018/978-1-5225-0474-0.ch007

Natarajan, M. (2017). Exploring Knowledge Sharing over Social Media. In R. Chugh (Ed.), *Harnessing Social Media as a Knowledge Management Tool* (pp. 55–73). Hershey, PA: IGI Global. doi:10.4018/978-1-5225-0495-5.ch003

Nazir, T. (2017). Preservation Initiatives in E-Environment to Protect Information Assets. In T. Ashraf & N. Kumar (Eds.), *Interdisciplinary Digital Preservation Tools and Technologies* (pp. 193–208). Hershey, PA: IGI Global. doi:10.4018/978-1-5225-1653-8.ch010

Ngulube, P. (2017). Embedding Indigenous Knowledge in Library and Information Science Education in Anglophone Eastern and Southern Africa. In P. Ngulube (Ed.), *Handbook of Research on Social, Cultural, and Educational Considerations of Indigenous Knowledge in Developing Countries* (pp. 92–115). Hershey, PA: IGI Global. doi:10.4018/978-1-5225-0838-0.ch006

Nicolajsen, H. W., Sørensen, F., & Scupola, A. (2016). The Potential of Workshops vs Blogs for User Involvement in Service Innovation. *International Journal of E-Services and Mobile Applications*, *8*(4), 1–19. doi:10.4018/IJESMA.2016100101

Nicolajsen, H. W., Sorensen, F., & Scupola, A. (2018). User Involvement in Service Innovation Processes. In M. Khosrow-Pour (Ed.), *Optimizing Current Practices in E-Services and Mobile Applications* (pp. 42–61). Hershey, PA: IGI Global. doi:10.4018/978-1-5225-5026-6.ch003

Nixon, M. L. (2016). Safety Doesn't Happen by Accident: Disaster Planning at the University of Pittsburgh. In E. Decker & J. Townes (Eds.), *Handbook of Research on Disaster Management and Contingency Planning in Modern Libraries* (pp. 184–206). Hershey, PA: IGI Global. doi:10.4018/978-1-4666-8624-3.ch009

Nwabueze, A. U., & Ibeh, B. O. (2016). Extent of ICT Literacy Possessed by Librarians in Federal University Libraries in South East Nigeria. *International Journal of Digital Literacy and Digital Competence*, *7*(3), 13–22. doi:10.4018/IJDLDC.2016070102

O'Grady, A. R. (2016). The Boston Library Consortium and RapidR: Partnering to Develop an Unmediated Book Sharing Module. In B. Doherty (Ed.), *Technology-Centered Academic Library Partnerships and Collaborations* (pp. 194–219). Hershey, PA: IGI Global. doi:10.4018/978-1-5225-0323-1.ch007

Ochonogor, W. C., & Okite-Amughoro, F. A. (2018). Building an Effective Digital Library in a University Teaching Hospital (UTH) in Nigeria. In A. Tella & T. Kwanya (Eds.), *Handbook of Research on Managing Intellectual Property in Digital Libraries* (pp. 184–204). Hershey, PA: IGI Global. doi:10.4018/978-1-5225-3093-0.ch010

Oladapo, Y. O. (2018). Open Access to Knowledge and Challenges in Digital Libraries. In A. Tella & T. Kwanya (Eds.), *Handbook of Research on Managing Intellectual Property in Digital Libraries* (pp. 260–291). Hershey, PA: IGI Global. doi:10.4018/978-1-5225-3093-0.ch014

Oladokun, O., & Zulu, S. F. (2017). Document Description and Coding as Key Elements in Knowledge, Records, and Information Management. In P. Jain & N. Mnjama (Eds.), *Managing Knowledge Resources and Records in Modern Organizations* (pp. 179–197). Hershey, PA: IGI Global. doi:10.4018/978-1-5225-1965-2.ch011

Olin, J. R. (2016). Libraries and Digital Media. In B. Guzzetti & M. Lesley (Eds.), *Handbook of Research on the Societal Impact of Digital Media* (pp. 163–177). Hershey, PA: IGI Global. doi:10.4018/978-1-4666-8310-5.ch007

Oluwaseun, A. A. (2016). Barriers to Information Seeking in the Digital Libraries. In A. Tella (Ed.), *Information Seeking Behavior and Challenges in Digital Libraries* (pp. 291–303). Hershey, PA: IGI Global. doi:10.4018/978-1-5225-0296-8.ch014

Omeluzor, S. U., Abayomi, I., & Gbemi-Ogunleye, P. (2018). Contemporary Media for Library Users' Instruction in Academic Libraries in South-West Nigeria: Contemporary Library Instruction in the Digital Age. In S. Bhattacharyya & K. Patnaik (Eds.), *Changing the Scope of Library Instruction in the Digital Age* (pp. 162–185). Hershey, PA: IGI Global. doi:10.4018/978-1-5225-2802-9.ch007

Ondari-Okemwa, E. (2016). Information-Seeking Behaviour of Users in the Digital Libraries' Environment in Sub-Saharan Africa. In A. Tella (Ed.), *Information Seeking Behavior and Challenges in Digital Libraries* (pp. 26–56). Hershey, PA: IGI Global. doi:10.4018/978-1-5225-0296-8.ch002

Oshilalu, A. H., & Ogochukwu, E. T. (2017). Modeling a Software for Library and Information Centers. *International Journal of Library and Information Services, 6*(2), 1–10. doi:10.4018/IJLIS.2017070101

Osterman, A. C., O'Gara, G., & Armstrong, A. M. (2016). The Evolution of Collaborative Collection Development within a Library Consortium: Data Analysis Applied in a Cultural Context. In B. Doherty (Ed.), *Space and Organizational Considerations in Academic Library Partnerships and Collaborations* (pp. 157–181). Hershey, PA: IGI Global. doi:10.4018/978-1-5225-0326-2.ch008

Oswal, S. K. (2017). Institutional, Legal, and Attitudinal Barriers to the Accessibility of University Digital Libraries: Implications for Retention of Disabled Students. In H. Alphin Jr, J. Lavine, & R. Chan (Eds.), *Disability and Equity in Higher Education Accessibility* (pp. 223–241). Hershey, PA: IGI Global. doi:10.4018/978-1-5225-2665-0.ch010

Otike, J. (2016). Legal Considerations of Providing Information in Support of Distance Learning by Digital Libraries in Universities in Kenya. In A. Tella (Ed.), *Information Seeking Behavior and Challenges in Digital Libraries* (pp. 57–69). Hershey, PA: IGI Global. doi:10.4018/978-1-5225-0296-8.ch003

Oukrich, J., & Bouikhalene, B. (2017). A Survey of Users' Satisfaction in the University Library by Using a Pareto Analysis and the Automatic Classification Methods. *International Journal of Library and Information Services*, *6*(1), 17–36. doi:10.4018/IJLIS.2017010102

Özel, N. (2018). Developing Visual Literacy Skills Through Library Instructions. In V. Osinska & G. Osinski (Eds.), *Information Visualization Techniques in the Social Sciences and Humanities* (pp. 32–48). Hershey, PA: IGI Global. doi:10.4018/978-1-5225-4990-1.ch003

Patel, D., & Thakur, D. (2017). Managing Open Access (OA) Scholarly Information Resources in a University. In A. Munigal (Ed.), *Scholarly Communication and the Publish or Perish Pressures of Academia* (pp. 224–255). Hershey, PA: IGI Global. doi:10.4018/978-1-5225-1697-2.ch011

Patnaik, K. R. (2018). Crafting a Framework for Copyright Literacy and Licensed Content: A Case Study at an Advanced Management Education and Research Library. In S. Bhattacharyya & K. Patnaik (Eds.), *Changing the Scope of Library Instruction in the Digital Age* (pp. 136–160). Hershey, PA: IGI Global. doi:10.4018/978-1-5225-2802-9.ch006

Paynter, K. (2017). Elementary Library Media Specialists' Roles in the Implementation of the Common Core State Standards. In M. Grassetti & S. Brookby (Eds.), *Advancing Next-Generation Teacher Education through Digital Tools and Applications* (pp. 262–283). Hershey, PA: IGI Global. doi:10.4018/978-1-5225-0965-3.ch014

Perez, M. J. (2016). Local Studies Centers in the Philippines: An Introductory Text. In J. Yap, M. Perez, M. Ayson, & G. Entico (Eds.), *Special Library Administration, Standardization and Technological Integration* (pp. 249–266). Hershey, PA: IGI Global. doi:10.4018/978-1-4666-9542-9.ch011

Perry, S. C., & Waggoner, J. (2018). Processes for User-Centered Design and Development: The Omeka Curator Dashboard Project. In L. Costello & M. Powers (Eds.), *Developing In-House Digital Tools in Library Spaces* (pp. 37–58). Hershey, PA: IGI Global. doi:10.4018/978-1-5225-2676-6.ch002

Phuritsabam, B., & Devi, A. B. (2017). Information Seeking Behavior of Medical Scientists at Jawaharlal Nehru Institute of Medical Science: A Study. In S. Ram (Ed.), *Library and Information Services for Bioinformatics Education and Research* (pp. 177–187). Hershey, PA: IGI Global. doi:10.4018/978-1-5225-1871-6.ch010

Pina, P. (2016). Copyright Issues in the Context of the Digital Library. In A. Tella (Ed.), *Information Seeking Behavior and Challenges in Digital Libraries* (pp. 70–83). Hershey, PA: IGI Global. doi:10.4018/978-1-5225-0296-8.ch004

Pionke, J. (2016). Disaster is in the Eye of the Beholder. In E. Decker & J. Townes (Eds.), *Handbook of Research on Disaster Management and Contingency Planning in Modern Libraries* (pp. 516–533). Hershey, PA: IGI Global. doi:10.4018/978-1-4666-8624-3.ch022

Quadri, R. F., & Sodiq, O. A. (2018). Managing Intellectual Property in Digital Libraries: The Roles of Digital Librarians. In A. Tella & T. Kwanya (Eds.), *Handbook of Research on Managing Intellectual Property in Digital Libraries* (pp. 337–355). Hershey, PA: IGI Global. doi:10.4018/978-1-5225-3093-0.ch017

Ram, S. (2017). Library Services for Bioinformatics: Establishing Synergy Data Information and Knowledge. In S. Ram (Ed.), *Library and Information Services for Bioinformatics Education and Research* (pp. 18–33). Hershey, PA: IGI Global. doi:10.4018/978-1-5225-1871-6.ch002

Rao, M. (2017). Use of Institutional Repository for Information Dissemination and Knowledge Management. In B. Gunjal (Ed.), *Managing Knowledge and Scholarly Assets in Academic Libraries* (pp. 156–173). Hershey, PA: IGI Global. doi:10.4018/978-1-5225-1741-2.ch007

Rao, Y., & Zhang, Y. (2017). The Construction and Development of Academic Library Digital Special Subject Databases. In L. Ruan, Q. Zhu, & Y. Ye (Eds.), *Academic Library Development and Administration in China* (pp. 163–183). Hershey, PA: IGI Global. doi:10.4018/978-1-5225-0550-1.ch010

Razip, S. N., Kadir, S. F., Saim, S. N., Dolhan, F. N., Jarmil, N., Salleh, N. H., & Rajin, G. (2017). Predicting Users' Intention towards Using Library Self-Issue and Return Systems. In N. Suki (Ed.), *Handbook of Research on Leveraging Consumer Psychology for Effective Customer Engagement* (pp. 102–115). Hershey, PA: IGI Global. doi:10.4018/978-1-5225-0746-8.ch007

Ress, A. D., McLaughlin, J. A., & Bertuca, C. (2016). Online Video Tutorials and Interlibrary Resource Sharing: A Model for Understanding the Role of Internet Video in Library Science and Education. In B. Doherty (Ed.), *Technology-Centered Academic Library Partnerships and Collaborations* (pp. 61–88). Hershey, PA: IGI Global. doi:10.4018/978-1-5225-0323-1.ch003

Rothwell, S. L. (2018). Librarians and Instructional Design Challenges: Concepts, Examples, and a Flexible Design Framework. In S. Bhattacharyya & K. Patnaik (Eds.), *Changing the Scope of Library Instruction in the Digital Age* (pp. 24–59). Hershey, PA: IGI Global. doi:10.4018/978-1-5225-2802-9.ch002

Roy, L., & Frydman, A. (2018). Community Outreach. In M. Khosrow-Pour, D.B.A. (Ed.), Encyclopedia of Information Science and Technology, Fourth Edition (pp. 6685-6694). Hershey, PA: IGI Global. doi:10.4018/978-1-5225-2255-3.ch579

Rutto, D., & Yudah, O. (2018). E-Books in University Libraries in Kenya: Trends, Usage, and Intellectual Property Issues. In A. Tella & T. Kwanya (Eds.), *Handbook of Research on Managing Intellectual Property in Digital Libraries* (pp. 120–141). Hershey, PA: IGI Global. doi:10.4018/978-1-5225-3093-0.ch007

Ryan, S. M., & Grubbs, W. T. (2016). Curricular Collaborations: Using Emerging Technologies to Foster Innovative Partnerships. In B. Doherty (Ed.), *Technology-Centered Academic Library Partnerships and Collaborations* (pp. 89–125). Hershey, PA: IGI Global. doi:10.4018/978-1-5225-0323-1.ch004

Sabharwal, A. (2017). The Transformative Role of Institutional Repositories in Academic Knowledge Management. In B. Gunjal (Ed.), *Managing Knowledge and Scholarly Assets in Academic Libraries* (pp. 127–155). Hershey, PA: IGI Global. doi:10.4018/978-1-5225-1741-2.ch006

Sadiku, S. A., Kpakiko, M. M., & Tsafe, A. G. (2018). Institutional Digital Repository and the Challenges of Global Visibility in Nigeria. In A. Tella & T. Kwanya (Eds.), *Handbook of Research on Managing Intellectual Property in Digital Libraries* (pp. 356–376). Hershey, PA: IGI Global. doi:10.4018/978-1-5225-3093-0.ch018

Sahu, M. K. (2018). Web-Scale Discovery Service in Academic Library Environment: A Birds Eye View. *International Journal of Library and Information Services*, *7*(1), 1–14. doi:10.4018/IJLIS.2018010101

Salim, F., Saigar, B., Armoham, P. K., Gobalakrishnan, S., Jap, M. Y., & Lim, N. A. (2017). Students' Information-Seeking Intention in Academic Digital Libraries. In N. Suki (Ed.), *Handbook of Research on Leveraging Consumer Psychology for Effective Customer Engagement* (pp. 259–273). Hershey, PA: IGI Global. doi:10.4018/978-1-5225-0746-8.ch017

San Kong, E. W., Chiu, D. K., & Ho, K. K. (2016). Applications of Social Media in Academic Library Services: A Case of the Hong Kong Polytechnic University Library. *International Journal of Systems and Service-Oriented Engineering*, *6*(2), 53–65. doi:10.4018/IJSSOE.2016040103

Saroja, G. (2017). Changing Face of Scholarly Communication and Its Impact on Library and Information Centres. In A. Munigal (Ed.), *Scholarly Communication and the Publish or Perish Pressures of Academia* (pp. 100–117). Hershey, PA: IGI Global. doi:10.4018/978-1-5225-1697-2.ch006

Sawant, S. (2016). Collaborative Online Learning Tools and Types: Few Perspectives of Its Use in Academic Library. In H. Rahman (Ed.), *Human Development and Interaction in the Age of Ubiquitous Technology* (pp. 94–119). Hershey, PA: IGI Global. doi:10.4018/978-1-5225-0556-3.ch005

Sawsaa, A. F., & Lu, J. (2017). Research Background on Ontology. In J. Lu & Q. Xu (Eds.), *Ontologies and Big Data Considerations for Effective Intelligence* (pp. 443–509). Hershey, PA: IGI Global. doi:10.4018/978-1-5225-2058-0.ch011

Schuster, D. W. (2017). Selection Process for Free Open Source Software. In E. Iglesias (Ed.), *Library Technology Funding, Planning, and Deployment* (pp. 55–71). Hershey, PA: IGI Global. doi:10.4018/978-1-5225-1735-1.ch004

Segaetsho, T. (2018). Environmental Consideration in the Preservation of Paper Materials in Heritage Institutions in the East and Southern African Region. In P. Ngulube (Ed.), *Handbook of Research on Heritage Management and Preservation* (pp. 183–212). Hershey, PA: IGI Global. doi:10.4018/978-1-5225-3137-1.ch010

Shakhsi, L. (2017). Cataloging Images in Library, Archive, and Museum. In T. Ashraf & N. Kumar (Eds.), *Interdisciplinary Digital Preservation Tools and Technologies* (pp. 119–141). Hershey, PA: IGI Global. doi:10.4018/978-1-5225-1653-8.ch007

Sharma, C. (2017). Digital Initiatives of the Indian Council of World Affairs' Library. In T. Ashraf & N. Kumar (Eds.), *Interdisciplinary Digital Preservation Tools and Technologies* (pp. 231–241). Hershey, PA: IGI Global. doi:10.4018/978-1-5225-1653-8.ch012

Shaw, M. D. (2016). Navigating Campus Disasters from Within the Library: Lessons and Implications from Gulf Coast Institutions. In E. Decker & J. Townes (Eds.), *Handbook of Research on Disaster Management and Contingency Planning in Modern Libraries* (pp. 340–365). Hershey, PA: IGI Global. doi:10.4018/978-1-4666-8624-3.ch015

Shawish, A., & Salama, M. (2016). Cloud-Based Digital Library Era. In J. Yap, M. Perez, M. Ayson, & G. Entico (Eds.), *Special Library Administration, Standardization and Technological Integration* (pp. 226–247). Hershey, PA: IGI Global. doi:10.4018/978-1-4666-9542-9.ch010

Siddaiah, D. K. (2018). Commonwealth Professional Fellowship: A Gateway for the Strategic Development of Libraries in India. In R. Bhardwaj (Ed.), *Digitizing the Modern Library and the Transition From Print to Electronic* (pp. 270–286). Hershey, PA: IGI Global. doi:10.4018/978-1-5225-2119-8.ch012

Silvana de Rosa, A. (2018). Mission, Tools, and Ongoing Developments in the So.Re. Com. "A.S. de Rosa" @-library. In M. Khosrow-Pour, D.B.A. (Ed.), Encyclopedia of Information Science and Technology, Fourth Edition (pp. 5237-5251). Hershey, PA: IGI Global. doi:10.4018/978-1-5225-2255-3.ch455

Silverman, R., Nakashima, T., Hunt, J. M., & Tuia, J. (2016). A Stitch in Time: Disaster Mitigation Strategies for Cultural Heritage Collections. In E. Decker & J. Townes (Eds.), *Handbook of Research on Disaster Management and Contingency Planning in Modern Libraries* (pp. 208–239). Hershey, PA: IGI Global. doi:10.4018/978-1-4666-8624-3.ch010

Smart, C. (2016). The Public Library's Role in Enabling E-Government: A View of Two Countries in the English-Speaking Caribbean. *International Journal of Public Administration in the Digital Age, 3*(3), 18–32. doi:10.4018/IJPADA.2016070102

Smolenski, N., Kostic, M., & Sofronijevic, A. M. (2018). Intrapreneurship and Enterprise 2.0 as Grounds for Developing In-House Digital Tools for Handling METS/ALTO Files at the University Library Belgrade. In L. Costello & M. Powers (Eds.), *Developing In-House Digital Tools in Library Spaces* (pp. 92–116). Hershey, PA: IGI Global. doi:10.4018/978-1-5225-2676-6.ch005

Sochay, L., & Junus, R. (2017). From Summon to SearchPlus: The RFP Process for a Discovery Tool at the MSU Libraries. In E. Iglesias (Ed.), *Library Technology Funding, Planning, and Deployment* (pp. 72–98). Hershey, PA: IGI Global. doi:10.4018/978-1-5225-1735-1.ch005

Sonawane, C. S. (2018). Library Catalogue in the Internet Age. In R. Bhardwaj (Ed.), *Digitizing the Modern Library and the Transition From Print to Electronic* (pp. 204–223). Hershey, PA: IGI Global. doi:10.4018/978-1-5225-2119-8.ch009

Sonawane, M. (2016). Creating an Agile Library. In E. de Smet & S. Dhamdhere (Eds.), *E-Discovery Tools and Applications in Modern Libraries* (pp. 109–121). Hershey, PA: IGI Global. doi:10.4018/978-1-5225-0474-0.ch006

Staley, C., Kenyon, R. S., & Marcovitz, D. M. (2018). Embedded Services: Going Beyond the Field of Dreams Model for Online Programs. In D. Polly, M. Putman, T. Petty, & A. Good (Eds.), *Innovative Practices in Teacher Preparation and Graduate-Level Teacher Education Programs* (pp. 368–381). Hershey, PA: IGI Global. doi:10.4018/978-1-5225-3068-8.ch020

Stavridi, S. V., & Hamada, D. R. (2016). Children and Youth Librarians: Competencies Required in Technology-Based Environment. In J. Yap, M. Perez, M. Ayson, & G. Entico (Eds.), *Special Library Administration, Standardization and Technological Integration* (pp. 25–50). Hershey, PA: IGI Global. doi:10.4018/978-1-4666-9542-9.ch002

Stewart, M. C., Atilano, M., & Arnold, C. L. (2017). Improving Customer Relations with Social Listening: A Case Study of an American Academic Library. *International Journal of Customer Relationship Marketing and Management*, *8*(1), 49–63. doi:10.4018/IJCRMM.2017010104

Sukula, S. K., & Bhardwaj, R. K. (2018). An Extensive Discussion on Transition of Libraries: The Panoramic View of Library Resources, Services, and Evolved Librarianship. In R. Bhardwaj (Ed.), *Digitizing the Modern Library and the Transition From Print to Electronic* (pp. 255–269). Hershey, PA: IGI Global. doi:10.4018/978-1-5225-2119-8.ch011

Taylor, L. N., Alteri, S. A., Minson, V. I., Walker, B., Hawley, E. H., Dinsmore, C. S., & Jefferson, R. J. (2016). Library Collaborative Networks Forging Scholarly Cyberinfrastructure and Radical Collaboration. In B. Doherty (Ed.), *Technology-Centered Academic Library Partnerships and Collaborations* (pp. 1–30). Hershey, PA: IGI Global. doi:10.4018/978-1-5225-0323-1.ch001

Tella, A., & Babatunde, B. J. (2017). Determinants of Continuance Intention of Facebook Usage Among Library and Information Science Female Undergraduates in Selected Nigerian Universities. *International Journal of E-Adoption*, *9*(2), 59–76. doi:10.4018/IJEA.2017070104

Tella, A., Okojie, V., & Olaniyi, O. T. (2018). Social Bookmarking Tools and Digital Libraries. In A. Tella & T. Kwanya (Eds.), *Handbook of Research on Managing Intellectual Property in Digital Libraries* (pp. 396–409). Hershey, PA: IGI Global. doi:10.4018/978-1-5225-3093-0.ch020

Tella, A., Oyeniran, S., & Ojo, O. J. (2016). Digital Libraries and Copyright Issues. In A. Tella (Ed.), *Information Seeking Behavior and Challenges in Digital Libraries* (pp. 108–126). Hershey, PA: IGI Global. doi:10.4018/978-1-5225-0296-8.ch006

Thull, J. J. (2018). Librarians and the Evolving Research Needs of Distance Students. In I. Oncioiu (Ed.), *Ethics and Decision-Making for Sustainable Business Practices* (pp. 203–216). Hershey, PA: IGI Global. doi:10.4018/978-1-5225-3773-1.ch012

Titilope, A. O. (2017). Ethical Issues in Library and Information Science Profession in Nigeria: An Appraisal. *International Journal of Library and Information Services, 6*(2), 11–22. doi:10.4018/IJLIS.2017070102

Tutu, J. M. (2018). Intellectual Property Challenges in Digital Library Environments. In A. Tella & T. Kwanya (Eds.), *Handbook of Research on Managing Intellectual Property in Digital Libraries* (pp. 225–240). Hershey, PA: IGI Global. doi:10.4018/978-1-5225-3093-0.ch012

Upev, M. T., Beetseh, K., & Idachaba, J. A. (2016). Usability of Digital Resources: A Study of Francis Sulemanu Idachaba Library University of Agriculture Makurdi. In A. Tella (Ed.), *Information Seeking Behavior and Challenges in Digital Libraries* (pp. 224–237). Hershey, PA: IGI Global. doi:10.4018/978-1-5225-0296-8.ch011

Verplaetse, A., Mascareñas, P., & O'Neill, K. (2016). Zen and the Art of Disaster Planning: Collaboration Challenges in Library Disaster Plan Design and Execution. In E. Decker & J. Townes (Eds.), *Handbook of Research on Disaster Management and Contingency Planning in Modern Libraries* (pp. 96–119). Hershey, PA: IGI Global. doi:10.4018/978-1-4666-8624-3.ch005

Walker, B., & Pursley, T. (2016). A Statewide Collaborative Storage and Print Repository Model: The Florida Academic Repository (FLARE). In B. Doherty (Ed.), *Space and Organizational Considerations in Academic Library Partnerships and Collaborations* (pp. 111–129). Hershey, PA: IGI Global. doi:10.4018/978-1-5225-0326-2.ch006

Wallace, D., & Hemment, M. (2018). Enabling Scholarship in the Digital Age: A Case for Libraries Creating Value at HBS. In S. Bhattacharyya & K. Patnaik (Eds.), *Changing the Scope of Library Instruction in the Digital Age* (pp. 86–117). Hershey, PA: IGI Global. doi:10.4018/978-1-5225-2802-9.ch004

Wani, Z. A., Zainab, T., & Hussain, S. (2018). Web 2.0 From Evolution to Revolutionary Impact in Library and Information Centers. In M. Khosrow-Pour, D.B.A. (Ed.), Encyclopedia of Information Science and Technology, Fourth Edition (pp. 5262-5271). Hershey, PA: IGI Global. doi:10.4018/978-1-5225-2255-3.ch457

Waring, S. M. (2016). Teaching with Primary Sources: Moving from Professional Development to a Model of Professional Learning. In T. Petty, A. Good, & S. Putman (Eds.), *Handbook of Research on Professional Development for Quality Teaching and Learning* (pp. 295–306). Hershey, PA: IGI Global. doi:10.4018/978-1-5225-0204-3.ch014

Weiss, A. P. (2018). Massive Digital Libraries (MDLs). In M. Khosrow-Pour, D.B.A. (Ed.), Encyclopedia of Information Science and Technology, Fourth Edition (pp. 5226-5236). Hershey, PA: IGI Global. doi:10.4018/978-1-5225-2255-3.ch454

Wentao, C., Jinyu, Z., & Zhonggen, Y. (2016). Learning Outcomes and Affective Factors of Blended Learning of English for Library Science. *International Journal of Information and Communication Technology Education*, *12*(3), 13–25. doi:10.4018/IJICTE.2016070102

White, G. W. (2016). The Library as a Center for Innovation: A Collaboration at the University of Maryland. In B. Doherty (Ed.), *Space and Organizational Considerations in Academic Library Partnerships and Collaborations* (pp. 68–86). Hershey, PA: IGI Global. doi:10.4018/978-1-5225-0326-2.ch004

Wu, S. K., Bess, M., & Price, B. R. (2018). Digitizing Library Outreach: Leveraging Bluetooth Beacons and Mobile Applications to Expand Library Outreach. In R. Bhardwaj (Ed.), *Digitizing the Modern Library and the Transition From Print to Electronic* (pp. 193–203). Hershey, PA: IGI Global. doi:10.4018/978-1-5225-2119-8.ch008

Wulff, E. (2018). Evaluation of Digital Collections and Political Visibility of the Library. In R. Bhardwaj (Ed.), *Digitizing the Modern Library and the Transition From Print to Electronic* (pp. 64–89). Hershey, PA: IGI Global. doi:10.4018/978-1-5225-2119-8.ch003

Xiao, L., & Liu, Y. (2017). Development of Innovative User Services. In L. Ruan, Q. Zhu, & Y. Ye (Eds.), *Academic Library Development and Administration in China* (pp. 56–73). Hershey, PA: IGI Global. doi:10.4018/978-1-5225-0550-1.ch004

Xin, X., & Wu, X. (2017). The Practice of Outreach Services in Chinese Special Libraries. In L. Ruan, Q. Zhu, & Y. Ye (Eds.), *Academic Library Development and Administration in China* (pp. 74–89). Hershey, PA: IGI Global. doi:10.4018/978-1-5225-0550-1.ch005

Yao, X., Zhu, Q., & Liu, J. (2017). The China Academic Library and Information System (CALIS). In L. Ruan, Q. Zhu, & Y. Ye (Eds.), *Academic Library Development and Administration in China* (pp. 1–19). Hershey, PA: IGI Global. doi:10.4018/978-1-5225-0550-1.ch001

Yap, J. M. (2016). Social Media Literacy of Agricultural Librarians in the Philippines. In J. Yap, M. Perez, M. Ayson, & G. Entico (Eds.), *Special Library Administration, Standardization and Technological Integration* (pp. 202–224). Hershey, PA: IGI Global. doi:10.4018/978-1-4666-9542-9.ch009

Yasue, A. (2016). Preservation Management in Company Libraries. In J. Yap, M. Perez, M. Ayson, & G. Entico (Eds.), *Special Library Administration, Standardization and Technological Integration* (pp. 305–314). Hershey, PA: IGI Global. doi:10.4018/978-1-4666-9542-9.ch013

Yin, Q., Yingying, W., Yan, Z., & Xiaojia, M. (2017). Resource Sharing and Mutually Beneficial Cooperation: A Look at the New United Model in Public and College Libraries. In L. Ruan, Q. Zhu, & Y. Ye (Eds.), *Academic Library Development and Administration in China* (pp. 334–352). Hershey, PA: IGI Global. doi:10.4018/978-1-5225-0550-1.ch019

Yuhua, F. (2018). Computer Information Library Clusters. In M. Khosrow-Pour, D.B.A. (Ed.), Encyclopedia of Information Science and Technology, Fourth Edition (pp. 4399-4403). Hershey, PA: IGI Global. doi:10.4018/978-1-5225-2255-3.ch382

Yusuf, F., Owolabi, S., Aregbesola, A., Oguntayo, S., Okocha, F., & Eyiolorunse, T. (2016). Demographics, Socio-Economic and Cognitive Skills as Barriers to Information Seeking in a Digital Library Environment. In A. Tella (Ed.), *Information Seeking Behavior and Challenges in Digital Libraries* (pp. 179–202). Hershey, PA: IGI Global. doi:10.4018/978-1-5225-0296-8.ch009

Yusuf, F., & Owolabi, S. E. (2018). Open Access to Knowledge and Challenges in Digital Libraries: Nigeria's Peculiarity. In A. Tella & T. Kwanya (Eds.), *Handbook of Research on Managing Intellectual Property in Digital Libraries* (pp. 241–259). Hershey, PA: IGI Global. doi:10.4018/978-1-5225-3093-0.ch013

Yuvaraj, M. (2016). Impact of Discovery Layers on Accessing E-Resources in Academic Libraries: A Case Study of Central University of Bihar. In E. de Smet & S. Dhamdhere (Eds.), *E-Discovery Tools and Applications in Modern Libraries* (pp. 181–200). Hershey, PA: IGI Global. doi:10.4018/978-1-5225-0474-0.ch010

Zaremohzzabieh, Z., Ahrari, S., Abu Samah, B., & Bolong, J. (2016). Researching Information Seeking in Digital Libraries through Information-Seeking Models. In A. Tella (Ed.), *Information Seeking Behavior and Challenges in Digital Libraries* (pp. 84–107). Hershey, PA: IGI Global. doi:10.4018/978-1-5225-0296-8.ch005

Zhu, S., & Shi, W. (2017). A Bibliometric Analysis of Research and Services in Chinese Academic Libraries. In L. Ruan, Q. Zhu, & Y. Ye (Eds.), *Academic Library Development and Administration in China* (pp. 253–262). Hershey, PA: IGI Global. doi:10.4018/978-1-5225-0550-1.ch015

Zimeras, S., Kostagiolas, P., & Lavranos, C. (2016). Dealing with the Uncertainty of Satisfaction Surveys in Organizations That Employ Interactive Multimedia: An Analysis of False Answers Statistical Models through a Digital Music Library Case Study. In I. Deliyannis, P. Kostagiolas, & C. Banou (Eds.), *Experimental Multimedia Systems for Interactivity and Strategic Innovation* (pp. 160–175). Hershey, PA: IGI Global. doi:10.4018/978-1-4666-8659-5.ch008

About the Contributors

Collence Takaingenhamo Chisita is a Principal Lecturer and Researcher based at Harare Polytechnic's School of Information Sciences. He is a holder of PHD Information Sciences, Masters of Science Information Sciences, BA English and Communication, Higher Diploma in Information Science. Chisita lecturers in a number of subjects namely, Information Storage Retrieval, Organisation of Knowledge, Digital Diplomatics and Resource sharing. Currently he is a Post Doctoral fellow (PDF) with UNISA. Chisita is a renowned writer and speaker who has presented papers at various fora including Euro Africa Partnership for Research in ICT's, Promoting African European Research Infrastructure Partnerships (PAERIP), IFLA, among others. He has also worked with Ubuntunet Alliance and other regional and international NRENS.

Alexander Madanha Rusero is a Senior Journalism and Political Studies Lecturer at Zimbabwe's pioneer journalism training institution of Harare Polytechnic – School of Journalism and Media Studies. Rusero is a holder of a Masters of Science in International Relations, a Bachelors of Science in Political Science, Bachelors of Mass Communication – Print Journalism as well as several diplomas, certificates and certifications. He is author to more than 8 text books on News Writing, Media, Democracy and Development, Public Relations, Marketing and Advertising as well as International Relations and Zimbabwe's History. Rusero is a prominent political analyst and resource person of various global media institutions, among them Al Jazeera, CNN, BBC and CGTV. Rusero is also currently a Doctoral Fellow with the University of Pretoria undertaking a PhD in International Relations.

***

Sindiso Bhebhe is a Principal Archivist at the National Archives of Zimbabwe. He is a part time tutor of records, archives and library courses at the Zimbabwe Open University. He holds a Master of Library and Information Science Degree from the National University of Science and Technology in Zimbabwe. He also hold a certificate on short course of modern library practices from the National Institute of Technical Teachers Training in Chennai, India. At the present moment he is doing a Doctorate in Information Science with the University of South Africa. He has attended and presented academic articles on numerous local and international conferences which deal mainly with the library and archival issues. He is part of the Africa research team in the International Research on Permanent Authentic Records in Electronic Systems [InterPARES] Trust. He is a member of the Oral History Association of South Africa. He has published academic articles on the issues of oral history, archival infrastructure and archival diplomatics in international journals.

Rupak Chakravarty is working as Associate Professor in the Department of Library & Information Science, Panjab University, Chandigarh, India for more than 10 years. Specialization areas include: Application of ICT in libraries including library automation, Free Open Source Software (FOSS), digital library, digital reference service, library portal development. Other areas of specialization include: Management of Library & Information Centres, Information & Communication, Dewey Decimal Classification, Information Sources, Open Access, Institutional Repositories (IRs), Web 2.0, Library 2.0. Also serving as Mendeley Advisor at Chandigarh region. Worked as Assistant Librarian, Panjab University Library for more than five years as the Reference Librarian and at Periodicals. Has contributed 5 lessons in the national OER project called ePGPathshala. Has written 5 book chapters with IGI Global.

Floribert Patrick C. Endong (PhD) is a research consultant in the humanities and social sciences. He is a reviewer and editor with many scientific journals in the social sciences. His current research interest focuses on culture, international communication, gender studies, digital media, media laws, international relations, and religious communication He is author of numerous peer-reviewed articles and book chapters in the above-mentioned areas of interest.

Tshepho Mosweu is a Lecturer in the Department of Library and Information Studies at the University of Botswana and a Doctoral Degree candidate in Information Science at the University of South Africa. She has a Master's Degree in Archives and Records Management where her research was on an ECM system implemented by the Administration of Justice in Botswana. Tshepho Mosweu is also a researcher at InterPARES Trust, Team Africa, a multi-disciplinary and multinational research project based in Canada concerned with digital records entrusted to the Internet.

She previously worked at Botswana National Archives and Records Services as an Archivist and Head of Kanye Records Centre. She has written and presented academic papers in electronic records management, Social Media, oral history and Cloud- Computing.

Darlington Musemburi is the Law Librarian at the University of Zimbabwe and a steering committee member for the Zimbabwe Legal Information Institute (ZIMLII), a nonprofit making Trust advocating for open and free access by public to the public legal information through electronic means. He is a holder of Master of Science in Library and Information Science and a facilitator in Open Access and Information Literacy Pedagogy. He has facilitated for IDS UK and INASP.

Arnold Mwanzu is the Head Librarian and Information Resource Centre Co-ordinator at International Centre of Insect Physiology & Ecology (icipe) in Nairobi Kenya. He holds a Masters in Library and Information Science (MLIS) from Kenyatta University, Kenya; an MSc in Organizational Development from USIU-Africa. He is currently pursuing a PhD in Information Science at Moi University, Kenya. Professionally, he is a Standing Committee member of the IFLA preservation & Conservation section 2017-2019; he is an executive board member in the Kenya Library & Information Science Consortium (KLISC). He is also the Country coordinator for INASP in charge of promotion and marketing of e-resources.

Mpho Ngoepe is a professor in the Department of Information Science at the University of South Africa (Unisa). Prior to his current position at Unisa, Prof Ngoepe has worked for the United Nations Children's Fund, Auditor-General South Africa and the National Archives of South Africa. Professor Ngoepe is serving in the national committee of the South African Society of Archivists (2009-2017) and the board of Eastern and Southern Regional Branch of the International Council on Archives (2009-2017) as the editor of the journals. Prof Ngoepe also serves on the advisory council of the National Archives of South Africa in his capacity as the chairperson of Gauteng Provincial Archives. He is the director of the African Team for the multi-national, interdisciplinary research project exploring issues concerning digital records called the International Research on Permanent Authentic Records in Electronic Systems (InterPARES Trust) (2013-2018).

Collen Nhendo is an Assistant Librarian at the University of Zimbabwe responsible for the Faculty of Engineering. He holds a Bachelor of Science Honours Degree in Library and Information Science. He has 5 years experience in librarianship. He has worked for Africa University Library before joining the University of Zimbabwe in 2012. His areas of research interest include Information Literacy, Open Access Publishing and Electronic Information Resources.

Ojinga Omiunu is a PhD student in Africa Regional Centre for Information Science, University of Ibadan, Ibadan, Oyo State, Nigeria. He is also the CEO of Unicorn Academics and organisation Developmental Research Centre, a registered NGO based in Nigeria, West Africa.

Lazarus Sauti is an information scientist, poet, short story writer, public relations as well as media practitioner based in Zimbabwe. Currently Lazarus is working fort the Ministry of Transport but also serves as an independent media practitioner for the Sunday Times.

Index

I

J

K

L

M

N

O

P

R

S

Z